Everyone's Guide to Maui

The Valley Isle:

The Best
The Bargains
The Unique

by Greg and Christie Stilson
art by W.C. Ballard

"Maui No Ka Oi"
(Maui is the best!!)

Our thanks to:

Francine "Scoop" Abolofia, Ava Hiegel, Diane Bazler, Deborah Tullis and Kris Bernard for their special contributions. To Ruby Kime and Tim Warren for the use of their magic machines. To Linda Owen Cooper for so many tiresome hours at the keyboard. To Elizabeth Farance and Grace Kammerer for proofreading. To Rick, Sue, Jenny and Kendra Miner for "adopting" Maren and a big thanks to Maren Stilson for being so patient with mom and dad.

Composition by Accucom Data Network, Inc.

© - Copyright 1985 Paradise Publications

No part of this publication may be reproduced or transmitted in any form without prior permission of the publisher, except for the purpose of a review written for inclusion in a magazine, newspaper or broadcast. Inquiries should be directed to : Paradise Publications, 8110 SW Wareham Circle, Portland, Or 97223. U.S.A.

ISBN #0-9614113-0-9
Printed in U.S.A.

TABLE OF CONTENTS

I.	INTRODUCTION	5
II.	A HISTORY OF MAUI IN BRIEF	7
III.	GENERAL INFORMATION	
	a. Our personal bests	11
	b. Maui's place names and their pronunciations	12
	c. Hawaiian words and their meanings	12
	d. Traveling with children	13
	e. Helpful information	14
	f. Getting there	15
	g. Getting around: bus, taxi and rental cars	16
	h. A few words about fish	22
	i. Annual Maui events	25
IV.	WHERE TO STAY AND WHAT TO SEE	
	a. Hotel and condo tips	26
	b. Condo & hotel index	28
	c. Kahului and Wailuku	30
	d. Lahaina and Kaanapali	35
	e. Kapalua, Napili and Kahana	49
	f. Kihei and Wailea	60
	g. Upcountry	76
	h. Hana	79
V.	RESTAURANTS	
	a. Restaurant Index	85
	b. Kahului/Wailuku	89
	c. Kaanapali/Lahaina	93
	d. Kapalua/Napili/Kahana	108
	e. Kihei and Wailea	113
	f. Upcountry	122
	g. Hana	124
	h. Sunsets and Nightlife	125
VI.	BEACHES AND BEACH ACTIVITIES	
	a. Makena area	129
	b. Wailea	132
	c. Kihei	134
	d. Maalaea to Lahaina	136
	e. Lahaina/Kaanapali	137
	f. Kahana/Napili, Kapalua and beyond	139
	g. Wailuku/Kahului	142

VII. RECREATION AND TOURS
    a. Land tours and sports 145
    b. Water tours and sports 146
    c. Air tours 153
    d. Golf 155
    e. Tennis 155
    f. Biking 156
    g. Hiking 158
    h. Running 158
    i. Horseback riding 159
    j. Shopping around the island 159

IX. BIBLIOGRAPHY

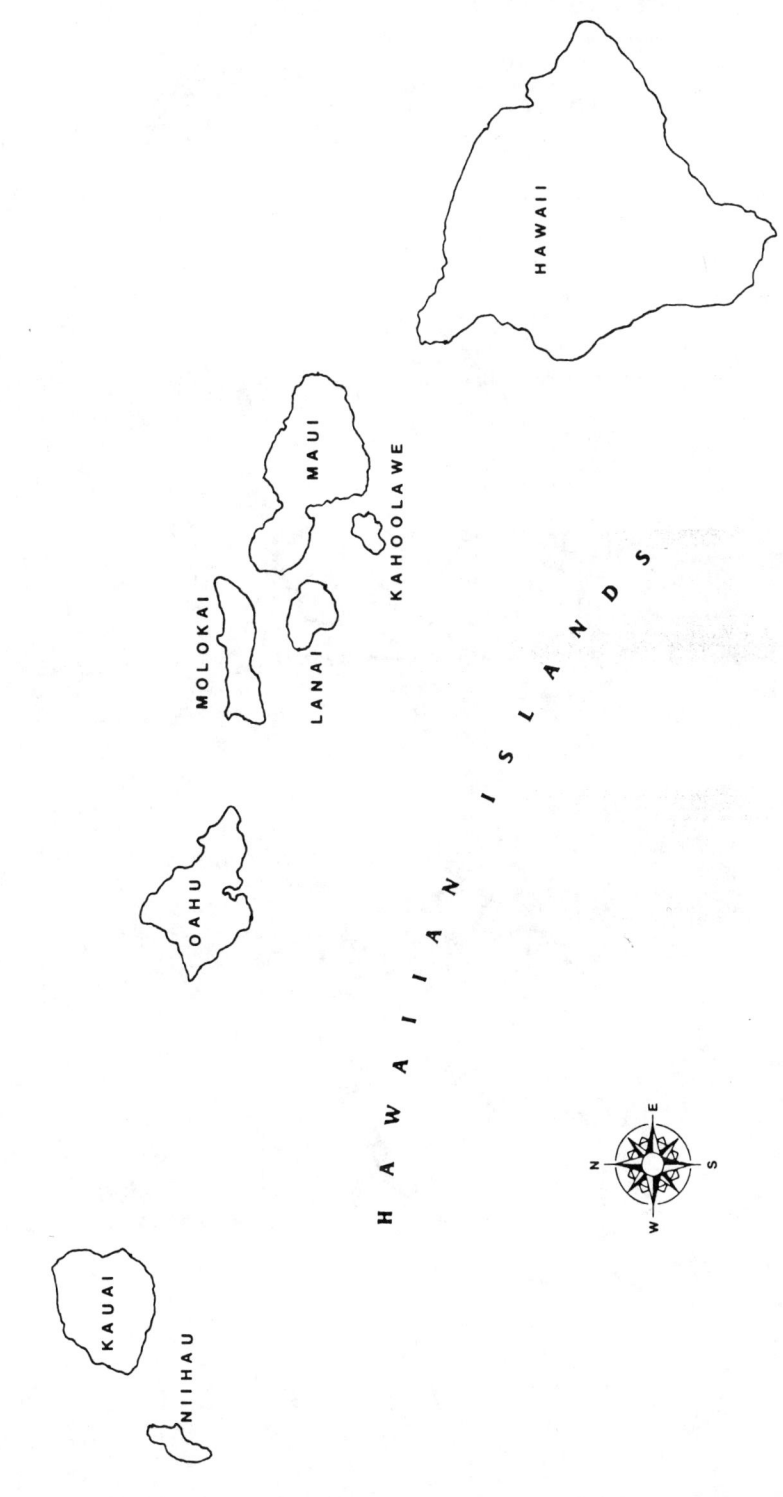

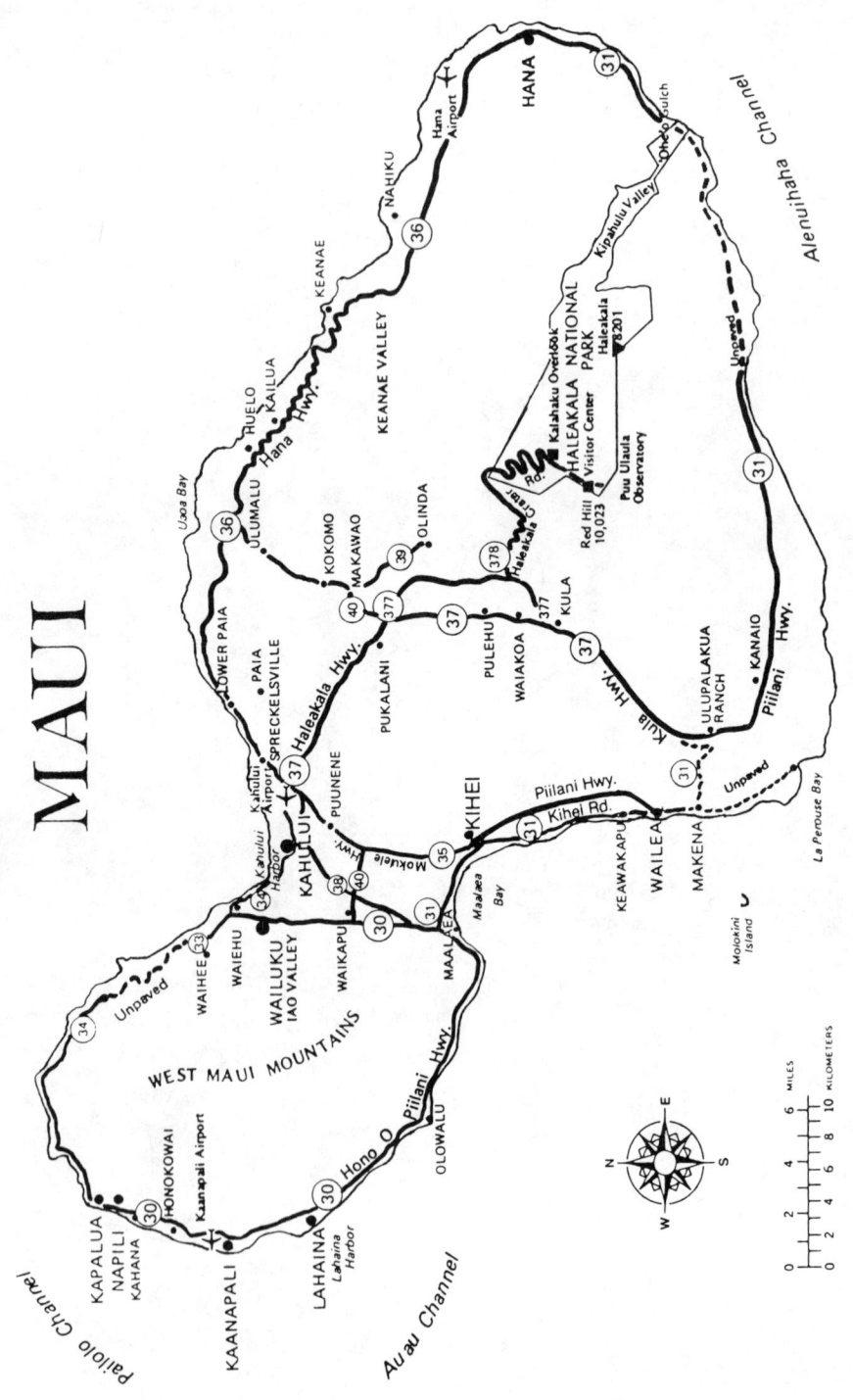

INTRODUCTION

Congratulations on choosing Maui as the site of your vacation. You will soon see why it has the deserved slogan, Maui No Ka Oi (Maui is the Best). The sun and lush tropicalness, and some of the finest accommodations blend sublimely together to create a perfect holiday paradise. There is something for everyone on Maui and prices to fit a variety of budgets. We hope our book will help make your stay a more enjoyable one. There is much to do and see on the island and we have endeavored to give complete descriptions so that you can choose the activities, accommodations and restaurants best suited to your needs. Even those of you who are making a return visit to Maui can discover new sights and activities on this magnificent island.

We don't live on the island, but visit frequently. We feel that gives us a fresh perspective in our research and writing. We have not been influenced by any form of remuneration from agencies, resorts, restaurants, rental companies, etc., so the opinions are all ours. We have tried to find positive aspects in all things, but felt it was your right to know, in certain cases, our bad experiences.

We have attempted to make our guide as accurate as possible at time of publication, however, the island is in a constant state of flux; restaurants open and close and re-open with name changes frequently. Prices of course, are always on the rise and there are new condominiums and hotels that open monthly. We cannot guarantee any of the prices listed, so while realizing that they may change, we have decided to include them to offer you this means of comparison.

For the purposes of organization, as well as geographical, climatic, and the distances involved, we have divided the restaurant and hotel-condominiums sections into six areas; Kahului and Wailuku on the North side, Hana on the eastern end, Kihei and Wailea which are on the southern shore, Kaanapali and Lahaina are on the western portion of the island, the Kahana, Napili and Kapalua areas which are beyond Kaanapali and lastly Upcountry. The chapter on beaches has also been divided in a similar manner. We hope this will make it easy for you to find the information you need. Remember that except for Hana, most of the areas are only a moderate drive away and worth a day of sight seeing or a meal at a fine restaurant.

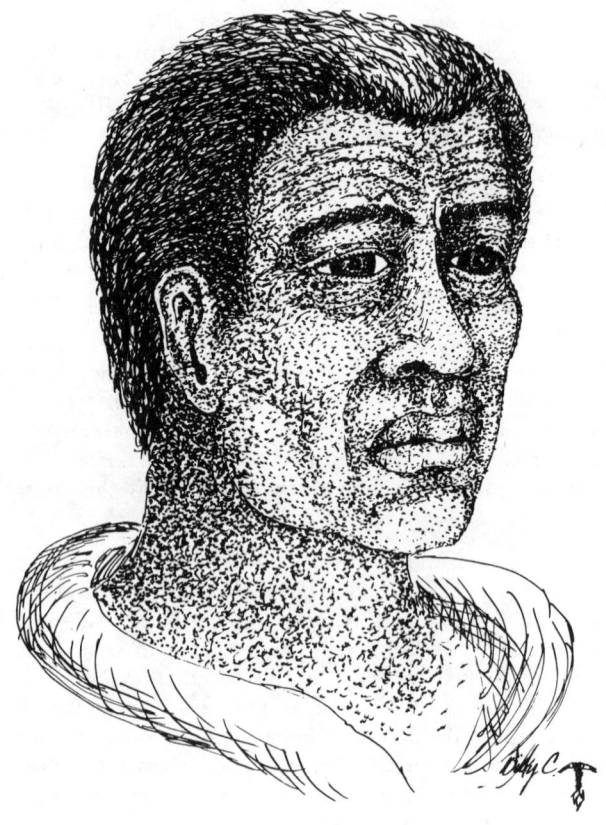

King Kamehameha I

EARLY HISTORY OF MAUI

Maui's beginnings were violent. Explosions of hot lava from two volcanos created the island. Puu Kukui (Poo'oo koo-KOO-ee) created the westerly section and the great Haleakala (HAH-leh-AH-kuh-LAH), now the world's largest dormant volcano, created the eastern portion of the island. A valley connects the two.

The first Hawaiians came from the Marquesa and Society Islands in the central Pacific. (Findings suggest that their ancestors came from the western Pacific, perhaps as far as Madagascar). The polynesians left the Marquesas in about the 8th century and were followed by natives from the Society Islands sometime between the 11th and 14th centuries.

The Hawaiian population may well have been as high as 300,000 by the 1700's, spread throughout the chain of islands. Fish and poi were diet basics, being supplemented by various fruits, and occasionally meat from chickens, pigs and even dogs. Four principal Gods formed the basis of their religion until the missionaries arrived. Hieaus, the ancient religions temples, can still be visited on Maui.

The major islands had a history of independent rule, with open warfare at times. Kahului and Hana were both sites of combat between the Maui islanders and the warriors from neighboring islands.

Kamehameha the First was born on the big island of Hawaii about 1758, and was the nephew of Kalaiopi the ruler. Following the King's death, Kalaiopi's son came to power, only to be subsequently defeated by Kamehameha in about 1794. The great chiefton Kahekili was Kamehameha's greatest rival ruling not only Maui, but Lanai and Molokai, and having kinship with the governing royalty of Oahu and Kaui. King Kahekili died in 1794, leaving control of the island to his son. It was a bloody battle in the Iao Valley which resulted in the defeat of Kahekili's son, Kalanikupule, in 1795.

Kamehameha united all the islands and made Lahaina the capitol of Hawaii in 1802. It remained there until the 1840's when Honolulu became the center for government affairs. Lahaina was a popular resort for the Hawaiian royalty who favored the beaches in the area. Kaahumanu, the favorite wife of Kamehameha was born in Hana, Maui, and spent much of her time there. Quiet Hana was another popular spot for vacationing royalty.

Liholiho, the heir of Kamehameha the Great, ruled as Kamehameha II from 1797 to 1824. Liholiho was not a strong ruler and Kaahumanu proclaimed herself prime minister during his reign. Liholiho and his wife succumbed to the measles while in London. Liholiho was succeeded by Kauikeaouli (the youngest son of Kamehameha the Great), who ruled under the title of Kamehameha the III from 1824 to 1854.

HISTORY

The islands were left undisturbed by western influence until 1778 with the arrival of James Cook. He first spotted and visited Kaui and Oahu and he is believed to have arrived on Maui about November 25 or 26, 1778. He was later killed in a brawl on the big island of Hawaii.

New England missionaries and their families arrived in Lahaina in the spring of 1823 at the invitation of Queen Keopuolani. They brought drastic changes to the island with the education of the natives both spiritually and scholastically. The first high school and printing press west of the Rockies was built just outside of Lahaina and remnants of Lahainaluna still stand for visitors to see. (See Lahaina sights for more details).

Beginning in 1819 and continuing for nearly 40 years, whaling ships became a frequent sight in the Lahaina Harbor. The whalers hunted their prey north and south of the islands and off the Japanese Coast. Fifty ships were generally anchored off Lahaina, but at the peak of whaling days over 400 ships could be counted at Lahaina and an additional 167 in Honolulu's harbor. Allowing 25 to 30 men per ship you can quickly see the enormous number of sailors who flooded the area. While missionaries brought their Christian beliefs, the whaling men lived under their own belief that there was "No God West of the Horn". This presented a tremendous conflict between the sailors and missionaries, with the islanders caught right in the middle. (In 1846, a Lahaina census reported 3,445 Hawaiians 112 foreigners, 600 seamen, 155 adobe houses, 822 grass houses, 59 stone and wooden houses as well as 528 dogs.)

After months at sea, sailors arrived in Lahaina anxious for the grog shops and the native women. It was the missionaries who put the island girls in muumuus and set up guidelines that forbid the native girls to visit the ships in the harbor. In 1832, a coral fort was erected near the Lahaina harbor following an incident with the unhappy crew of one vessel. The story goes that a captain, disgruntled when he was detained in Lahaina for enticing "base women", ordered his crew to fire shots at the homes of some Lahaina area missionaries. Although the fort was demolished in 1854, remnants of the coral were re-excavated and a corner of the old fort reconstructed. You'll find it at the harbor side of the Banyan Tree.

A combination of things brought the downfall of the whaling industry. The onset of the Civil War depleted men and ships, (one Confederate warship reportedly set 24 whaling vessels ablaze) and the growth of the petroleum industry lessened the need for whale oil. Lastly the arctic freezes of 1871 and 1876 resulted in ships being crushed by the ice. In 1871 alone 33 whaling ships were lost in the Arctic Ocean. Lahaina, however, continues to maintain the charm and history of those bygone days.

The whaling era strengthened Hawaii's ties with the United States economically and the presence of the missionaries further strengthened this bond. The United States supported the islands in their desire to maintain their independence against other nations who tried to dominate. The last monarch was Lilokalani, who ruled from 1891 to 1893. Hawaii became a territory of the United States in 1900 and achieved statehood in 1959.

Sugar cane brought by the first Hawaiians was developed into a major industry on Maui. Two sons of missionaries, Henry P. Baldwin and Samuel T. Alexander played notable roles, and their construction of a water pipeline secured the future of the sugar industry and other agricultural development on the island.

Pineapple, another major agricultural industry, had its origins in 1813 when Don Marin planted the first pineapples. Later, in 1885 the smooth Cayenne variety, which is now the major crop, was introduced.

It was about 100 years ago that the Macadamia Nut tree arrived from Australia. It was intended to be an ornamental tree, having nuts that were most unagreeable to open. It was not until the 1950's that the development of the trees began to take a commercial course. Today, some sugar cane fields are being converted to Macadamia. It takes seven years for the grafted root, they do not grow from seed, to become a producing tree. A slow process, but much less polluting than the sugar cane industry. However, beware of their hazards, 1/2 ounce of nuts is 100 calories!

The Kula area of Maui has become the center for many delicious fruits and vegetables as well as the unusual Protea flower. Wineries are also making a comeback with the opening of the Tedeschi Winery a few years ago. They first began producing an unusual pineapple wine. In 1984 they introduced to the market a champagne that is already in great demand. Be sure to also sample the very sweet Maui onions which are grown in this area and are available for shipping home.

Early Whaling Days

GENERAL

OUR PERSONAL BESTS

BEST SPLURGE; Raffles Buffet Sunday Brunch at Stouffer's Wailea Resort

BEST SUNSET; COCKTAILS AND COMPLIMENTARY PU-PUS; Kapalua Bay Resort Lobby Bar

BEST BREAKFAST BUFFET VALUE; The Maui Surf at their Eight Bells Restaurant

BEST FRESH FISH; Island Fish House in Kihei and Kahului

BEST SALAD BAR; Royal Ocean Terrace

BEST DINNER VALUES; The early bird specials at the Moana Terrace at the Marriott Hotel, also at Leilani's at Whaler's Village. Sometimes early bird specials are also available at Chuck's in Kihei and Island Fish House

BEST RESTAURANT ATMOSPHERE; Swan Court at the Hyatt Regency Hotel

BEST DESSERT; The Chocoholic Bar at the Lahaina Provision Company located at the Hyatt Regency

BEST SHOPPING; A) Touristy — Lahaina waterfront B) Practical — Kaahumanu Shopping Center in Kahului C) Extravagant — Hyatt Regency shops

BEST HOTEL VALUE; The Marriott Hotel or Stouffer's Wailea Resort with a 50% off coupon from Entertainment '85

BEST HOTEL VALUE AT REGULAR PRICE; Maui Surf Hotel at Kaanapali

MOST SPECTACULAR HOTEL GROUNDS; Hyatt Regency at Kaanapali — Runners up: Kapalua Bay Resort and Stouffers Wailea

EXCURSIONS; Most spectacular — a helicopter tour. Most unusual — a bike trip down Haleakala. Best sailing — a day long snorkel and picnic to Lanai with the congenial crew on the Trilogy.

BEST BEACHES; A) Beautiful and safe — Kapalua Bay B) Unspoiled — Oneloa (Makena Beach)

BEST BODY SURFING; Slaughterhouse in winter

BEST SURFING; Honolua Bay and Hookipa Beach Park

BEST WINDSURFING; Hookipa Beach Park

BEST SNORKELING; A) North end — Honolua Bay in summer B) Kapalua area — Kapalua Bay C) Kaanapali — Black Rock at Sheraton D) Kihei/Wailea — Ulua/Mokapu Beach E) South end — Ahihi Kinau Natural Reserve F) Of Maui County — The island of Lanai at Hulopoe Beach Park (also called White Sand Manele Beach)

GENERAL _____

PRONUNCIATION OF MAUI'S PLACES, NAMES AND AREAS

Haleakala (HAH-leh-AH-kuh-LAH) means house of the sun

Hana (HAH-nuh) means rainy land

Honoapiilani (HOH-noh-AH-PEE-'ee-LAH-nee)

Iao (EE-AH-oh) means cloud supreme

Kaanapali (KAH-AH-nuh-PAH-lee) means land divided by cliffs

Kahana (Kuh-HAH-nuh) meaning unknown, of Tahitian origin

Kapalua (KAH-puh-LOO-uh) means two borders

Kihei (KEE-HEH-ee)

Kahului (Kah-hoo-LOO-ee) winning

Kula (koo-LUH)

Lahaina (LAH-HAH-ee-NAH) means unmerciful sun

Maalaea (MAH-'uh-LAHeh-uh) area of red dirt

Makawao (mah-kah-wah-oh) means forest beginning

Napili (NAH-PEE-lee) pili grass

Olowalu (oh-loh-wah-loo) means many hills

Paia (PAH-EE-uh) meaning unknown

Pukalani (poo-kah-lah-nee) means sky opening

Ulupalakua (OO-loo-PAH-luh-KOO-uh) ripe breadfruit

Wailea (WAH-ee-LEH-uh) water Lea (Lea was the canoe makers goddess)

Wailuku (WAHee-LOO-KOO) water of slaughter

COMMONLY USED HAWAIIAN WORDS AND THEIR MEANINGS

alii (ah-lee-ee) chief

aloha (ah-loh-hah) greetings

hale (Hah-lay) house

Heiau (heh-ee-ah-oo) temple

kai (kye) ocean

Kamaaina (Kah-mah-ai-nuh) native born

kane (kah-nay) man

kapu (kah-poo) keep out

keiki (kayee-kee) child

lanai (lah-nah-ee) porch or patio

luau (loo-ah-oo) feast

makai (mah-kah-ee) toward the ocean

mauka (mah-oo-kah) toward the mountain

menehune (may-nay-hoo-nee) Hawaiian dwarf or elf

moana (moh-ah-nah) ocean

ono (oh-no) delicious

paniolo (pah-nee-ou-loh) Hawaiian cowboy

pau (pow) finished

pupus (poo-poos) appetizers

wahine (wah-hee-nay) woman

wiki wiki (wee-kee, wee-kee) hurry

TRAVELING WITH CHILDREN

A few pointers may help make your vacation with your young family members a safer and more enjoyable one.

CAR SEATS: By law, children must travel in child safety seats. You may wish to bring your own with you. Several styles are permitted by airlines for use in the airline seats. It may also be checked as a piece of baggage. While most rental agencies do have car seats, you need to request them well in advance as they have a limited number.

BABYSITTING: Most hotels have some form of babysitting service and it will run about $5.00 an hour. There is also an independent babysitting service which will send a person to your hotel or condominium. They charge $5.00 an hour with a three hour minimum for one to two children, and an additional 50 cents an hour for each additional child. After contacting them and requesting the date and time, they will locate a sitter and call you back giving you the background information on the sitter who will be caring for your children. The sitters are 20 - 60 years and are male and female. They also have persons capable of working with handicapped children or adults. A 24 hour notice is appreciated and they service between the hours of 6 a.m. and 2 a.m. For more information contact BABYSITTING SERVICES OF MAUI PO Box 1595, Kihei, Maui, HI 96753. Phone: 661-4118 8a.m. - 5 p.m. Monday thru Friday or 879-6371

GENERAL

7 p.m. - 9 p.m. daily. Also check with your condo office as they sometimes have numbers of local sitters.

CRIBS: Most condos and hotels offer cribs for a rental fee that may vary from $2 a night to $10 per night.

EMERGENCIES: There is a clinic in Lahaina that will take walk-in patients. It is located at 130 Prison Street, phone 661-0051. In the Kihei/Wailea area there are doctor offices located at 1325 S. Kihei Rd., phone 879-7781. Kaiser Permanente Medical Care Facilities are located in Wailuku, phone 242-6622 or in Lahaina at 661-0081.

A new island service is a children's day camp, Kamp Keiki O' Kai for children aged 5-12. A half or full day of camp includes island tours, snorkeling, or beach activities. Hotel pickups provided in the Lahaina to Kapalua area. Phone 661-0846. During the summer months many of the resort hotels offer partial or full day activities for children.

HELPFUL INFORMATION

Booths located at the shopping areas can provide you with helpful information and lots of brochures!

Hawaii Visitors Bureau, 26 N. Puuene Avenue, Wailuku, phone 877-7822.

KBPC Cable Television, channel 7, in the Kihei/Wailea area is designed especially with tourists in mind. Information on recreation, real estate, shopping, restaurants and other points of interest are covered.

The Guide to Maui — a weekly published magazine that is free at newstands. It covers where to go, what to do, dining out, entertainment and shopping. It also has a number of discount coupons.

This Week Maui — published each Friday is also free. Activities, shopping, entertainment, maps and coupons are featured.

Rent a car Drive Guide — This free bi-monthly publication will accompany your rental car. It also has a variety of discounts for local area merchants.

Maui Beach Press — Published each Friday, this free publication in a newspaper format has informative local stories, maps, entertainment, restaurant information and, you guessed it, more coupons!

Maui News — This is the local area newspaper, published Monday thru Friday and available for 25 cents.

Maui Gold — Published four times yearly, this is also a free publication.

The Bulletin — This is primarily a T.V. guide which is published newspaper style and available at no charge. However, it does have features on some local events and is very popular among the residents. You may have a little more trouble locating a copy of this one.

NOTE: Most of these free publications offer coupons which will give you discounts on everything from meals to sporting activities to clothing. It may save you a bit to search through these in advance of making your purchases.

HELPFUL PHONE NUMBERS

Ambulance-Police-Fire	911
Poison Control	1-941-4411
Helpline (suicide & crisis center)	244-7407
State Parks (camping permits)	244-4354
County Parks (camping permits)	244-5514
Hawaii Visitors Bureau in Kahului	877-7822
Time of Day	242-0212
Information and Complaint Office	244-7756
Haleakala National Park	572-7749 572-9306
Weather-Maui	877-5111
Weather-Marine	877-3477
Weather-Recreational Area	877-5124

GETTING THERE

CLIMATE:

First a few words to the new-comer about Maui's climate. The weather is fair here year-round, with the winter months having more rainfall than summer. The temperatures remain quite constant. Following are the average daily highs and lows for each month.

January	80/64	May	84/67	September	87/70
February	79/64	June	86/69	October	86/69
March	80/64	July	86/70	November	83/68
April	82/66	August	87/71	December	80/66

Summer type wear is suitable all year round. However, a warm sweater or light-weight jacket is a good idea for evenings and trips such as to Haleakala.

ARRIVAL:

Generally, visitors arrive via the largest of Maui's three airports, which is located in Kahului. There are currently five airlines which service the island; Hawaiian, Aloha, Mid-Pacific, Royal Hawaiian and in 1983 United Airlines began a direct mainland flight. The other airlines serve as inter-island carriers. If you plan to stay in the Lahaina to Kapalua areas and are flying over from one of the other islands, we would suggest you try flying Royal Hawaiian Airlines into the smaller Kaanapali airport. Their small twin engine planes allow you a seat up front with the pilot, who will provide you with a first class scenic air tour. There are direct flights from Oahu to Maui, but we chose one with a

GENERAL

stop over on Molokai. It allowed us to take advantage of a close up view of the fabulous volcanic cliffs located there. Although the price of this inter-island trip is slightly higher than on the other inter-island jets (about $50 each way), consider an air tour of Maui on one of the helicopter services which would run $125. (Royal Hawaiian also offers senior citizen discounts which could save you as much as 30%). Also, by arriving in Kaanapali you save the half-hour drive from Kahului. There are rental car agencies located here, however, you won't have the selection that you have at the Kahului airport. The Kaanapali airport is currently on prime beachfront property and is scheduled to be closed, but hopefully, will be moved just across the road. With the introduction of the new United direct service, other major airlines are offering very good package deals which include your transportation from Oahu to Maui.

GETTING AROUND:

After arriving there are several options. Taxi cabs, because of the distances between areas, can be very costly. (i.e., $30 to travel from Kahului to Kaanapali) There are several bus/limo services to transport you to your hotel also. The third option is a rental car.

From the airport :
The Grayline airport, phone 887-5507 for reservations, provides the Kahului airport with service to Lahaina, Kaanapali, Kihei and Wailea. The charge to the Lahaina or Kaanapali areas is $6.75 and to Kihei or Wailea $5.50.

Mita Inc. is a local taxi company, phone 871-4622. They can provide service from the Kahului airport to the Lahaina area for $25 - $30 per car and to Kihei-Wailea for about $10-$18. Service from the Kaanapali airport to either Kaanapali or Kapalua would be much less expensive.

Local transportation:
If you don't choose a rental car, you may find limited public transportation. The Maui Transit System, phone 661-3827, runs between Lahaina and Kaanapali every 15 minutes between 8 a.m. and 5 p.m., then every half hour between 5 p.m. and 10 p.m. It also runs from Lahaina to Napili and Kapalua. One way rate is $1.50 no matter how far you travel. Three round trips are made daily between Lahaina and Wailea and points in-between. The price depending on the distance you travel. The Kaanapali jitney runs through the Kaanapali Beach Resort area daily between 9 a.m. and 9 p.m. and is $2.00 for an all day pass. In the Wailea resort area a complimentary shuttle runs every 15-20 minutes between 6:30 a.m. and 10:30 p.m., making stops at condos and shopping centers. In Kapalua, their shuttle is on call from 7 a.m. to 11 p.m. Several restaurants in the Kaanapali area offer free local hotel pickup. (See Restaurant section) Most tours offer pickup at your hotel.

GENERAL

RENTAL CARS AND TRUCKS:

A choice of more than 30 car rental agencies await you on Maui. Some are local island operations, others are nation-wide chains, but all are very competitive. The prices listed will give you a basic idea, but you may be pleasantly surprised to find the rates even lower if you time your arrival in the middle of a price war, or a super summer discount. We would highly recommend all visitors take advantage of one of the island's best bargains, a rental car.

The policies of all the rental car agencies are basically the same. Most require a minimum age which ranges from 21 to 25 years and a maximum age of 70 is also established by many. All feature unlimited mileage with you buying the gas (it runs 35-40 cents per liter). A few require a deposit or major credit card to hold your reservation. Insurance is an option you may wish, which will run you an additional $3 - $7 a day. A few agencies will require insurance for those under age 25. Add to the rental price a 4% sales tax. The Kahului airport has a large courtesy phone board in the main terminal (not at the United terminal). This free phone is for those rental agencies who do not have an airport booth so you can call for a shuttle pick up. A pay phone is available in the United terminal. A few agencies will take your flight information when your car reservation is made and will meet you and your luggage at the airport with your car.

AAA RENT A CAR 150 Hana Hwy, Kahului, Maui, HI 96732 _PHONE:_ 1-808-871-4610 or 1-808-871-7473 _SERVICE:_ Kahului Airport, courtesy phone #32 for pickup _TYPE OF CARS:_ Toyota Tercels, Chevy Chevettes, Chevy Malibu 4-dr., with air conditioning, vans and wagons. All are late models. _RATES:_ High season - used compacts $13.95 daily, ($83.70 weekly), late model compacts $18.95 daily, ($113.70), midsize with air $20.95 daily ($125.70), station wagons with air $20.95 daily ($179.70), vans $59.95 daily ($359.70). Low season - rates are discounted. Mastercard and Visa are accepted.

ALAMO RENT A CAR Kahului Airport _PHONE:_ 1-800-327-9633 _SERVICE:_ Kahului Airport _TYPE OF CARS:_ GM products _RATES:_ Compact cars $99.95 a week, no compact wagons, mid-size cars $34.95 a day, $189.95 a week.

AMERICAN INTERNATIONAL PO Box 1647, Kahului, Maui, HI 96732 _PHONE:_ 1-800-527-0160 or at Kahului 1-808-877-7604 or at Kaanapali 1-808-661-4808 _SERVICE:_ Kahului and Kaanapali airports _TYPE OF CARS:_ new and late model Chevrolet, Ford, Datsuns. Compacts, midsize, station wagons all offer air conditioning options. _RATES:_ High season - compacts $21.95 daily ($119.95 weekly), midsize $30.95 daily ($179.95). Low season - prices quoted at time of rental.

ANDRES RENT A CAR Kahului Airport _PHONE:_ 1-808-877-5378 _SERVICE:_ Kahului airport, check in at airport booth. _TYPE OF CARS:_ Compact Toyotas and Datsuns, also Ford Fairmonts _RATES:_ High Season - Compact automatic $26.95 daily, $33.95 daily for wagon without airconditioning. Midsize without air conditioning $35.95 daily. Low season - compacts $17.95 daily, wagon $27.95 daily, midsize $31.95 daily.

ATLAS U DRIVE P.O. Box 126 Puunene, Maui, HI 96784 _PHONE:_ 1-808-877-7208 _SERVICE:_ Kahului airport: car delivered to you at terminal. _TYPE OF CARS:_ Late model Toyota Tercels with a choice of 2 door standard transmissions or 4 door automatic, also Ford

GENERAL

Escort compact wagons, sedans, 6 passenger wagons, 9 passenger vans. *RATES:* Low season — Summer specials are promoted which include the rental price, tax and insurance. A compact standard runs $115 weekly, automatic $130.50 weekly, compact wagon $145 weekly, sedans $188.95 weekly, 6 passenger wagons $203.50, 9 passengers $254.50. Call for high season rates. Mastercard or Visa accepted.

AVIS
PHONE: 1-800-331-2212 or locally at Kahului airport 1-808-871-7575 and at Kaanapali 1-808-661-4588. *SERVICE:* Kahului airport and Kaanapali area. Check in at Kahului airport booth. *TYPE OF CARS:* late model featuring GM and imports RATES: compacts $27 daily ($129 for 5 - 7 days), midsize $35 daily ($169 weekly), convertibles (Sunbird or LeBaron) $59 daily ($259 weekly). Prices vary seasonally. Mastercard, VISA, Diners, American Express and Cart Blanche are all accepted.

BEACH BOY CAMPERS 1765 S. Kihei Rd., Kihei, Maui *PHONE:* 1-808-879-5292 *SERVICE:* Kahului airport, pickup provided *RATES:* All campers are Toyota or Datsun and sleep 4. Three sizes are offered. Minicabs offer a stove, sink, icebox, sheets, towels, blankets, kitchen accessories and run $45 a day plus 6 cents a mile. A 16 foot camper features gas refrigerator, hot water and shower for $55 a daily plus 6 cents a mile. A 19 foot camper runs $60 a day plus 6 cents a mile.

BUDGET
PHONE: 1-800-527-0700 — Kaanapali 1-808-661-4660 — Wailea 1-808-879-9150 — Kahului 1-808-871-8811

CHARTON U DRIVE 456 Dairy Road, Kahului, Maui, HI *PHONE:* 1-808-877-7836 in Kahului or 1-808-661-3489 in Kaanapali. After hours 1-800-244-0008. *SERVICE:* Kahului airport with a booth also at the Maui Eldorado Resort in Kaanapali *TYPE OF CARS:* Compact, sedans and wagons *RATES:* Compact automatic $19.95 daily ($119 weekly), compact wagons $21.95 daily ($133). Sedan with no air conditioning $24.95 daily ($154), with air conditioning add $3 per day. Wagon with air conditioning $30.95 daily ($189). Add $2 a day extra from December 1 to April 15. A one week minimum reservation is required December 1 - April 15 and $50 is required to hold reservations.

CONVERTIBLES HAWAII 552 Keolani Place *PHONE:* 1-800-367-5230 or 1-808-877-0031 *SERVICE:* Kahului airport, also Kaanapali (by reservation only). Kahului courtesy phone #15 for pick up. *TYPE OF CARS:* Fords, sedans and convertibles; Datsuns, sedans, coupes and convertibles; VW Rabbit convertibles, also vans and station wagons. (All with air conditioning options.) *RATES:* USED - compact standard $13.95 daily ($89 weekly), compact automatic $15.95 ($99), compact station wagon automatic $16.95 ($110), midsized four door with air $19.95 ($125). NEW MODELS - compact standard $19.95 ($125), compact automatic $21.95 ($139), midsize four door air conditioned $26.95 ($175), wagons and vans $26.95 to $34.95 ($175 - $220), Mustang convertible $49.95 ($325), VW convertibles $38.95 ($240). Mastercard, Visa, Diners, American Express, Carte Blanche are all accepted.

DOLLAR RENT A CAR 2270 Kalakaua Avenue #1010, Honolulu, Hawaii 96815 *PHONE:* 1-800-926-4200 or Kahului 1-808-877-6526 or Kaanapali 1-808-661-3037 *SERVICE:* Kahului airport and Kaanapali airport with rental cars also available at the Maui Surf Hotel, Kaanapali Shores and the Napili Kai Beach Club. *TYPE OF CARS:* Most offer air conditioning as an option. Featured are compact Datsuns or Toyotas, Buick, Ford, Cadillac, Dodge. *RATES:* Compact standard $22.95 ($126.25), automatic $24.95 ($137.25), compact wagon $29.95 ($164.75), midsize sedan $34.95 ($192.25), midsize wagon $39.95 ($219.75), T-Bird

GENERAL

or Monte Carlo $44.95 ($274.75), 4 wheel drive jeep or VW convertible $49.95 ($274.75), 9 passenger wagon or van $54.95 ($302.25), luxury sedan (i.e. Cadillac) $59.95 ($329.75), Mustang convertible or 12 passenger van $69.96 ($384.75). Mastercard, Visa, Diners and American Express accepted.

EL CHEAPO P.O. Box 1065, Puuene, Maui, HI 96784 *PHONE:* 1-808-877-5851 *SERVICE:* Kahului Airport, for pickup use courtesy phone #24 *TYPE OF CARS:* Toyotas Tercels, Suzuki Jeeps, all late model *RATES:* High season - $14.95 daily ($95 weekly) Low season - $13.95 ($89.95). Jeeps $30 daily. No air conditioning. Mastercard and Visa accepted.

FORD RENT A CAR PO Box 2123, Kahului, Maui, HI *PHONE:* 1-808-871-7721

FOX CAR RENTALS 335 Wakea Avenue, Kahului Maui, HI *PHONE:* 1-800-367-2924 *SERVICE:* Kahului airport *RATES:* Economy cars $103.95 per week, compacts $113.95/week, Wagons $137.95/week.

HERTZ
PHONE: 1-800-654-8200 *SERVICE:* Kahului airport, Kaanapali Beach Hotel, Sheraton, Hyatt Regency, Marriott at Kaanapali and the Wailea Resort.

HOLIDAY Kahului Airport, Kahului, Maui, HI 96793 *PHONE:* 1-800-367-2631 or 1-808-877-2464 *SERVICE:* Kahului airport, check in at terminal booth *TYPE OF CARS:* Chevrolet chevettes, Ford Fairmonts with air conditioning, Mercury Marquis, six and nine passenger wagons. *RATES:* Compact standard $18.95 daily ($89.50 weekly), compact automatic $19.95 ($99.50), sedan with air $27.95 ($159.50), six passenger wagon $34.95 ($189.50), Lincoln or nine passenger wagon $39.95 ($219.50). Visa, Mastercard and American Express are accepted.

ISLAND RENT A CAR 110 S. Hana Hwy *PHONE:* 1-808-871-6246 *SERVICE:* Kahului Airport, call for pick up *RATES:* Compact with standard transmission $89.95/week, Cutlas Supreme $195/week.

JBJ RENT A CAR PO Box 1043 Paia, Maui, HI 96779 *PHONE:* 1-808-579-8188 *SERVICE:* Kahului Airport *TYPE OF CARS:* Aspens, Plymouth Champs, Chevettes *RATES:* Compacts $11.95 - $14.95, Champs $13.95, Midsize with air conditioning $14.95 daily.

KAMAAINA RENT A CAR P.O. Box 1851, Kahului, Maui, HI 96732 *PHONE:* 1-808-877-5460 *SERVICE:* Kahului airport, use courtesy phone #2 *TYPE OF CARS:* Toyota Tercels, Ford Escorts, Ford Fairmonts, all new to three years old. *RATES:* Subcompact automatic or standard $18.50 for 24 hours, $16.50 per day for 7 - 27 days, $14 per day for 28 days or longer. Midsize $22.50 per 24 hours, $2 discount for use 7 - 27 days, $18 per day for use 28 days or longer. Master card and Visa accepted.

KAMAOLE RENT A CAR Located in Kihei at Kai Nani Village *PHONE:* 1-808-879-1103 *SERVICE:* From the Kihei area *TYPE OF CARS:* Late model Toyota Tercels only *RATES:* $126 weekly. Visa and Mastercard accepted.

KIHEI HOLIDAZE 1979 S. Kihei Rd., Kihei, Maui, HI *PHONE:* 1-808-879-1905 *SERVICE:* Kihei and Wailea area *TYPE OF CARS:* New compacts, intermediates, wagons, jeeps, convertibles. *RATES:* Compact standard $16.50, automatic $18.50, intermediate $25, six passenger wagon $29.95, Mustang convertible or Jeep CJ7 $45. M.C., Visa, A.E. honored.

KIHEI U DRIVE Did not wish to be included

KLUNKERS USED CARS 456 Dairy Road, Kahului, Maui, HI 96732 *PHONE:* 1-808-877

GENERAL

-3197 SERVICE: Kahului Airport TYPE OF CARS: Late model Fords, Toyotas, Datsuns, Subaru and others RATES: Vary seasonally. Three day minimum rental required. No rentals or rental turn in on Sundays. Cars picked up and dropped off at Kahului Base lot. Phone between the hours of 8 a.m. and 4:30 p.m. Monday thru Saturday. Visa and Mastercard accepted.

LUXURY SPORTS CAR RENTAL
PHONE: 1-808-661-5646 TYPE OF CARS: Mercedes, Porsche, Corvettes, Camaros RATES: $49 - $195 per day

MAUI AIRPORT RENT A CAR 905 W. Mokuea Place, Kahului, Maui, HI 96732 PHONE: 1-808-877-7368 (office) 1-808-877-0488 (airport) SERVICE: Kahului airport TYPE OF CARS: 4 dr. Toyota Tercels. Ford Fairmont, all new models RATES: Compact $22.95 daily ($137.70 weekly), Intermediate $31.95 ($191.70), 6 passenger wagon $35.95 ($215.70), 12 and 15 passenger wagons $62 - $76 daily. Master card, Visa, Diners, American Express, and Carte Blanche accepted.

MAUI CAR RENTALS 353 Hanamau, Kahului, Maui, HI 96732 PHONE: 1-808-877-2081 or 1-800-367-2952 SERVICE: Kahului airport TYPE OF CARS: New and late models RATES: Compact automatic $17.95 ($107.95 weekly), compact wagon $23.95 ($143.95), Intermediate with air conditioning $27.95 ($167.95), Intermediate wagon $30.95 ($185.95), seven and twelve passenger vans $44.95 - $55.95 ($269.95 - $335.95). Master card, Visa, Diners, American Express, and Carte Blanche are all honored.

MAUI RENT A JEEP 450 Dairy Rd., Kahului, Maui 96732 PHONE: 1-808-877-6626 SERVICE: Kahului Airport RATES: $29.95/day for two week drive, $34.95 for four wheel drive (CJ-7 or Suzuki), $39.95 for Renegade. A $5 per day discount is offered for their weekly rate.

MAUI SAILING CENTER Sugar Beach Condominiums in Kihei, 1-808-877-3065 Jeep rentals only

NATIONAL
PHONE: 1-800-328-6321 toll free or Kahului 1-808-877-5347 SERVICE: Kahului Airport, call direct on courtesy phone TYPE OF CARS: new Toyotas, Mazdas, Nissan and just about everything else! RATES: Vary according to season. Economy sedan with standard transmission $69 weekly, automatic $79 weekly, compact sedan with air conditioning $119, intermediate with air conditioning and automatic $149. Also available are full size cars, wagons, jeeps and vans. Mastercard, Visa, Diners, American Express, Carte Blanche and National Car Rental credit cards are accepted.

PACIFIC RENT A CAR Kahului Airport, Kahului, Maui, HI 96753 PHONE: 1-808-877-3065 SERVICE: Kahului Airport RATES: Compacts $80 per week, Toyotas or Datsuns, Intermediates $140.95 per week, Mustangs, Zepher or Granada, Compact wagons, $98.50 per week.

PARADISE RENT A CAR 1939 S. Kihei Rd., Kihei, Maui, HI 96753 PHONE: 1-808-879-8788 SERVICE: Kahului airport, use courtesy phone #3 for pickup TYPE OF CARS: Datsun, Mazda, Toyota, Ford, Suzuki Jeep (late models) RATES: High season - compact $17.95 daily, $15.95 per day for three day rental or $89 weekly. Low season - compact $15.95 or $13.95 for three day rental. Fords run $20.95 daily. Mastercard, Visa and American Express accepted.

RAINBOW P.O. Box 426, 161 Dickenson Street, Lahaina, Maui 96761 PHONE: 1-808-661

-8734 SERVICE: Kaanapali airport TYPE OF CARS: Late model Toyotas, trucks, no air conditioning available. RATES: Compacts $14.50 daily, $87 weekly, $325 monthly, or 1/2 ton trucks $28.00 daily. Mastercard, Visa, and American Express accepted.

RENT A WRECK 522 Keolani Place PHONE: 1-808-877-5600 or 1-800-367-5230 TYPE OF CARS: later models as well as some new RATES: Compact, standard $13.95/day, $89/week; compact wagon $16/day, $110/week. Intermediate with air $19.95/day, $125/week

ROBERTS Kahului Airport PHONE: 1-808-877-5038 SERVICE: Kahului Airport TYPE OF CARS: New models, Toyota RATES: Year round rates for compact $20.95 with standard, $22.95 with automatic transmission. All midsize are Fords with air conditioning $30.95. Compact and full size wagons also available. Mastercard and Visa accepted.

SOUTH SEAS P.O. Box 440, Kahului, Maui, HI 96732 PHONE: 1-808-877-6768 / Hours: 8 a.m. - 5 p.m. unless prior arrangements are made SERVICE: Kahului airport, phone #18 on courtesy board for pickup RATES: High season - compacts with standard or automatic $20.95 ($125.95 weekly), compact wagons $27.95 ($165.95), large wagons with air conditioning $34.95 ($207.95). Low season rates deduct $3.00 per day from daily rate. A $50 deposit is required to confirm and hold your reservation. Visa, Mastercard and American Express are honored.

SUNSHINE RENT A CAR Kahului Airport, Kahului, Maui, HI 96732 PHONE: 1-808-871-6222 SERVICE: Kahului airport RATES: Compact Toyota $89.95/week, Ford Tempo with air conditioning $135/week.

THRIFTY 532 Keolani PHONE: 1-800-367-2277 or 1-808-871-7596 SERVICE: Kahului and Kaanapali airports TYPE OF CARS: Toyota, Datsuns, and Chrysler products RATES: compacts $21.95 manual, $25.95 automatic, midsize with air $26.95. Major credit cards accepted.

TOM'S RENT A CAR P.O. Box 2123, Kahului, Maui, HI 96732 PHONE: 1-800-367-5224 or 1-808-871-7721 SERVICE: Kahului Airport use courtesy phone #16 & #20 TYPE OF CARS: Fords, Datsuns, Toyotas RATES: Compact standard $19.95 ($119.95 weekly), automatic $21.95, ($128.95) with air $24.95 ($152.95), standard sedan with air $28.95 ($152.95), convertibles such as VW or station wagons $34.95 ($209). Also luxury cars, wagons, vans and jeeps available. Mastercard, Visa and American Express honored.

TRANS MAUI RENT A CAR Kahului Airport, Kahului, Maui, HI 96732 PHONE: 1-800-367-5228 or 1-808-877-5222 SERVICE: Kahului Airport, check in at airport booth TYPE OF CARS: New and late model Toyota Tercels, AMC concords, Ford Granada wagons. RATES: Compact automatic or standard $18.45 daily ($108.45 weekly), intermediate sedan with air conditioning $27.45 ($164.50), station wagons $29.45 ($185.50). Mastercard, Visa and American Express honored.

TROPICAL RENT A CAR 41 Hana Hwy, Kahului, Maui, HI 96732 PHONE: 1-800-367-5140 toll free or Kahului 1-808-877-0002, Kaanapali 1-808-661-0061, Kihei 1-808-879-1514 SERVICE: Kaanapali and Kahului airports. At Kahului call on courtesy phone for van to pick you up TYPE OF CARS: Lots of Toyotas and Datsuns, also midsized, wagons and more RATES: Economy $19.95 ($119.95 weekly), subcompact $22.95 ($129.95), compact $24.95 ($139.95), intermediate $28.95 ($174.95), wagon $38.95 ($209.95). Mastercard, Visa, Diners, American Express and Carte Blanche honored. SPECIAL NOTE: This is our preferred rental agency. We have always had a reliable car and they offer some of the

GENERAL

best super bonus priced deals you can find. One occasion found an economy car going for $75 a week. This one is definitely worth checking out!

24 KARAT CARS Located at Kaanapali Transportation Center PHONE: 1-808-667-6289 RATES: VW Rabbit convertibles $49.95/day, $299.75/week; VW Vanagon $59.95/day, $359.75/week: Porsche 911 Targa $195/day, $1170/week. Mercedes convertibles for $175.95/day. Rates may be higher during holidays or peak periods.

UNITED CAR RENTAL 542 Keolani Place, Kahului, Maui, HI 96732 PHONE: 1-808-871-7328 SERVICE: Kahului and Kaanapali airports. Also in Lahaina at 672 Wainee Street TYPE OF CARS: New and late models, compact, midsize, full size, vans and jeeps. Air conditioning available on cars that are midsized and up. RATES: Compact standard $18.95 daily ($113.70 weekly), automatic $21.95 ($131.70), midsize with air $28.95 ($173.70), 6 passenger wagon with air conditioning $34.95 ($209.70), 9 passenger wagon with air conditioning $44.95 vans $69.96 - $79.95 ($419.70 - $479.70), Suzuki jeep $38.95, ($233.70). Major credit cards accepted.

UPTOWN SERVICE 2085 Main Street, Wailuku, Maui, HI PHONE: 1-808-244-0869 SERVICE: Kahului airport pickup available TYPE OF CARS: A limited number of Datsuns and Toyotas. No rentals on Saturday or Sunday.

VIP CAR RENTAL Dairy Road, Kahului, Maui SERVICE: Kahului Airport TYPE OF CARS: Datsun, Mazda, Toyota, Nova and Fairmont RATES: Compact automatic $21.95 ($129.95), standard $17.95 ($119.95), wagon $25, ($119.95), midsize older models $25 ($155), new models $29.95 ($189). Low season rates are discounted. Mastercard, Visa and American Express are accepted.

WORD OF MOUTH RENT A CAR Dairy Road, Kahului, Maui, HI 96732 PHONE: 1-808-877-2436 SERVICE: Kahului airport, use courtesy phone TYPE OF CARS: Datsun, Toyota, also midsize, AMC Concord wagons. Most intermediates offer air conditioning. All cars are late model. RATES: 1980 - 1982 models $85 weekly, midsize $115 weekly. Mastercard and Visa accepted.

A WORD OR TWO ABOUT ISLAND FISH

Whether cooking fish at your condominium or eating out, the names of the island fish can be confusing. While local shore fishermen catch shallow water fish such as goatfish or papio for their dinner table, commercial fishermen angle for two types. The steakfish are caught trolling in deep waters and include Ahi, Ono, Mahi, which sometimes provide a healthy struggle before being landed. The more delicate bottom fish include Opakapaka or Onaga and they are caught on ledges or shelves off Maui's west shorelines with lines dropped as deep as 1,500 feet. Here is a little background on the popular fish you might find on your menu.

A'U — The broadbill swordfish averages 250 pounds in Hawaiian waters. The broadbill is hard to locate, difficult to hook and a challenge to land. It would be classified as a steakfish.

AHI — The yellow fin tuna (Allison tuna) is caught in deep waters off the Kauai coast. The pinkish red meat is firm yet flakey. This fish is popular for

GENERAL

sashimi. They weigh in between 60 and 280 pounds.

ALBACORE — This smaller version of the Ahi averages 40 - 50 pounds and is lighter in both texture and color.

AKU — This is the blue fin tuna.

EHU — Snapper

HAPU — Hawaiian Sea Bass

KAMAKAMAKA — Island catfish is a very tasty and popular dish, however, a little difficult to find at most restaurants.

LEHI — This fish is a newer addition to restaurant menus with a growing popularity for it's similarity to Mahi Mahi.

MAHI MAHI — Although called the dolphin fish, this is no relation to Flipper or his friends. It is caught while trolling and weighs between 10 and 65 pounds. This is a seasonal fish which causes it to command a high price when fresh. BEWARE, while excellent fresh, it is often served in restaurants having arrived from the Phillipines frozen and is far less pleasing. A clue as to whether fresh or frozen may be the price tag. If it runs less than $10 it is probably the frozen variety. Fresh Mahi will run $14 - $20 a dinner. This fish has excellent white meat that is moist and light. It is very good sauteed.

MU'U — We tried this mild white fish at the Makawao Steak House. They serve it quite often and we were told there is no common name for this fish.

ONAGA — (ULA ULA) Red snapper is a local favorite. Caught in holes that are 1,000 feet or deeper this fish has an attractive hot pink exterior with tender juicy white meat inside.

ONO — A game fish also known as Wahoo. The word ONO means very good in Hawaiian. A member of the Barracuda family, it's white meat is flakey and moist. Caught at depths of 25 - 100 fathoms while trolling. It weighs between 15 and 65 pounds.

OPAKAPAKA — Is otherwise known as pink snapper and one of our favorites. The meat is very light and flakey with a delicate flavor.

PAPIO — This fish is a baby Ulua and is caught in shallow waters weighing 5 - 25 pounds.

UKU — The meat of this grey snapper is light and firm white meat with a slight texture. It is very popular with local residents. This fish is caught off Kauai, usually in the deep Paka Holes. The texture of this fish varies with it's size.

ULUA — Also known as Pompano, this fish is firm and flakey with a steaklike textured white meat. It is caught trolling, bottom fishing or speared by divers. It weighs between 15 and 110 pounds.

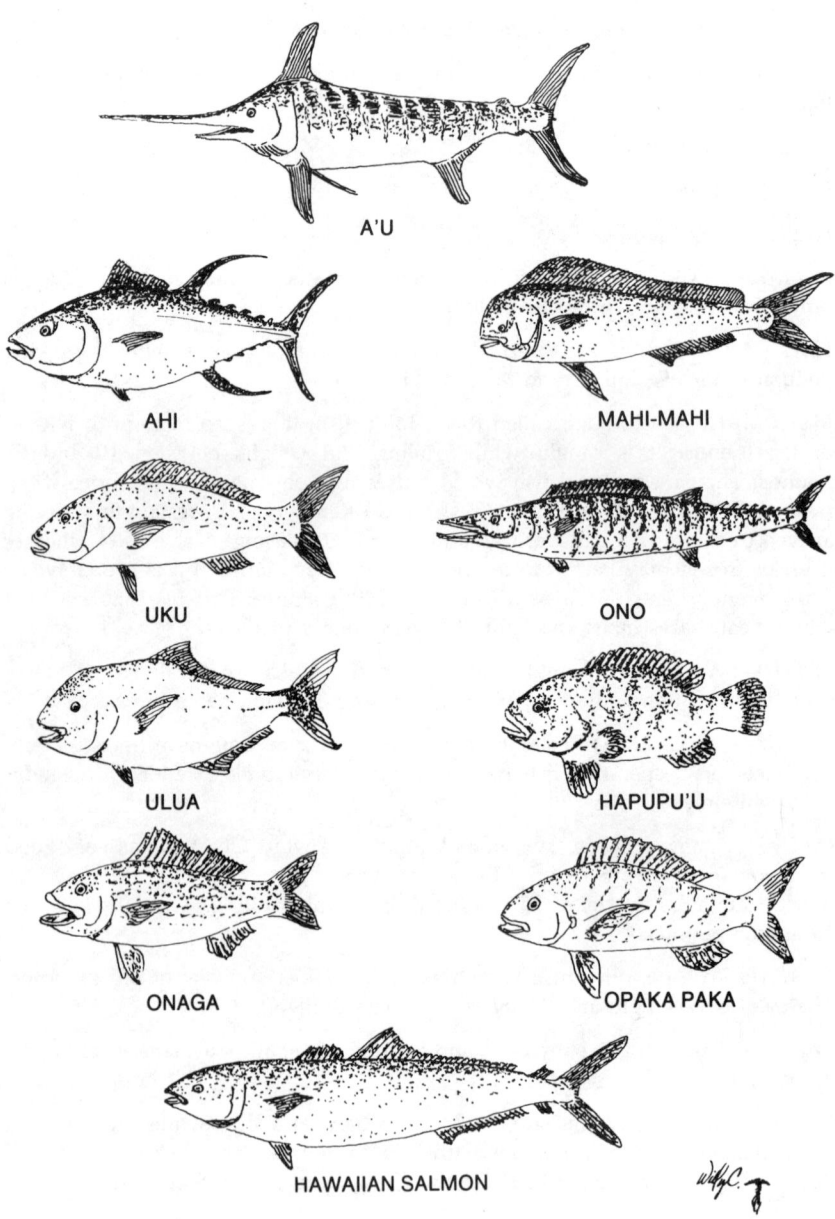

GENERAL

ANNUAL MAUI EVENTS

JANUARY

FEBRUARY

MARCH
—Annual Maui Marathon from Wailuku to Lahaina Sponsored by Valley Isle Road Runners —Annual Kukini Run - along the Kahakuloa Valley Trail —26th Prince Kuhio Day - A State Holiday —LPGA Womens Kemper Open at Kaanapali Golf Course

APRIL

MAY
—May Day celebration in Wailea

JUNE
—King Kamehameha Day Celebration —Maui Upcountry Fair

JULY
—4th Annual 4th of July Rodeo & Parade in Makawao —Canoe races at Hookipa State Park —Maui Jaycees Carnival at Kahului Fairground — Annual Sausa Cup races in Lahaina, sponsored by the Lahaina Yacht Club —Victoria to Maui Yacht Race

AUGUST
—Kapalua Music Festival —Run to the Sun Marathon - A grueling trek from sea level up to the 10,000 foot level of Haleakala Crater —21st Admissions Day - A State Holiday

SEPTEMBER
—Maui County Rodeo in Makawao

OCTOBER
—Aloha Week Festival —Maui County Fair at the Kahului Fairgrounds

NOVEMBER
—Na Mele O'Maui Festival at Lahaina & Kaanapali Beach Resorts —Kapalua International Championship of Golf —Queen Kaahumanu Festival at Maui High School —Sand Castle contest at Kaanapali Beach in front of Whaler's Village

DECEMBER

For exact dates of these events write the: Hawaii Visitors Bureau Honolulu, Hawaii 96815 and request the Hawaii Special Events Calendar. The calendar gives non annual information on who to contact as well.

WHERE TO STAY-WHAT TO SEE

Maui has two "price" seasons. Off or low season is generally considered to be April 15 until December 1 and the rates are discounted at some places as much as 30%. However, different resorts and condominiums may vary these dates by as much as two weeks, one way or the other. A few resorts are going to a flat year round rate. Ironically some of the best weather is during the fall. Temperatures are cooler than summer and it is less rainy than the spring months. (See Getting Around section for year round temperatures).

For a long term stay on the island of Maui, accommodations with a kitchen or kitchenette is almost a requirement. The cost of having a unit with cooking facilities will result in significant savings on your food bill. There are several large chain grocery stores around the island with fairly competitive prices, although things at the store will run slightly higher than on the mainland. (See Shopping Section for more information.)

Following in this chapter are a listing of most of the condominiums and hotels on the island. Condos are prolific, and the prices and facilities they offer can be quite varied. We have tried to indicate our own personal comments and *'s by the ones we felt were the best buys or special in some way. However, it was impossible for us to view all the units and since condominiums are privately owned, each unit can vary in it's furnishings and it's condition.

Money can be saved by using the following tips when choosing a place to settle. First, it is less expensive to stay during the off or low season. Secondly, there are some areas that are much less expensive. Although Kahului has some very inexpensive motel units, we can't recommend this area as a place to headquarter your stay. The weather is wetter in winter and hotter in summer than the other side of the island and there are few good beaches. There are some terrific condo buys in the Kihei area and if you prefer, the northern area above Lahaina has some older complexes that are reasonably good values. Thirdly, some condo type units without kitchens are less expensive, but you must weigh the cost savings versus doing your own cooking. We found some pleasant condo units either across the road from the beach, or on a rocky, less attractive beach. This can represent a tremendous savings and there are good beaches a short walk or drive away. Also, hotel rooms or condos with garden or mountain views are less costly than oceanview or oceanfront rooms. We find the mountain view, especially in Kaanapali to be in fact, superior. Not only are the mountains gorgeous, but your room does not get full day sunlight and stays cooler.

WHERE TO STAY — WHAT TO SEE
Wailuku & Kahului

There is a growing trend to offer only limited maid service in the condominiums, perhaps only on check out or once a week. Additional maid service is usually available for an extra charge. Rooms without telephones or color televisions usually have lower prices and a few condominiums do not have pools. Lastly, many condominiums have a no credit card policy and even request payment in full as much as four weeks prior to your arrival. We have indicated toll free 800 numbers when available. Look for an 808 area code preceeding the non-toll free numbers. Travel agents will be able to book your stay in the Maui hotels and also in most condominiums. We have listed the contacts for each condominium which offered the lesser prices. Some condominium rental agencies can book you, but with slightly higher prices. A few words of caution, condominium units within one complex can differ greatly and if a phone is important to you ask! We were astonished at how few condominium units had telephones, however, most offer a courtesy phone or pay phone at the office. Some units have washers and dryers in the rooms, while others do not. Prices we have listed do not include the 4% sales tax.

As for choosing the area of the island in which you stay, we offer these suggestions. The Lahaina and Kaanapali areas offer the visitor the hub of the island's activities, and are a little more costly to stay. The beaches are especially good at Kaanapali. The values and choice of condos are more extensive a little beyond Kaanapali in the Kahana (Lower Honoapiilani Hwy. area) and further at Napili. However, there are fewer restaurants here and slightly cooler temperatures. Some of the condominiums in this area, while very adequate, may be less than new and a little overdue for redecorating. Many condominiums in this area are on nice beaches, however, a few are pebbly or rocky. Kapalua offers high class and high price condominium and hotel accommodations.

Kihei and Wailea are a half-hour drive from Lahaina and offer some nice newer condo units at excellent prices. It is much quieter and while there are not as many restaurants, they do offer some excellent ones. The beaches here are beautiful and well kept, suitable for a variety of water activities.

We have divided the units by area of the island and also by price groupings. Luxury units we list run $85 and up, deluxe units are $65 - $85 nightly, moderate facilities are $40 - $65 and bargain units $40 or less per night. We have based these categories on a standard room at off season rates. Some condominiums will offer weekly and monthly discounts and we have listed them whenever possible. The rates are current at time of publication, but may not reflect recent price increases.

WHERE TO STAY – WHAT TO SEE
Wailuku & Kahului

CONDOMINIUM & HOTEL INDEX

Bed and Breakfast 29	Kealia 63
Hale Hui Kai 65	Keanae (YMCA) 84
Hale Kai 51	Kihei Alii Kai 67
Hale Kai O Kihei 65	Kihei Akahi 67
Hale Kamaole 66	Kihei Bay Surf 63
Hale Napili 51	Kihei Beach Resort 67
Hale Ono Loa 51	Kihei Kai 64
Hale Pau Hana 66	Kihei Kai Nani 64
Haleakala Shores 66	Kihei Resort 68
Hana Bayview 84	Kihei Sands 68
Hana Kai Resort Apts 84	Kihei Surfside 68
Heavenly Hana Inn 84	Koa Lagoon 68
Hono Kai 65	Koa Resort 69
Honokeana Cove 52	Kula Lodge 78
Honokowai East 59	Kulakane 52
Honokowai Palms 51	Kuleana I and II 53
Honolani 52	Lahaina Roads 44
Hotel Hana Maui 84	Lahaina Shores 44
Hotel Intercontinental 61	Lahainaluna 40
Hoyochi Nikko 52	Laule'a 69
Hyatt Regency Hotel 41	Lauloa 69
International Colony Club 45	Leilani Kai Resort 64
Islands Sands 66	Leinaala 69
Island Surf 63	Leinani Apartments 59
Kaanapali Alii 46	Lihi Kai 64
Kaanapali Beach Hotel 41	Lokelani 53
Kaanapali Plantation 44	Luana Kai 70
Kaanapali Royal 46	Maalaea Banyans 70
Kaanapali Shores 47	Maalaea Kai 70
Kamaole Beach Royale 66	Maalaea Surf 73
Kamaole Nalu 67	Mahana 45
Kahana Beach Hotel 50	Mahina Surf 53
Kahana Outrigger 58	Makani a Kai 70
Kahana Reef 52	Makani Sands 53
Kahana Sunset 57	Makena Surf 61
Kahana Village 58	Mana Kai 71
Kana'i a Halu 67	Marriott Hotel 42
Kapalua Bay and Golf Villas ... 57	Maui Beach Hotel 33
Kapalua Bay Resort 50	Maui Beachfront Resort 73
Kapulanikai 63	Maui Eldorado 45
Kauhale Makai 63	Maui Hill 74
Kauiki Cabin 84	Maui Hukilau 33

28

WHERE TO STAY — WHAT TO SEE
Wailuku & Kahului

Maui Islander	40	Pioneer Inn	40
Maui Kaanapali Villas	47	Pohailani	56
Maui Kai	45	Polo Beach Club	74
Maui Lu Resort	74	Polynesian Shores	56
Maui Palms	33	Pualani	65
Maui Parkshore	71	Puamana	46
Maui Sands	54	Royal Kahana	56
Maui Seaside	33	Royal Lahaina Resort	42
Maui Sunset	74	Royal Mauian	72
Maui Surf Hotel	41	Sands of Kahana	58
Maui Vista	71	Sheraton Hotel	43
Mauian	54	Shores of Maui	72
Menehune Shores	72	Silversword Inn	78
Nani Kai Hale	64	Stouffers Wailea Resort	62
Napili Bay	54	Sugar Beach	73
Napili Kai	58	Sunseeker Resort	65
Napili Point	57	Surf and Sand Motel	61
Napili Puamala	54	Travelodge	40
Napili Sands	59	Valley Isle Resort	56
Napili Shores	54	Waianapanapa State Park	83
Napili Sunset	55	Wailana Sands	65
Napili Surf	55	Waiohuli Beach Hale	73
Napili Village	55	Wailea Luxury Condominiums	75
Noelani	55	Ekolu Village	75
Nohonani	55	Ekahi Village	75
Nona Lani	65	Elua Village	75
Paki Maui	56	Whaler	47
Papakea	57		

BED AND BREAKFAST

One alternative to condominiums or hotels is the "Bed and Breakfast Hawaii" organization. It offers homes in various areas around Maui at some very reasonable rates. For example in the Lahaina area they list: "A stunning architectually designed home right on the ocean. Walking distance to the center of the charming and lively old whaling village of Lahaina...Two double rooms available, one has a pullman kitchen and opens onto an outdoor sitting area. Cable TV with HBO ... Both rooms share the bath, but have private entrances. $35 without a kitchen and $45 with a kitchen". Some accommodations are as low as $19 a night for a single. To become a member and receive their directory, which also includes the other islands, Send $5 to: Bed and Breakfast Hawaii, Directory of Homes, Box 449, Kapaa Hi 96746.

WHERE TO STAY – WHAT TO SEE
Wailuku & Kahului

INTRODUCTION

Wailuku and Kahului are located on the northern side of the island. Wailuku is the county seat of Maui, and Kahului houses not only the largest residental population on the island, but also the main airport terminal.

Kahului has a very colorful history, beginning with the arrival of King Kamehameha I in the 1790's from the big island if Hawaii. The meaning of Kahului is "winning" and may have had it's origins in the battle which ensued between Kamehameha and the Maui chieftain. The shoreline of Kahului Bay began it's development in 1863 with the construction of a warehouse by Thomas Hogan. By 1879 the sugar cane industry had grown and created the need for a landing at the bay, and in 1881 the Kahului Railroad Company was set up. The city of Kahului grew rapidly until 1900 when it was purposely burned down to destroy the spreading of a bubonic plague outbreak. The reconstruction of Kahului created a full-scale commercial harbor, which was bombed along with Pearl Harbor on December 7, 1947. After World War II, a housing boom began with the development of reasonably priced homes for the increasing number of people moving to the island. The expansion has continued ever since.

While we feel there is little reason to headquarter your stay in the Kahului/Wailuku area if you are a short term visitor, there are a few good reasons to linger.

WHAT TO SEE

Some historic sights you might not want to miss on this side of Maui include:

Kaahumanu Church, Maui's oldest remaining church was built in 1837 at High and Main Streets in Wailuku.

Hale Hoikeike in Wailuku houses the Maui Historical Society and is known as the Bailey House (circa 1834). To reach it follow the signs to Iao Gorge and you will see the historical landmark sign on the left side of the road. It is open daily from 9 a.m. to 3:30 p.m., and a $2.00 admission is charged. Here you will find the Bailey Gallery, (once a dining room for the female seminary that was located at this site), with paintings of Edward Bailey done during the 19th century. His work depicts many aspects of Hawaiian life during earlier days. Also on display are early Hawaiian artifacts and memorabilia from the missionary days. The staff is extremely knowledgeable and friendly. They also have for sale an array of Hawaiian history, art, craft and photographic books available at prices LESS than local area bookstores. Originally the Royal Historical Society was established in 1841, but it was not reactivated until 1956.

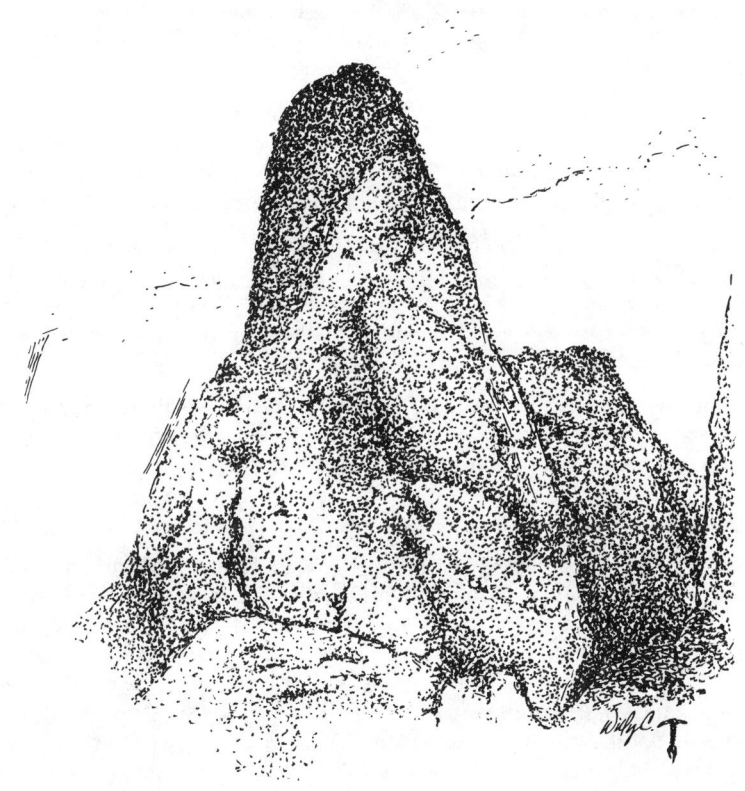

Iao Needle

WHERE TO STAY – WHAT TO SEE
Wailuku & Kahului

The museum was dedicated on July 6, 1957, then closed for restoration on December 31, 1973 to be re-opened on July 13, 1975. Of special interest are the impressive 20" thick walls that are made of plaster using a special missonary recipe including goat hair. These thick walls provided the inhabitants with a natural means of air conditioning.

BALDWIN BEACH - see section on Beaches for Baldwin Beach and others located in the area.

The Iao Valley is a short drive beyond Hale Hoikeike. Within the valley is an awesome volanic peak that rises 2,250 feet and is known as the Iao Needle. Parking facilities are available and there are a number of hiking trails which can be followed.

The Hawaiian Tropical Plantation is a new addition to the Wailuku area. Fifty acres have been planted with sugar cane, bananas, guava and other island products. A ten acre visitor center will include exhibits, marketplace, nursery and restaurant. Admission is free with a slight charge for ground tours.

The Maui Zoological and Botanical Gardens are open 9-4 daily with FREE admission. Go up Kaahumanu to Kanaloa Street and turn by the Wailuku War Memorial Center. The zoo is on the right hand side. This is a zoo Maui style, with a few pigmy donkeys, sheep, goats, monkeys, Galapogos turtles, birds and picnic tables.

The Kahana Wildlife Sanctuary is off Route 32, near the Kahului Airport, and was once a royal fish pond. Now a lookout is located here for those interested in viewing the stilt and other birds which inhabit the area.

WHERE TO SHOP

There are three large shopping centers in Kahului. The Maui Mall which is on Kaahumanu Street, only a two minute drive from the airport is relatively new. It offers several large grocery stores, the Star and Safeway, and a nice Long's Drug store which is great for picking up those sundry items as well as sovenirs. They also have a variety of small shops and restaurants. The older Kahului Shopping Center is also on Kaahumanu. Monkey pod trees line this mall which is filled with local residents playing cards. This mall did not appear to be as well kept up, but you will find an interesting drug store (TODA) that has a very reasonable luncheonette and some assorted shops. The largest shopping center is Kaahumanu, which ironically is also on Kaahumanu Street. With 47 shops and restaurants it offers the largest selection of clothing, gift and department stores (Sears and Liberty House included). If you don't have accommodations with a kitchen, you might want to pick up a styrofoam type ice chest at one of these centers and stock it with juices, lunch meats and what not to enjoy in your hotel room. Hopefully, your accomodations will offer complimentary ice. Wailuku has no large shopping centers, but a cluster of shops down their Main Street makes for interesting strolling.

WHERE TO STAY – WHAT TO SEE
Wailuku & Kahului

ACCOMMODATIONS

One advantage to choosing this area for headquarters is it's proximity to the main Kahului airport and it's somewhat central location to all other parts of the island. Room rates are very economical also. The motels are clustered around the Kahului harbor and include the Maui Hukilau, Maui Palms, Maui Beach and the Maui Seaside. The Maui Hukilau's reservation phone number 1-808-877-3311. The Maui Palms offer free airport pickup, color TV and pool, phone 1-808-877-0051. The Maui Beach features air-conditioned rooms, color TV and pool as well as free airport service, phone 1-808-877-0051. Our preference is the newer Maui Seaside which has spacious rooms with refrigerators and also a pool. (The beach in this area is not suitable for swimming.) The Maui Seaside's reservation number is toll free 1-800-367-7000. All of the room rates are comparable and run $25 - $35 a night. In Wailuku there are no short term places to stay.

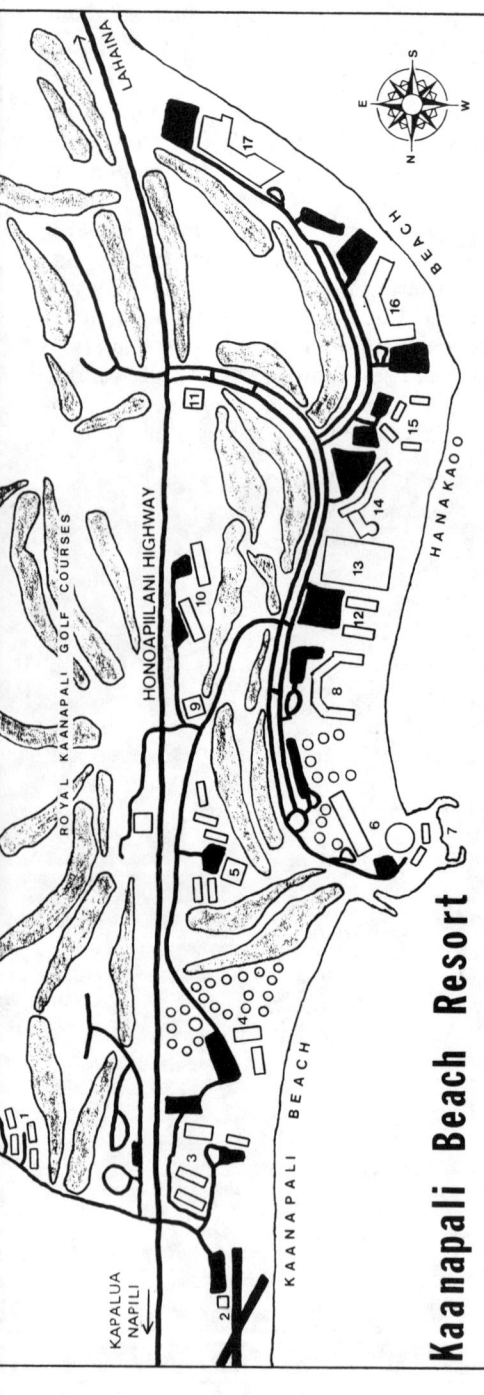

WHERE TO STAY – WHAT TO SEE
Lahaina & Kaanapali

INTRODUCTION

An idyllic combination of old and new are blended into a sunny setting making a vacation area to suit the needs of most any visitor. Under the watchful eye of the Lahaina Restoration Foundation, the small seaport of Lahaina continues to reflect the image of a 19th century whaling port. Grog shops have been replaced with fine restaurants and cocktail lounges, and it is now tourists and not the natives who sport the muu-muus. Kaanapali is an Amfac development that began in the early 1960's and can boast of an array of fine hotel and condominium units, distributed along one of the finer Maui beachfronts.

WHAT TO DO AND SEE

In the middle of Kaanapali is the shopping area known as Whalers Village. 1984 found it getting a facelift and the addition of more shops and restaurants. They also feature an exhibit of early whaling memorabilia.

The Hyatt Regency Hotel at Kaanapali must be put at the top of everyone's list of things to see. It is a small city in itself. Few hotels can boast that they need their own wildlife manager, but upon entry you'll see why the Hyatt does. Without spoiling the surprises too much, just envision palm trees growing through the lobby with peacocks strolling by and parrots perched amid extraordinary pieces of oriental art. The lagoon and black swans are spectacular and the swimming pool is indescribable. Occupying a two acre area it offers two swim through waterfalls and a cavern in the middle of them features a swim up bar. A swinging bridge is suspended over one of the two pools and a huge slide offers added thrills for hotel guests. If only Robinson Crusoe could have had it so good.

There is much to see and do in busy Lahaina town. The word Lahaina means "merciless sun" and it does tend to become quite warm, especially in the afternoon. Parking can be somewhat irksome. An all day lot is located at the corner of Wainee and Dickenson (only a couple blocks off Front Street) and charges $1.50 for all day. However, it as all lots fill up early in the day. The Lahaina Shopping Center has a three hour (free) parking area, but it also is very crowded. (See the Lahaina map for locations of other parking areas.) On street parking is very limited and if you are fortunate enough to find a spot, many are only a one hour limit. BEWARE, the police here are quite prompt and efficient at towing. Now that you have arrived, lets get started. Historical memorabilia abounds in Lahaina.

The Banyan tree is at the south end of Lahaina and an easy spot to sight on Front Street. Planted on April 24, 1873, by Sheriff William Owen Smith, it was to commemorate the 50th anniversary of Lahaina's first Protestant Christian Mission. It's boughs are now so weighty that they require support.

The stone ruins of the old fort can be found harborside near the Banyan Tree. The fort was constructed in the 1830's to protect the missionary's homes from

WHERE TO STAY – WHAT TO SEE
Lahaina & Kaanapali

the whaling ships and the occasional cannon ball that would be shot off when the sailors were arroused. The fort was later torn down, and the coral blocks reused elsewhere. However, a few have been excavated in the area and the corner was rebuilt as a landmark.

Pioneer Inn, built in 1901, is the distinquished green and white structure just North of the Banyan Tree. It was a haven for inter-island travelers during the early days of the 20th century. Having survived the dry years of prohibition, it added a new wing in 1966 along with a center garden-pool area. Two restaurants still operate here and accommodations are available in the original and the new structure as well. (See "Lahaina Restaurants" and "Lahaina Where to Stay" for additional information).

The Lahaina Courthouse was built in 1858 of wood and stone taken from the palace of Kamehameha II, which was never completed. You'll find it is located near the Lahaina harbor and currently houses the district court and assorted offices.

In front of the Pioneer Inn is the Lahaina harbor. You can stroll down and see the ships and visit stalls where a wide variety of water sports and tours can be arranged. (See Water Recreation.)

The Carthinagin is anchored in the harbor and is actually a replica of the first Carthinagin, which went aground in 1920 during an attempt to tow it to Honolulu. The Carthingin has been used in the filming of several movies, including Hawaii. It is open for public inspection daily from 9 a.m. to 4:30 p.m., with admission $2.00 for adults and accompanying children free. Proceeds go to the Restoration Foundation.

The Hauola Stone or Healing Rock can be found near the Lahaina harbor. Look for the cluster of rocks marked with a visitors bureau warrior sign. The rock resembling a modern chair was believed by Hawaiians to have healing abilities, which could be gained by merely sitting in it with feet dangling in the surf. Also in this area are remnants of the Brick Palace of Kamehameha the Great.

The Baldwin House is across Front Street from Pioneer Inn. Built during 1834 - 1835, it housed the Reverand Dwight Baldwin and his family from 1837 to 1871. Tours are given every 15 minutes between the hours of 9:30 and 4:30. Adults are charged $2, no charge for children. The empty lot adjacent was once the home of Reverand William Richards, and a target of attack by cannonballs from angry sailors during the heydey of whaling. On the other side of the Baldwin Home is the Master's Reading Room. Built in 1833 it is the oldest structure on Maui. It's original purpose was to provide a place of leisure for visiting sea captains. It now houses the Lahaina Restoration Foundation and is not open to the public.

Whale watching is always an exciting past-time in Lahaina, especially for those

WHERE TO STAY – WHAT TO SEE
Lahaina & Kaanapali

who make a sighting. The whales usually arrive in November and December and breed in the warm waters off Maui. At the desk of the Carthinagin you will find a chart showing where whale sightings have occurred this season. There is also a number to call to report any sightings you make. WHALE WATCH HOTLINE 879-6530. Many whaling watching excursions are available, for more information see WATER TOURS in Chapter VII.

The old jail (Hale Paaho) is located on Prison Street, just off Wainee and only a short trek from Front Street. The remains of the old jail were reconstructed in 1959. Originally it was built in 1852 to house the unruly sailors from the whaling vessels and it replaced the old fort. The prison house was first built and then a few years later the coral walls, (the blocks taken from the old fort) were added.

The Wo Hing Temple on Front street re-opened in late 1984. Build in 1912 it has been recently restored and converted into a museum featuring the influence of the chinese population on Maui. Hours 9-9 with a small admission charged.

The Lahaina Jodo Mission is located a moderate walk from Lahaina on Ala Moana Street near the Mala Wharf. The great Buddah commemorated the 100th anniversary of the Japanese immigration to the islands which was celebrated in 1968. None of the buildings are open to the public.

Construction of the Waiola Church began in 1828 on what was then called the Wainee Church. Made of stone, it was the first of it's kind. The church, unfortunately did not survive the destructive forces of nature and man and finally succumbed in 1859. The current structure dates from only 1953. In the neighboring cemetary you will find tombs for several notable members of Hawaiian royalty, including Queen Keopulani wife of Kamehameha the Great and mother of Kamehameha I and II. The church is located on Wainee and Shaw Streets.

Maria Lanakila Church is on the corner of Wainee and Dickenson. Built in 1928, it is a replica of the 1858 church. Next door is the seamen's cemetary.

The Sugar Cane Train is just outside Lahaina and will transport you between Kaanapali and Lahaina. One way for adults is $4.25, and children $2.00. Round trip for adults runs $6.50 and children $3.25. Babes in arms are free. Special package options include train trips combined with lunch in Lahaina, a visit to the Baldwin House and the Carthinagin or a trip in the glass bottom boat the Lin Wai. Make your plans early as space is limited and sometimes the return trips are booked. The red double decker bus stops at the Wharf Shopping Center and in front of the Pioneer Inn to transport you to the Sugar Cane Depot.

Just outside Lahaina at Olowalu is the site of an early Hawaiian village and the Petrogylphs. These rock carvings are believed to be the Hawaiian's first attempt at a written language. The area is under the auspices of the Lahaina Restoration Foundation.

WHERE TO STAY – WHAT TO SEE
Lahaina & Kaanapali

WHERE TO SHOP

Shopping is a prime facination in Lahaina. The shops frequently change names and most sport the same aloha wear and tourist memorabilia, however, there are several which are favorites of ours and might be of special interest to you.

The Macadamia Nut Factory is a very special stop for all tourists visiting Lahaina. Located at the Pioneer Inn they offer tasty nuts in soup mixes, dark chocolate, clusters and more. A very popular gift to take home. Phone 661-4855 or toll free from the U.S. 1-800-367-5150.

The Gallery Ltd. is at 716 Front Street, 661-0695. It is only open weekdays and features Oriental new and antique items as well as an array of fine jewelry.

The Lahaina Print Sellers is located on the second floor of the Wharf Shopping Center with another office at the Whaler's Village. They specialize in framed antique maps and old prints from around the world. An interesting place to browse. Phone 667-7617 Whaler's Village or 661-3579 at the Wharf. The items differ at each location.

Emeralds International features nothing but that. If you like emeralds in any form, from rough to finished pieces, stop in here. You'll find it at 858-1 Front Street. Phone 661-8705.

Claire the ring lady is right next door at 858-4 Front Street, phone 667-9288. Claire, who learned her craft in Florence, can take your stone or choose one of hundreds of hers and make it up to your specifications.

The Sea Breeze is located at 855 Front Street and doesn't feature classy atmosphere, but it has been around for awhile and it's prices tend to be a little less for some things than the other shops along the waterfront. Phone 661-0863.

The Kite Store at 703 Front St., phone 661-3159, has a fine array of flying paraphernalia from small to enormous kites.

Superwhale, at Pioneer Inn, phone 661-3424. We had difficulty finding children's clothing in certain sizes, but here they specialize in children's wear and the selection is large.

Waikiki Fragrance and Cosmetic Factory is at 637 Front St., Lahaina, phone 667-6905. All their items are made on the islands. Many of their fragrances are made from native flowers. They also carry a line of suntan products designed for the islands. Their Medic, at $8.50 a tube, is terrific on itchy sun rashes and handy to have back at home for bites.

Upstart and Crow, upper level of the Wharf Shopping Center, phone 667-9544, offers an assortment of coffees and a good selection of books.

BE FOREWARNED!!! If you have the time, do a lot of window shopping before you buy. The prices can vary significantly on some items from one store to another.

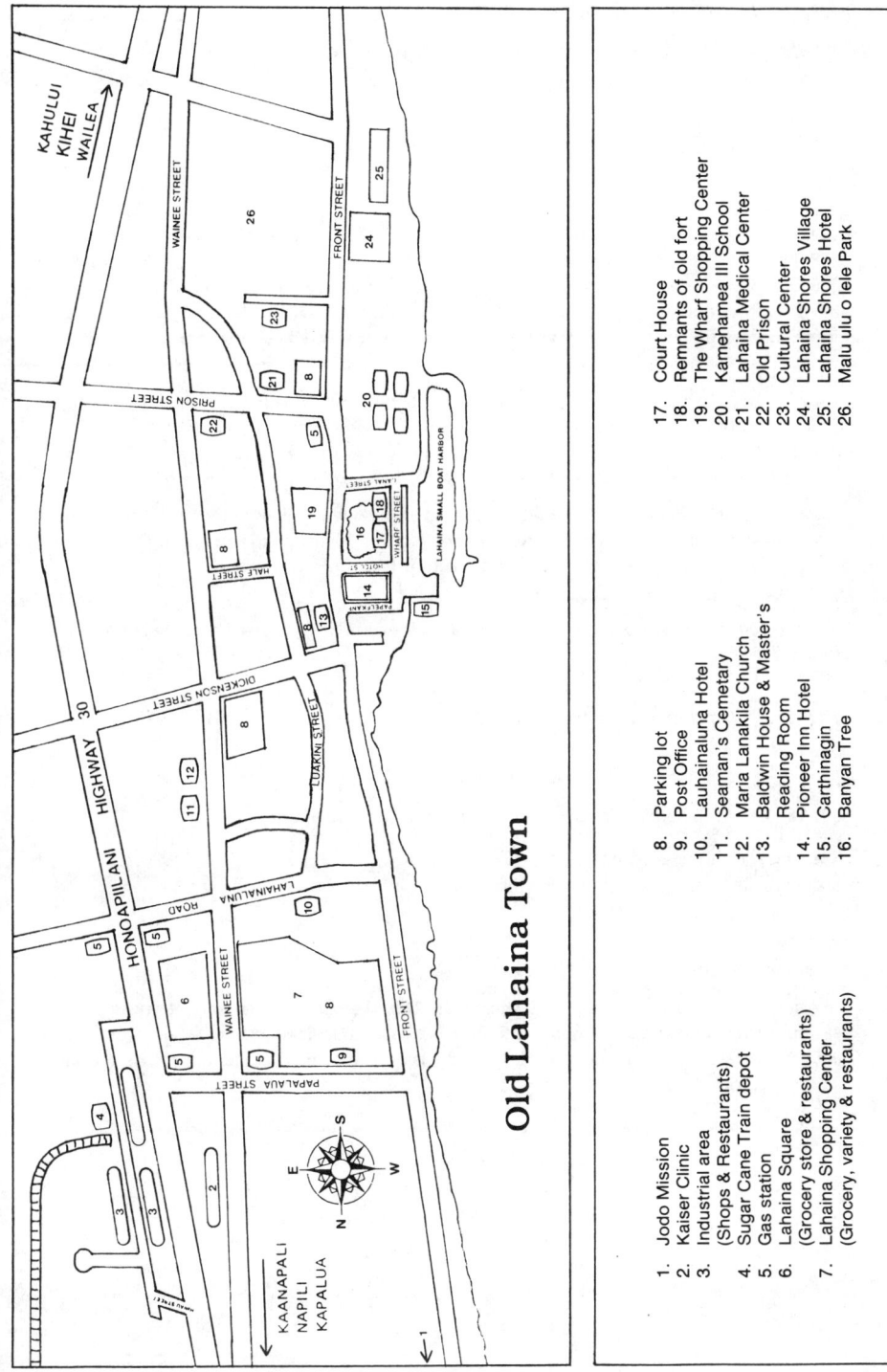

WHERE TO STAY – WHAT TO SEE
Kaanapali/Lahaina   Hotels

"BARGAIN RANGE"

LAHAINALUNA
Downtown Lahaina at 127 Lahainaluna Rd., Lahaina, Maui, HI 96761. Phone 1-808-661-0577. $29.95 single or double, mountain or ocean view, rooms with two single beds and a lanai. $27.50 room is inside, no view. Hotel has three units with double beds. Air conditioned, bath and shower, black and white television. Two-night minimum stay, no maid service for less than three-day stay. Visa, Mastercard, or travelers checks accepted.

PIONEER INN
658 Wharf St., Lahaina, Maui, HI 96764-4295. Phone 1-808-661-3636. Original building: single $18, double $21 with a shared bath. Rooms with own bath $22-$24 single, and $25-$27 double. New wing has lanais, private bath, air conditioning. Single $36 outside, $39 courtyard. Double $39 outside, $42 courtyard, $52 superior.

If you want rustic, this is it. Don't let the "new" in new wing give you ideas of grandeur. This is an old building and the furnishings are "quaint". However, you are in the hub of activity and sounds of the music downstairs will drift you off to sleep.

TRAVELODGE
Phone 1-800-255-3050 toll free, or locally at 1-808-661-3661. Located in Lahaina at 888 Wainee St.

"MODERATE RANGE"

MAUI ISLANDER
660 Wainee St., Lahaina, Maui, HI 96761. Phone 1-808-667-9766.

Hotel room for 2, no kitchen	$ 42
Studio for up to 3	55
1 bedroom (4)	65
2 bedroom, 2 bath (5)	90
3 bedroom, 3 bath (7)	115

This is a nice complex located only a short walk from Lahaina, yet far enough away to be peaceful. They offer planned daily activities, such as hula lessons, etc. Maid service is daily, pool, telephones, laundry facilities, television, kitchens, and tennis courts are all added amenities.

Hotels | *WHERE TO STAY – WHAT TO SEE*
Kaanapali/Lahaina

"DELUXE RANGE"

KAANAPALI BEACH HOTEL
P.O. Box 637, Lahaina, Maui, HI 96761. Phone 1-808-661-0011. Contact: Amfac Hotels by phoning 1-800-227-4700 or toll free in California 1-800-622-0838.

	High Season:	Low Season:
Standard room	$ 70	$ 65
Superior	80	75
Deluxe	90	85
Deluxe ocean front	100	95
Junior suite (4)	100	95
Oceanfront	140	130
Governor suite	180	170

Add $15 each additional person. Tennis available at nearby Royal Lahaina. Try their whale-shaped swimming pool!

MAUI SURF**
At Kaanapali Beach. Phone 1-800-367-5360

Mountain view standard room	$ 79
Mountain view superior	90
Deluxe oceanview	105
Surf deluxe	115

This is our favorite of the Kaanapali Resort hotels for the accommodations and the prices. The beach is excellent and their grounds are large, nicely landscaped, and offer a large grassy sunning area and two pools. An outdoor snack bar and cocktail bar provide close-hand refreshments. There are three restaurants in the complex, a nice open lobby, and one of the better parking facilities. The rooms are in tropical greens and yellows and haven't been recently refurbished, but are still more than adequate. Each room offers a lanai with a mountain or ocean view. We prefer the mountain view for the price savings, and for the spectacular view of the hillside. The rooms also have a small refrigerator. Free scuba instruction is daily at the pool and scuba as well as snorkel equipment is available. They enjoy your patronage, greeting your arrival with a fresh pineapple in your room, and a Christmas card at holiday time.

"LUXURY RANGE"

HYATT REGENCY***
200 Nohea Kai Drive, Lahaina, Maui, HI 96761. Phone 1-800-228-9000. Direct to the hotel Phone 1-808-667-7474. Located at Kaanapali Beach.

Garden view $125, Golf suite $200, Golf/mountain view 145, Ocean suite 325, Oceanfront 165, Deluxe 475, Regency Club* (mtn. view) 185, Regency 750, Regency Club* (oceanfrt.) 195, Presidential 1,200

WHERE TO STAY — WHAT TO SEE
Kaanapali/Lahaina   Hotels

No off-season discount rates are offered. This magnificent complex is located on 18 beachfront acres and offers 815 rooms and suites. *The Regency Club are special floors that feature special services, including continental breakfast, evening cocktails and appetizers, and a complimentary health club membership. There is a $15 per night charge for children on the Regency floors over the age of four. Other rooms, children over the age of 13 are charged $15 per night. Three adults maximum per room. Numerous fine restaurants and an outstanding pool area are featured as well as an array of fine shops. It's worth coming here just to look around!

MARRIOTT***
Located at Kaanapali Beach. Phone 1-800-228-9290.

Mountain view	$ 95	(double occupancy)
Mountain/ocean view	125	"
Corporate	120	
Oceanview/oceanfront	140 - 165	
Parlors	125	
Suites	325/425/800	

The Marriott offers a 50% discount coupon in the Entertainment coupon books. The 1985 coupon is good on any room, but reservations cannot be made through a travel agent or their toll free number, so call 1-808-667-1200 to take advantage of this offer. It is based on space available, and while you may get the room at a discount on weekdays, the price may be full-scale on weekends. The 1985 discount is good between April 15 and December 15 with a maximum stay of 7 nights. This complex has a nice, large, and open lobby. The rooms have an historical Hawaiian theme. The beachfront in this area is a little corally, but good for swimming.

ROYAL LAHAINA RESORT
Located at Kaanapali Beach. Write: Amfac, P.O. Box 8519, Honolulu, HI 96815. Phone 1-800-227-4700 for reservations. The hotel's direct phone is 1-808-661-3611. No off-season rates are offered.

Standard	$ 80	Cottage suites:	
Superior	95	Ocean view	$350*
Deluxe	110	Garden view	275*
Deluxe ocean front	120	3 bdrm. garden	355*
Garden cottage	100	Royal suite	650*
Ocean front cottage	125		
Deluxe 1 bdrm. ocean front	300	* indicates kitchen facilities	
Deluxe 2 bdrm. ocean front	420		

$15 extra person charged. A tennis center is located here offering 11 courts. Reservations from California call 1-800-622-0838. From San Francisco area call 1-415-772-3080.

WHERE TO STAY – WHAT TO SEE

Hotels   Kaanapali/Lahaina

SHERATON
Located at Kaanapali Beach. Phone 1-808-661-0031 or toll free 1-800-325-3535.

Mountain view cottage	$ 95
Garden cottage	105
Partial ocean view	110
Full ocean view	120
Deluxe ocean view	130
Deluxe ocean front	150
Suites	190

This hotel was one of the first completed in the Kaanapali Development. It winds around the side of Black Rock. There are cottages which have grounds around them and have eight units per building, and there are rooms in the main hotel building. We found the complex confusing to find our way around. The beachfront here is excellent for snorkeling and generally everyone from all around comes here to enjoy it.

Kaanapali Resort

WHERE TO STAY − WHAT TO SEE
Kaanapali/Lahaina   Condominiums

"MODERATE RANGE"

KAANAPALI PLANTATION
Located at 150 Puukolii Rd., mailing address: P.O. Box 845, Lahaina, Maui, HI 96761. Phone: 1-808-661-4446. Toll free, phone Condo Resorts International at 1-800-854-3823. In California phone 1-800-432-7059. Sixty-two units in a garden setting set upon a hill with unobstructed view of the ocean.

1 bdrm. units (1-2)	$ 80 (double occupancy)
2 bdrm. units (up to 4)	95 "
3 bdrm. units (up to 6)	110 "

Each unit has at least two baths. $10 per night discount for two weeks or longer. $6 each person per night extra. Daily maid services except Sundays and holidays. $100 deposit required with 10-day notice of cancellation for refund. Three-day minimum stay except December to March when it is a seven-day minimum stay. During December, full payment must be made 30 days prior to arrival to hold reservations. NO CREDIT CARDS. Units offer washer/dryers, ice makers, color televisions, phones, complimentary daily paper. No air conditioning, only ceiling fans. Pool, tennis court, BBQ, shuffleboard, and pool table located in the complex which overlooks the Royal Kaanapali golf course.

LAHAINA ROADS
1403 Front St., Lahaina, Maui, HI 96761.

	High Season:	Low Season:
1 bdrm. (1-4) (double occupancy)	$ 55	$48
2 bdrm. (1-6) "	63	54
Penthouse (for 4 persons)	110	96

Each additional person $6. Three-night minimum stay during low season, one-week stay during high season. NO CREDIT CARDS. Units offer fully equipped kitchens, televisions, and maid service is available upon request. Covered parking and elevator to upper levels. These 34 units are on the beach in Lahaina.

LAHAINA SHORES
475 Front Street, Lahaina, Maui, HI 96761. Phone 1-808-661-4835

Studio single	$55 mountain view;	$61 ocean view
Studio double	$58 " "	$64 " "
One bedroom	$77 " "	$90 " "
Penthouse	$100 " "	$110 " "

Children six years and under no charge, extra persons charged $6 a day. 200 ocean front units in this building of Victorian style offer air conditioning, lanais, kitchens, daily maid service and laundry facilities on each floor. Swimming pool is located off the lobby. The beach here is fair and the water calm due to off shore reefs. Lahaina is a short walk away. This complex is neighboring the Lahaina Shores Village which offers several restaurants and a small grocery store.

Condominiums

WHERE TO STAY — WHAT TO SEE
Kaanapali/Lahaina

"DELUXE RANGE"

INTERNATIONAL COLONY CLUB
Write: Manager, 2750 Klapui Dr., Lahaina, Maui, HI 96761. Phone: 1-808-661-4070. Forty-four individual cottages offer ocean view, located near Kaanapali. One-bedroom units for two, $70; two-bedroom units for two, $80. Each additional person add $10 during high season, low season $5. Minimum stay four days. Two-day deposit required within 10 days of reservations with a two-week notice for refund; 5% weekly discount. Some units offer washer/dryers, but coin-op laundry is on premises. Units have separate bedroom, living room, and kitchen. Some units have terraces, others lanais. All have phones and televisions. Maid service every fourth day. Two swimming pools. Located across from the Kaanapali air strip.

MAHANA
Located at Kaanapali Beach. Write: Hotel Corporation of Pacific, 2299 Kuhio Ave., Honolulu, HI 96815. Phone: 1-800-367-5124.

Studio (1-2)	$ 75
1 bdrm., 1 bath (1-4)	100
1 bdrm., 2 bath (1-4)	100
2 bdrm., 2 bath (1-6)	140

Two tennis courts, heated pool, central air conditioning, saunas, elevators, and food service is available. Some units offer kitchens.

MAUI ELDORADO
Located at Kaanapali on golf course. Phone: 1-800-367-2967 (6 a..m. - 5 p..m. Hawaii time).

	High season:	Low season:
Studio	$ 69 - $ 80	$ 59 - $ 80
1 bdrm.	90 - 110	80 - 100
2 bdrm.	130 - 170	120 - 160

Weekly and monthly discounts are available. Units feature kitchens, daily maid service, and central air conditioning.

MAUI KAI
106 Kaanapali Shores Place. Write: Manager, Maui Kai Resort, RR 1, Box 9, Lahaina, Maui, HI 96761. Phone: 1-808-661-0002 or 1-800-367-5635.

High season:		
Studio (1-3)	$ 69 daily,	$420 weekly
1 bdrm. (1-4)	89 daily,	$539 weekly
Low season:		
Studio (1-3)	$ 62 daily,	$364 weekly
1 bdrm. (1-4)	75 daily,	455 weekly

Fifth person $6 per night extra. Visa and Mastercard are accepted. Two-day minimum stay required. Units offer color televisions, kitchens, central air conditioning, lanais. Pool, therapy pool, ping pong, paddle tennis, a paperback library, and laundry facilities on each floor. A two-night deposit is required within 10 days of booking reservation.

WHERE TO STAY – WHAT TO SEE
Kaanapali/Lahaina   Condominiums

PUAMANA*
Contact: Manager, P.O. Box 515, Lahaina, Maui, HI 96767. Phone: 1-808-667-2551 or 1-800-367-5630.

	High season:	Low season:
1 bdrm. (4)	$ 68 - $120	$ 58 - $104
2 bdrm. (6)	126 - 173	110 - 153
3 bdrm. (8)	147	129
3 bdrm. ocean front	215	191

The large variation in price reflects location in the complex, ocean front to garden view. This resembles a residential community much more than a vacation resort. Located ocean-side, it is a series of duplexes and four-plexes in a garden setting. The management office, and also where you check in, is located in Lahaina proper at 910 Honoapiilani, Unit #11, while the complex is one mile south of Lahaina. All units offer full kitchens. Minimum stay is three days. For a car, add $12 per day.

"LUXURY RANGE"

KAANAPALI ALII* NA
Kaanapali Beach at 50 Nohea Kai Dr., Lahaina, Maui, HI 96761. Phone 1-800-367-6090. Canada and Hawaii call 1-808-667-1400.

	High season:	Low season:
1 bdrm. (2)	$100 - $130	$105 - $125
2 bdrm. (4)	$150 - $175, $225	$185 - $210, $275

Four-night minimum stay required. This is the newest condo development on Kaanapali with 264 condos. The units are beautifully furnished, offer full kitchens, daily maid service and washer/dryers. All are air conditioned. Lighted tennis courts, pool, and exercise room. They still have units for sale, so if you have an extra million, check them out!

KAANAPALI ROYAL
On golf course overlooking Kaanapali Resorts. 2560 Kekaa Dr., Lahaina, Maui, HI 96761. Phone: 1-808-667-7200 or contact Hawaiian Resorts, 1100 Ward Ave., Suite 1100, Honolulu, HI 96814. Phone: 1-808-523-7785 or 1-800-367-7040.

One-bedroom, garden view $90; golf view $95; ocean view $105. Two-bedroom garden view $120; golf view $125; ocean view $140. One-bedroom sleeps a maximum of four people, the two bedroom units sleep six. Low season: discounts weekly 15%, monthly 20%. Three-night minimum stay required. The two-bedroom units offer washer/dryers. These spacious codos offer 1,600 - 2,000 square feet, lanais, color televisions, complete kitchens, and maid service.

WHERE TO STAY – WHAT TO SEE

Condominiums   Kaanapali/Lahaina

KAANAPALI SHORES UP
100 Kaanapali Shores Place. Contact: Hotel Corporation of Pacific, 2299 Kuhio Ave., Honolulu, HI 96815. Phone: 1-808-922-3368 or 1-800-367-5124.

High season:

Studio: Garden view	$ 95	Ocean view	$100
1 bdrm. "	110	"	120
2 bdrm. "	140	"	155
Penthouse	N/A	"	235

Low season:

Studio: Garden view	$ 80	Ocean view	$ 85
1 bdrm. "	95	"	105
2 bdrm. "	125	"	140
Penthouse	N/A	"	220

Extra person $9 nightly. Under 18 free in existing beds. Seven-night minimum stay required over Christmas holiday. 926 units in this complex, all offer kitchens, telephones, free tennis, daily maid service, air conditioning, and color television.

MAUI KAANAPALI VILLAS
2805 Honoapiilani Hwy., Lahaina. Phone: 1-808-667-7791.

High season:

Hotel room (1-2)	$ 74
Studio superior (1-2)	94 (maximum 3 persons)
Studio deluxe (1-2)	104 " " "
1 bdrm. superior (1-4)	124 (maximum 4 persons)
1 bdrm. deluxe (1-4)	139 " " "
2 bdrm. superior (1-6)	189 (maximum 6 persons)
2 bdrm. deluxe (1-6)	199 " " "

Low season: deduct $9 per night. Extra person, extra bed or crib is an additional $9 per night. Seven-night minimum stay 12/25- 1/1. Located beachfront at Kaanapali, this was until recently a part of the Royal Lahaina Resort, and before that the Hilton. It is now refurbished and has been converted into condominiums.

*THE WHALER**
Located on Kaanapali Beach at 2481 Kaanapali Parkway. Phone: 1-800-367-2963 or 1-808-661-4861.

	High season:	Low season:
Garden units—		
Studio	$ 84	$ 79
1 bdrm., 1 bath (4)	125	120
1 bdrm., 2 bath (4)	135	130
2 bdrm., 2 bath (6)	200	190
Ocean front—		
1 bdrm., 2 bath (4)	$155	$150
2 bdrm., 2 bath (6)	230	215
Suite (4)	320	305

Located in the heart of Kaanapali next to the Whaler's Village shopping center. Excellent beach front, pool, kitchens.

WHERE TO STAY – WHAT TO SEE
Lahaina/Kaapapali   Long-term

Contact: Ho'Oli Hale, 278 Wili Ko Place #2, Lahaina, Maui, HI 96761. Phone: 1-808-667-7971. $500 - $600 studios and one-bedrooms. Usually 100% occupancy, so plan ahead. They also offer short-term facilities in various areas between Lahaina and Napili, as well as in Kihei.

WHERE TO STAY – WHAT TO SEE
Kapalua/Napili/Kahana

INTRODUCTION

Colin Cameron chose 750 ocean view acres of his family's 20,000-plus acre pineapple plantation for the development of a high-class resort. The result was the Kapalua Bay Resort which opened in 1979 under the management of Rockresort, headed by Laurence Rockefeller. The grounds are spacious and sport flowering poinsettias in abundance near holiday time. The bay here and at next door Napili have lovely, white sand beaches, and are very safe for swimming and snorkeling.

There are pros and cons about staying in the Kapalua, Kahana, or Napili areas. The weather tends to be a little cooler and more breezy with more rain. The afternoons especially, tend to cool off more rapidly than in the Kaanapali and Lahaina areas. This may be an advantage to those of you who find hotter climates uncomfortable. It is also a quieter, slower-paced atmosphere than in the busy hub of Lahaina, while still being very close to all the action. There are a greater selection of condos from which to choose here and the prices are pretty copetitive, however, hotel accommodations are very limited and expensive.

WHAT TO SEE

Kapalua Resort has a shopping mall located just outside the hotel itself. The road beyond Kapalua is in excellent condition, however, while it does offer some magnificent shoreline views, it finally turns to a rough trail, passable only with four-wheel drive. Slaughterhouse Beach is located along this road, and you may find it interesting to watch the body surfers challenge the waves. Just beyond is Honolua Bay where winter swells make excellent board surfing conditions. A good viewing point is along the roadside on the cliffs beyond the bay.

WHERE TO SHOP

Kapalua offers an excellent shopping mall which includes the Kapalua Shop (phone 669-4172) where everything from men's and women's resort wear to glassware display the Kapalua butterfly logo.

Auntie Nani Children's Boutique, phone 669-5282, features children's fashions from infants to teens.

The Market Cafe has fresh pastries, wines, gourmet items to go, or enjoy breakfast, lunch, or dinner at their restaurant phone: 669-4888.

WHERE TO STAY – WHAT TO SEE
Kapalua/Kahana/Napili   Hotels

"DELUXE RANGE"

KAHANA BEACH HOTEL
Located in Kahana. Contact: Kahana Resort Condominium Hotel, 2404 Townsgate Rd., Westlake Village, CA 91361. Phone: 1-213-991-3390. Toll-free: 1-800-2-HAWAII in southern California; 1-800-8-HAWAII in northern California; 1-800-235-7070 nationwide.

Studio ocean front $49, double occupancy; studio ocean view $45, double occupancy; one-bedroom ocean front suite $69, double occupancy.

Add $8 per additional person. One night's deposit required in advance. All units offer ocean view. The studio sleeps up to four and has kitchenette. The suites have two balcony lanais, a living room with queen-size sofa bed. The bedroom offers two queen beds, also two full-size bathrooms, dressing room, and will accommodate seven. A kitchen is featured. Units offer color televisions, maid service daily, and telephones. Coin-op laundry and pool on premises. Visa, Mastercard, and American Express accepted.

"LUXURY RANGE"

KAPALUA BAY RESORT***
One Bay Drive, Kapalua, Maui, HI 96761. Phone: 1-800-367-6082 or 1-808-669-5656.

Ocean view $183 single or double occupancy. Garden view $143 single or double occupancy. Suites $350.

Additional persons $35 per night. Add $37 a night per person for Modified American Plan. Deposit during high season of three nights required. During low season, a one night's deposit required. Full refund upon 14-day notice of cancellation. Units have small refrigerators no kitchens. Lovely grounds and located on an excellent beach front.

Condominiums   *WHERE TO STAY – WHAT TO SEE*   Kapalua/Napili/Kahana

"BARGAIN RANGE"

HONOKOWAI PALMS
3666 Lower Honoapiilani Hwy., Lahaina, Maui, HI 96761. Phone: 1-808-669-6130.

Forty units are located across the road from Honokowai Beachfront Park. High season: one-bedroom units $37 - $40 for 2 persons; two-bedroom $52 for four persons. Low season: one-bedroom units $29 - $32 for two persons; two-bedroom units $41 for four in room.

Weekly and monthly discounts are available. $6 is charged for one additional person in room, $10 for two. A three-night minimum stay is required. $100 deposit is required and refundable upon one month's notice. All units have electric kitchens and maid service is available only at extra fee. A pool is located in the rear of the complex.

"MODERATE RANGE"

HALE KAI
3691 Lower Honoapiilani Hwy., Lahaina. Phone: 1-808-669-6333. For information, write: Manager, RR 1, Box 500, Lahaina, Maui, HI 96761.

Forty units located in the Honokowai area. High season: one-bedroom $45 daily, $260 - $370 weekly rate. Two-bedroom units for four, daily $75, weekly $430 - $550. Extra person charged $6. Low season: $100 deposit required with a one-month notice for refund.

A three-night minimum stay required, excepting over Christmas when it is a two-week minimum. The beach is rocky, but the units do have lanais, kitchens, and a pool.

HALE NAPILI
65 Hui Rd., Napili, Maui, HI 96761. Phone: 1-808-669-6184.

Eighteen units are all ocean front on Napili Bay. High season: garden studio (maximum three persons) $48; studio ocean front $60; one-bedroom ocean front $70.

Three-day minimum stay and a $100 deposit required. Seven days notice for deposit refund. Units have daily maid service, color television, lanai, and all electric kitchens. NO CREDIT CARDS ACCEPTED. No pool.

*HALE ONO LOA**
3823 Lower Honoapiilani. Phone: 1-808-669-6362. Write: Manager, Rt. 1, Box 300, Lahaina, Maui, HI 96761. Ocean front condominiums and ocean view units available. Honokowai area.

Rates: 1-bedroom, first floor (2 persons) $50; (3 persons) $58; (4 persons) $66. One-bedroom, second, third, fourth floors (2) $55; (3) $63; (4) $71. Two-bedroom, two bath (4) $85; (5) $93; (6) $101.

A three-day minimum stay and three-day deposit required. NO CREDIT CARDS. The units have complete kitchens, some units have phones. A pool is on the premises. The units we toured were roomy and nicely furnished. The Honokowai General Store is also nearby.

WHERE TO STAY – WHAT TO SEE
Kapalua/Napili/Kahana   Condominiums

HONOKEANA COVE
5255 Lower Honoapiilani Hwy. Phone 1-808-669-6441. Write: Manager, RR 1, Box 200, Lahaina, Maui, HI 96761.

Thirty-eight units near Napili, all ocean view, on cove. Rates: one-bedroom (2) $60; two-bedroom (4) $84; two-bedroom, two bath (4) $90; three-bedroom, two bath (4) $99. Townhouse A $119; Townhouse B $109. Extra person charges $6 in bedroom units, $8 - $10 in townhouse units.

Weekly and monthly rates available. Three-night minimum stay, three-night deposit required. NO CREDIT CARDS. Nice grounds, pool, televisions.

HONOLANI
Sixty-three units at Kahana, ocean front. Write: Honolani Resort Condos, RR 1, Lahaina, Maui, HI 96761. Phone: 1-808-669-8021.

Rates: two-bedroom, 2 bath units sleep a maximum of six persons. High season: $70; low season: $60. During high season, add $10 per day for each person over two. Low season add $6 each.

$100 deposit required with four-week notice for refund. Full payment is required 30 days prior to arrival. Minimum stay is three days during low season, seven days during high season. NO CREDIT CARDS. Units are ocean front on sandy, reef protected beach. A grocery store is on the premises. Maid service is weekly. Pool.

HOYOCHI NIKKO
Kahana area. Write: Manager, RR 1, Lahaina, Maui, HI 96761. Phone: 1-808-669-8343.

Rates: High season—one-bedroom $60 (has 495 sq. ft.); large one-bedroom $65 (has 593 sq. ft.); extra large one-bedroom $70 (has 667 sq. ft.). Extra persons above two add $15 per day. Low season—1-bedroom $50; large $55; extra large $60.

Extra persons $7 per day. $100 deposit required with 30-day notice during low season; 60-day notice during high season. Prepayment required. NO CREDIT CARDS. Cars are available upon request with a minimum 14-day rental. Rooms have extra long twin beds and some have doubles. Pool. Maid service on check-out only. Kitchens in units.

KAHANA REEF**
4471 Honoapiilani Hwy., Lahaina, Maui, HI 96761. Phone: 1-808-669-6491. Eighty-eight units on ocean, all with ocean view.

Rates: High season—studio (3 maximum) $57; one-bedroom (5 maximum) $62. Low season—studio $52; one-bedroom $57. Extra persons above two add $6.

$100 deposit required 10 days following confirmation of reservations. 15% monthly discounts available. Units offer maid service Monday - Saturday, kitchens include dishwasher. All rooms with television. Pool. A one-bedroom unit including car runs $74 during low season and $79 during high season. The units are well kept & nicely furnished. The beachfront is sandy, but fair for swimming and snorkeling. A good value.

KULAKANE
3741 Lower Honoapiilani Hwy., Honokowai area. Phone 1-800-367-6088 or 1-808-669-6119. Write P.O. Box 5238, Lahaina, Maui, HI 96761.

Rates: one-bedroom (1-2 persons) $65; one-bedroom extra wide unit $70; two-bedroom, two bath (1-4 persons) $90; two-bedroom, 2 bath extra wide $95.

WHERE TO STAY – WHAT TO SEE

Condominiums   Kapalua/Napili/Kahana

10% discount for 28-day stay or longer. Minimum three nights. $100 deposit required to hold room with one-month notice for refund. NO CREDIT CARDS. The first and second floor units are all one-bedroom. The third floor are two-bedroom townhouses that sleep up to six. Units have kitchens and lanais.

KULEANA I AND II
3959 Lower Honoapiilani Hwy., Lahaina, Maui, HI 96761. Phone: 1-808-669-8080 or 1-800-367-5176.

Rates: garden view units $55, weekly $330. Oceanfront $60, weekly $360. Extra persons $6. Children under two years, no charge. Cribs $2 a night. Two nights deposit due within 14 days following confirmation. Full prepayment required 30 days prior to arrival, 14-day notice for deposit refund. Large pool, tennis court, volleyball, and activity center.

LOKELANI
Write: Manager, 3833 Lower Honoapiilani Hwy., Lahaina. Phone 1-808-669-8110. Thirty-six units.

Rates: one-bedroom (2) $55 per day, $350 per week, $1350 per month. Two-bedroom (4) $80 per day, $525 per week, $2100 per month.

Extra persons $5 with minimum three-day stay. Three nights deposit required and 30-day notice for refund. NO CREDIT CARDS. Kitchens include dishwashers, washer/dryers. No pool. On beach front.

MAHINA SURF
4057 Lower Honoapiilani Hwy., Lahaina. Phone: 1-800-669-6086 or 1-808-669-6068. Write: Manager, RR 1, Box 100, Lahaina, Maui, HI 96761.

Rates: High season—one-bedroom (2) $55 day, $366 week, $1,309 month. Extra persons $6. Low season—$50 day, $333 week, $1,190 month. $150 deposit refundable on two-week notice. Two bedroom units add $5 for 1 bath units add $10 for 2 bath units.

Pool, electric kitchens with dishwashers, color television, TELEPHONES!, maid service available at hour charge, no pets allowed. NO CREDIT CARDS. Located on an area with no beach. The nearest sandy ones are a short drive to Kahana.

MAKANI SANDS
3765 Lower Honoapiilani Hwy., Lahaina. Phone: 1-808-669-8223. Write: Manager, Route 1, Box 600, Lahaina, Maui, HI 96761.

1 bedroom (2)	$ 55 day	$350 week	$1,350 month
2 bedroom (4)	75	475	1,840
3 bedroom (6)	100	650	2,400
Penthouse (6)	120	760	2,750

$6 extra person charged. Three-day minimum stay required. Deposit varies based on length of stay and room size. Televisions, dishwashers, washer/dryers, trash compactors, elevator. On ocean with pool, weekly maid service.

WHERE TO STAY – WHAT TO SEE
Kapalua/Napili/Kahana   Condominiums

MAUI SANDS
3559 Lower Honoapiilani Hwy., Lahaina. Phone: 1-808-669-4811, or 1-800-367-5037. Write: Manager, Maui Sands, Honokowai, Maui, HI 96761 or Maui Resort Management, P.O. Box 208, Lahaina, Maui, HI 96761.

	standard	garden	ocean
1 bedroom	$49	$62	$75
2 bedroom	69	81	98

Above two persons $6 each, 13% monthly discounts. Units have air conditioning, all electric kitchens with dishwashers.

MAUIAN
Napili Bay. Phone: 1-808-669-6205. Office open 8 a.m. - 5 p.m. and closed for lunch (12 - 1). Studio apartments with kitchenettes on bay.

High season: standard $55; premium $60. Low season: standard $45; premium $55.

Three-day minimum stay with 5% after 14 days and 12% monthly discounts. Extra person $6, rental crib also $6 night. $100 deposit required within 10 days after placing reservation. Fourteen-day notice for refund. NO CREDIT CARDS. Located on Napili Bay, the rooms feature one queen and two twin day beds, kitchens. BBQ area, and pool. Courtesy phone in office and television only in recreation center.

NAPILI BAY
Located on Napili Bay. Write: 33 Hui Drive, Lahaina Maui, HI 96761. Phone: 1-808-669-6044

On ocean $55 for 2, $6 extra person charged
Off ocean $44 for 2, $6 extra person charged

Two night deposit to hold reservation. 7 day notice to cancel. Minimum 3 day stay. Studio apartments offer 1 queen and 2 single beds. Lanais and Kitchens. Daily maid service. Coin operated laundromat. Public phones in laundromat. Major credit cards accepted.

NAPILI PUAMALA
Napili Bay, Route 1, Lahaina, Maui, HI 96761. Phone: 1-808-669-8002. Studios $51 double occupancy, $8 each additional person. $100 deposit required. Eighteen units located behind the Napili Surf and only a short walk to the beach.

NAPILI SHORES
5315 Honoapiilani Hwy., Lahaina, Maui, HI 96761. Contact: Colony Resorts at 1-800-367-6046.

Studio garden (1-2)	$ 65	maximum occupancy	3
Studio ocean view (1-2)	75	" "	3
Studio ocean front (1-2)	85	" "	3
1 bedroom garden (1-4)	80	" "	4
1 bedroom ocean (1-4)	95	" "	4

Weekly 15% discount. Additional persons $8 nightly. No minimum stay, daily maid service provided. Rooms offer lanais and televisions, and the one-bedroom units have dishwashers. Laundry facilities on premises as well as two pools, an adult hot tub, croquet, and BBQ area. CREDIT CARDS ACCEPTED.

Condominiums　　　　　　　　　　_WHERE TO STAY – WHAT TO SEE_
　　　　　　　　　　　　　　　　　　Kapalua/Napili/Kahana

NAPILI SUNSET*
Write: Manager, Napili Sunset, Napili Bay, Lahaina, Maui, HI 96761. Phone: 1-808-669-8083.

Studio: $53 double; one-bedroom: $92 double; two-bedroom, one bath: $140 for four persons. Additional persons $7 per night. 10% discount for four-week stay. Minimum three-day stay. Deposit required: studios $150; one-bedroom $200; two bedroom $300. NO CREDIT CARDS. Located on Napili Bay, which is excellent for swimming. These units have great ocean views and are nicely maintained.

NAPILI SURF
50 Napili Place, Napili Hwy., Lahaina, Maui, HI 96761. Phone: 1-808-669-8002. Studio: 2-3 persons $61; one-bedroom (2-5 persons) $79; additional persons $8.

Four weeks or longer 10% discount. Deposit $150, 14-day notice of cancellation to receive refund. Three-night minimum stay except during Christmas which requires a 10-day minimum. NO CREDIT CARDS. Two pools, BBQ, shuffleboard, lanais, daily maid service, kitchens, color televisions, and guest laundry facilities. Located on Napili Bay, excellent white sand beach.

NAPILI VILLAGE
5425 Honoapiilani Hwy., Lahaina, Maui, HI 96761. Phone: 1-808-669-6228.

High season: double studio $55, low season $50. Extra persons $5.

All rooms have king size beds, daily maid service. Kitchens include garbage disposals. Free laundry facilities on premises. Pool, access to Napili Bay. One-night deposit is required within 15 days of placing reservation. 72-hour notice required for refund.

NOELANI
4095 Lower Honoapiilani Rd. Phone: 1-808-669-8375.

Studio (2) $50, one-bedroom (2) $65, two-bedroom, two bath (4) $65, three-bedroom two and one-half bath $100. Extra persons $7. Weekly and monthly discounts available. A three-day deposit is required and refund only with two-week notice of cancellation. Fifty ocean front units located on a rock beach. Complex has two pools, and has weekly maid service. Units have color televisions, kitchens with dishwashers only in one, two, and three-bedroom units. LOW SEASON SPECIAL: no extra person charge when occupying existing beds. Located above area of boulders, no sandy beach. Nearest sand beach is short drive to Kahana.

NOHONANI
3723 Lower Honoapiilani Hwy., Phone 1-808-669-8208. Office open 8 a.m. - 5 p.m. Monday through Saturday. Write: Nohonani, RR 1, Lahaina, Maui, HI 96761.

High season:　one-bedroom (1-2) $66　　two-bedroom (1-4) $82
Low season:　　　　"　　　　　$58　　　　　　"　　　　$77

Weekly discounts, extra persons $7. $100 deposit required and 60-day notice of cancellation to receive refund. NO CREDIT CARDS. Complex has large pool, televisions, phones, and is one block to grocery store. Maid service on checkout only.

WHERE TO STAY – WHAT TO SEE
Kapalua/Napili/Kahana   Condominiums

PAKI MAUI
Route 1, Box 490, Lahaina, Maui, HI 96761. Phone: 1-808-669-8235.

Garden waterfall one-bedroom (2) $48; ocean front studio (2) $53; one-bedroom (2) $63; two-bedroom $78; two-bedroom deluxe $84; suite for four has two-bedrooms, two baths and large living room $92.

Children under two at no charge; crib rental $2 per night. This complex centers around a garden waterfall area. All units have kitchens. Deposit required for two nights stay to be mailed within 10 days of confirmation. Pool. No air conditioning.

POHAILANI
4435 Honoapiilani Hwy., Lahaina, Maui, HI 96761. Phone: 1-808-669-6125 or 1-800-367-6038.

High season: Studio beach front (2) $55, deluxe studio (2) $65, two-bedroom (4) $80. Low season: Studio beach front (2) $45, deluxe studio (2) $55, two-bedroom (4) $65.

Deposit varies with the room size, and is refundable with 14-day notice of cancellation. Additional persons $5, under age 2 no charge. 10% monthly discounts. Minimum stay high season is five days, low season is three days. Weekly maid service. Visa and Mastercard accepted. Rooms have kitchens and televisions, complex has two pools, two tennis courts, two paddle tennis areas, an activity center, and four shuffleboard courts.

POLYNESIAN SHORES
3975 Lower Honoapiilani Rd., Lahaina, Maui, HI 96761. Phone 1-808-669-6065.

High season: One-bedroom (2) 3-6 day stay $65; 7-27 day stay $60; 28 or more days $50. Two-bedroom, two bath (2) 3-6 day stay $75; 7-27 day stay $70; 28 or more days $60. Two bedroom, two bath (4) 3-6 day stay $100; 7-27 day stay $90; 28 or more days $80. Three-bedroom, two bath (4) $125; 7-27 day stay $115; 28 or more days $100. Additional persons $8.

Three-day minimum stay, with deposit of $100 for one-bedroom or $150 for two-bedroom units. Thirty-day notice for refund.

ROYAL KAHANA
4365 Honoapiilani Hwy. Phone 1-808-669-8051.

High season: Studio (2-3) $56; one-bedroom (1-4) $72; two-bedroom (1-6) $120.

Low season: Studio (2-3) $49; one-bedroom (1-4) $59; two-bedroom (1-6) $96.

Two nights deposit required within 10 days of confirmation, refundable with 15 days notice. High-rise complex with 236 beach front units, all with view. Underground parking, nice pool area, sauna and pool open 9 a.m. - 9 p.m., tennis 7 a.m. - 7 p.m., ping pong, and central air conditioning.

VALLEY ISLE RESORT
4327 Lower Honoapiilani Hwy., Lahaina, Maui, HI 96761. Phone: 1-808-669-5511. Studio units $49; one-bedroom $59; two-bedroom $79. Three-night minimum stay, deposit required and refundable with 14-day notice.

WHERE TO STAY – WHAT TO SEE
Condominiums   Kapalua/Napili/Kahana

"DELUXE RANGE"

KAHANA SUNSET   *Call during day*
P.O. Box 10219, Lahaina, Maui, HI 96761. Phone 1-808-668-8011 or 1-800-367-5224.

One-bedroom (2) $75; two-bedroom (2) $95; two-bedroom, two and one-half bath $95; ocean front $125.

Monthly discounts are 10%. Additional persons $6. Ninety units on nice white sand beach, all with ocean view.

NAPILI POINT
P.O. Box 5183 Lahaina, Maui, HI 96761. Phone: 1-808-669-5611. Located on Lower Honoapiilani Hwy. Contact: Hotel Corp. at 1-800-367-5124.

	High season:	Low season:
1 bdrm. 1 bath superior ocean view (1-4)	$ 88	$ 73
1 bdrm. 1 bath deluxe ocean view (1-4)	98	83
2 bdrm. 2 bath superior ocean view (1-6)	105	90
2 bdrm. 2 bath deluxe ocean view (1-6)	115	100

$8 additional persons. Located on rocky beach, but is next door to beautiful Napili Bay.

PAPAKEA**   *N/A*
Honokowai area. Write: Maui Resort Management, 3559 Lower Honoapiilani Hwy., Lahaina, Maui, HI 96761. Phone: 1-800-367-5037.

Garden: studio (3) $75; one-bedroom (4) $95; one-bedroom with loft (4) $110; two-bedroom (6) $150; two-bedroom with loft (6) $165. Ocean front: one-bedroom (4) $110; one-bedroom with loft (4) $125; two-bedroom (6) $170.

Weekly, monthly discounts available, i.e. studio weekly ($60), monthly ($52.50). Cribs or roll-away $6 day.

Two nights deposit required with refund upon seven days notice. Christmas holiday 14-day minimum stay with no refunds after October 1. Two pools, two jacuzzi's, two saunas, tennis court, putting green, washer/dryers, BBQ area, nice beach area.

"LUXURY RANGE"

KAPALUA BAY AND GOLF VILLAS**
Located at Kapalua. Phone: 1-800-367-5035 or 1-808-669-7110.

One-bedroom mountain view $110; fairway view $135; golf view $155; ocean front $230; ocean view $200. Two-bedroom mountain view $165; fairway view $205; golf view $240; ocean front $375; and ocean view $325.

Over 300 units are in these combined complexes that are lavishly furnished. A two-night deposit is required to hold your reservation. Units include kitchens, and washer/dryers. Complex offers several pools, tennis, and daily maid service.

WHERE TO STAY – WHAT TO SEE
Kapalua/Napili/Kahana   Condominiums

KAHANA OUTRIGGER
4521 Honoapiilani Hwy., Lahaina, Maui, HI 96761. Contact: Hotel Corp. at 1-808-922-3368.

High season: $198. Low season: $189. Extra persons $9. Complex offers pool, and units have televisions, kitchens with dishwashers.

Three bedroom ocean view penthouse suites sleep six. Located on the ocean.

KAHANA VILLAGE   No   N/A   1-800-824-3065
4531 Honoapiilani Hwy., Lahaina, Maui, HI 96761. Phone: 1-808-669-5111.

High season: two-bedroom ocean front unit on second level $110; ground level ocean front with two bedrooms and study or three bedrooms $130. Ocean view two bedroom $90. Poolside three-bedroom $110. Low season: deduct $10. Units sleep four persons. 10% discount for 30 days or more. $200 deposit to hold reservation with balance paid prior to arrival. NO CREDIT CARDS. Weekly maid service. All second level units feature a 1,200 square foot room. Ground level three-bedroom units have 1,700 square feet with a wet bar and sunken tub in master bath. Televisions, phones, Jenn-aire ranges, lanais, and washer/dryers provided.   Sandy Beach

NAPILI KAI*   No   N/A
5900 Honoapiilani Hwy., Lahaina, Maui, HI 96761. Phone: 1-800-367-5030 or 1-808-669-6291. (NAPILI LANI is their ocean front wing.)

Standard room for 2 $100;	deluxe $115;	for 3-4 persons $135
Deluxe ocean view 115	(2) 130	155
Deluxe ocean front 135	160	180

Additional persons over age three $8 per night. First and last night's deposit required and no refund of deposit if cancellation made later than 14 days prior to arrival. NO CREDIT CARDS. The grounds are extensive and the area very quiet. Restaurant is located on the grounds. A nice beach fronts the resort. Complimentary tennis equipment, beach equipment, croquet, putters, and snorkel gear are available. Units feature kitchenettes, lanais, telephones, and washer/dryer facilities.

SANDS OF KAHANA**   No   N/A
Honoapiilani Hwy. Contact: Hotel Corp. at 1-800-367-5124.

High season: One-bedroom garden (4) $99; ocean view (4) $114; one-bedroom ocean front (4) $124; two-bedroom ocean view (1-6) $134; two-bedroom ocean front $159; three-bedroom ocean view (1-6) $198; three-bedroom ocean front or penthouse $219.

Low season: deduct $9 per night. Extra persons $9. Under age 18 free in existing space. Located on nice beach, this highrise complex features nice grounds and pool. Units all have fully equipped kitchens.

WHERE TO STAY – WHAT TO SEE
Long-term Stays — Kapalua/Kahana/Napili

HONOKOWAI EAST
Contact: Manager, Honokowai, Maui, HI 96761. Minimum three-month stay, Kahana Beach.

LEINANI APARTMENTS
Write: Manager, Leinani Apartments, Honokowai, Lahaina, Maui, HI 96761. Long-term only. Phone: 1-808-669-6230.

NAPILI SANDS
Hui F. Rd. 132 units on hill, 1,000 feet mauka of beach road. Only long-term stay. $275 to $350 per month for studios; $375 to $450 for one-bedrooms. One block from shopping facilities and a walking distance to beach or bus stop. Includes swimming pool and laundry area. Contact: Ho'oli Hale, 278 Wiliko Place - 2, Lahaina, Maui, HI 96761. Phone: 1-808-667-7971.

WHERE TO STAY – WHAT TO SEE
Kihei/Wailea

INTRODUCTION

The Kihei/Wailea area began its growth after the onset of the West Maui development. Kihei was the first to develop and it now sprawls a distance of six miles with one condominium complex following another. Just south of Kihei is the more thoughtfully designed area of Wailea. This area was well laid out with two golf courses first appearing. Finally, two high-class resorts were built in the late 1970's. Stouffer's Wailea (changed from the Westin Wailea in November, 1983) and the Maui Intercontinental both add fine accommodations and restaurants to this end of Maui.

This section of East Maui has a much different feel than the West Maui or Lahaina areas. It is much quieter and runs at a more leisurely pace. Accommodations are generally a much better value here. The beaches are very nice with good public access, so no need to worry if your accommodations are not beach front. Restaurant selections are more limited, and many vacationers stay in condominiums and utilize their kitchens. There are several large grocery stores along South Kihei Road that make shopping for food simple.

WHAT TO SEE

The road beyond Wailea offers some interesting scenery, unspoiled beaches and rough roads (see "Makena Area Beaches"). This section is currently being developed, but about four miles past Polo Beach you will arrive at and can drive through an old lava flow. Just past this, the road ends at the lovely La Perouse Bay.

The Wailea area beaches are well planned, nicely maintained and worth a stop for beach afficionados. The Stouffer's Resort also offers lovely grounds you might want to enjoy.

WHERE TO SHOP

Wailea Shopping Center is located at the southern end of Wailea. It offers a nice mall of shops and a restaurant. The Stouffer's Resort and the Maui Intercontinental both offer nice shopping areas within their resorts.

The Rainbow Mall is a new small center on the Mauka side (towards the mountain) of South Kihei Road offering an ice cream shop, restaurant, and a limited number of small assorted clothing and souvenir shops.

The Kihei Town Center offers a selection of shops including sporting goods, (which offer rental equipment), novelty shops, grocery, and clothing. Located on South Kihei Road by McDonald's.

Azeka's Place shopping center is where you can pick up Azeka's famous ribs at the market to cook up yourself. Also, International House of Pancakes and Sailmaker Annie's are among the restaurants to be found. We enjoyed prowling through the very good bookstore they have as well as the sporting, clothing, and souvenir shops.

Hotels   WHERE TO STAY – WHAT TO SEE
                                                                  Kihei/Wailea

"BARGAIN RANGE"

SURF AND SAND HOTEL
2980 S. Kihei Beach Rd., Kihei, Maui, HI 96753. Phone: 1-800-367-2958.

Rates:				
Garden view (single/double)	$30;	suite (1-4)	$58
Ocean view	"	$35;	"	$68
Ocean front	"	$40	"	$78

Kitchenettes add $10. Room and car special $39.90 for two people. Direct-dial phones, televisions, air conditioning, daily maid service. Deposit of one night's rental within 10 days of reservation and 72 hours' notice required to receive refund. No elevator to second floor. The exterior of these units are an Oriental brown and orange. The room we viewed was very small and, while ocean front, there was only one small window from which to view the surf and no lanais. There was a small refrigerator, toaster, and hotplate. A shower, but no bathtub. The room appeared very clean, but the furnishings had seen a better day.

"LUXURY RANGE"

HOTEL INTERCONTINENTAL***
Wailea. Contact: Hotel Intercontinental at 1-800-367-2960 from the Mainland or from Honolulu toll free at 1-800-537-5589.

High season:
  Minimum accommodation $95; moderate $115; maximum $125.

Low season:
  Minimum accommodation $70; moderate $ 90; maximum $100.

Third person in room add $10. Suites run from $130 - $525. Full American Plan add $44 per person, Modified American Plan add $35 per person. Deposit equal to one night required to guarantee reservation with 72-hour cancellation notice for refund. Also offered are an assortment of package plans: family, room and car, golfer's paradise, tennis paradise, and honeymoon paradise. Three pools and four restaurants in this Spanish style resort. The fronting beach is rocky, but resort adjacent to nice white sand beach.

MAKENA SURF
Contact: Makena Surf, ~~841 Bishop St., #1000, Honolulu, Hi 96813~~ Phone: ~~1-800-367-7052~~ or 1-808-531-5323.   *879-5764*   *No*

	RATES: First floor units-	2 bedroom, 2 Bath (1-4) $225
		2 bedroom, 2 Bath with study (1-6) $250
	Second floor units-	2 bedroom, 2 bath (1-4) $200
	Third floor units-	2 bedroom, 2 Bath (1-4) $175
		3 bedroom, 3 bath (1-6) $300

WHERE TO STAY – WHAT TO SEE
Kihei/Wailea — Hotels

Located 2 miles past Wailea. These rates include the 4% sales tax and a mid-size rental car. A two night deposit is required 15 days after reservation confirmation. Refund only if cancellations is made two weeks prior to arrival. Holiday periods require payment in full 30 days prior to arrival. All units are ocean front and feature central air conditioning, fully equipped kitchens, washers and dryers, wet bar, whirlpool spa in the master bath, telephones, T.V. and daily maid service. Two pools, and four tennis courts are set in nicely landscaped grounds. Three historic sites found on location have been preserved. The nearest restaurants are located in Wailea.

STOUFFER'S WAILEA RESORT***
Contact: Stouffer's at 1-800-385-5000. Rates: mountain view $95; garden view $105; ocean view $135; beach front $180.

Five restaurants, excellent beach, good snorkeling and swimming. Beautiful jungly grounds and nice pool area. We have heard the beach front cottages are marvelous.

Entertainment 1985 coupon books offer a 50% discount on ocean view rooms between April 15 and December 15. Your stay with this coupon is limited to four days.

Condominiums _WHERE TO STAY — WHAT TO SEE_
Kihei/Wailea

"BARGAIN RANGE"

ISLAND SURF
Contact: Maui Beachfront Rentals, 1993 S. Kihei Rd., Kihei, Maui, HI 96753. Phone: 1-808-879-1683 or 1-800-367-5232.

High season: one-bedroom $55; two-bedroom $65.
Low season: one-bedroom $37; two-bedroom $45. (Hotel room unit $27.)

$100 deposit with refund upon 30-day notice of cancellation. Eighty-two units are across the road, all with ocean view, pool, shops on lower level. Rooms are air conditioned and have washer/dryers. Located near Kamaole I Park. Older complex.

KAPULANIKAI
73 Kapu Place, Kihei, Maui, HI 96753. Contact: Manager, P.O. Box 716, Kihei, Maui, HI 96753. Phone: 1-808-879-1607. High season: $50. Low season: $35. Kitchens in units and pool.

KAUHALE MAKAI (Village by the Sea)
930-938 S. Kihei Rd. Contact: Maui Beachfront Rentals, 1993 S. Kihei Rd., Kihei, Maui, HI 96753. Phone: 1-808-879-1683 or 1-800-367-5232.

High season: studio (2) $35 - $40; one-bedroom (2) $45 - $60; two-bedroom $75 - $80; two-bedroom deluxe (4) $85 - $90.

Low season: studio (2) $32 - $35; one-bedroom (2) $40 - $50, two-bedroom (4) $60 - $65; two-bedroom deluxe (4) $75- $80.

$7.50 additional person. 169 units are located in two six-floor buildings. On beach front, with nearby quick market. Complex features putting green, gas BBQ, pool, children's pool, sauna, laundry center. Units are air conditioned with kitchens and telephones. The beach here is fair, but was strewn with coral rubble when we visited.

KEALIA
191 N. Kihei Rd., Kihei, Maui, HI 96753. Phone 1-800-367-5222 or 1-808-9159.

High season:	studio $45;	one-bedroom $55;	two-bedroom $75
Low season:	" $37;	" $45;	" $55

Prices based on double occupancy, extra person $5 per night. No charge for children under five. $100 deposit. 100% payment required 14 days prior to arrival. NO CREDIT CARDS ACCEPTED. Fifty-one units located on the ocean. Units are air conditioned with lanais, kitchens, washer/dryers, and dishwashers. Pool, nice beach, good value.

KIHEI BAY SURF
Kihei Rd. Contact: Maui Beachfront Rentals at 1-808-879-5455 or 1-800-367-5242.

High season: $35. Low season $30. Double occupancy studio units.

118 units across from the beach. Two-story structure has no elevator. Jacuzzi, pool, recreation area, 1 gas BBQ, laundry area, tennis. Air conditioned units have kitchens.

WHERE TO STAY – WHAT TO SEE
Kihei/Wailea   Condominiums

KIHEI KAI
61 N. Kihei Rd., Kihei, Maui, HI 96753. Contact: Manager. Phone 1-808-879-2357.

High season: $40 - $45 minimum seven-day stay. Low season: $30 - $35 with four-day minimum stay.

Prices on double occupancy, third and fourth guests $5 a day. Maximum occupancy four. Fourteen-day stay entitles 10% discount, one month—20% discount. $100 deposit within 10 days and a 30-day notice of cancellation for full refund. Twenty-five units are beach front at Maalaea Bay. Pool, recreation area, and laundry room. Units have complete kitchens, televisions, air conditioning or ceiling fans.

KIHEI KAI NANI
2495 S. Kihei Rd., Kihei, Maui, HI 96753. Phone: 1-808-879-9088 or 1-808-879-1430.

One-bedroom units. High season: $45; low season $35.

Minimum four-night stay. This complex has 180 units and is older looking than most along Kihei Rd. It boasts having the second largest pool on Maui, offers a laundry room, recreation center, and kitchens.

LEILANI KAI RESORT
1226 Uluniu St. Contact: P.O. Box 296, Kihei, Maui, HI 96753. Phone: 1-808-879-2606.

High season: studio (2) $42; one-bedroom (2) $55; one-bedroom deluxe (4) $68; two-bedroom (4) $68. Low season: studio $29; one-bedroom $37; one-bedroom deluxe $45; two-bedroom $45.

Nine garden apartments, however, no pool. Televisions, crib and rollaway rentals available. Deposit $50 - $100 with 30-day cancellation notice. Five-day minimum stay. Units have lanais and kitchens.

LIHI KAI
2121 Ilili Rd., Kihei, Maui, HI 96753. Contact: Manager at 1-808-879-2335.

Double or single occupancy $35 daily, $175 weekly, $465 monthly.

This appears to be one of the earlier condo developments. It does not have a pool.

*NANI KAI HALE***
73 N. Kihei Rd., Kihei, Maui, HI 96753. Contact: Manager at 1-808-879-9120 or toll free at 1-800-367-6032.

High season: room with bath only for two persons $29; studio with kitchen $42; one-bedroom, two bath (2) oceanview $55, ocean front $65; two-bedroom, two bath (1-4) $80; deluxe ocean front one-bedroom $65. Low season: room with bath only for two persons $22; studio with kitchen $30; one-bedroom, two bath (2) ocean view $40, ocean front $50; two bedroom, two bath (1-4) $50. High season seven-day minimum stay and $8 extra person charge. Low season three-day minimum stay and $6 extra person charge. Monthly 10% discounts. $100 deposit and 30-day notice to cancel. No charge for children under five. Located on nice sand beach, under building parking, pool, laundry on each floor, elevator (six story building). Nice patio and BBQ by beach. Lanais have ocean and mountain view.

Condominiums

WHERE TO STAY – WHAT TO SEE
Kihei/Wailea

NONA LANI
455 S. Kihei Rd. Contact: Manager, P.O. Box 655, Kihei, Maui, HI 96753. Phone: 1-808-879-2497.

High season: $48 a night for seven nights, $45 a night for 14-night stay. Third person charge $6. Low season: $38, minimum three-night stay.

Eight cottages on large grounds. Laundry facilities and public phone on premises. Large refrigerator and oven. Units have queen bed plus a day bed, full bath with tub and shower, lanais. Two BBQ's on grounds. These units are across the road from the beach.

PUALANI
Kihei Rd. Contact: Manager, P.O. Box 716, Kihei, Maui, HI 96753. Phone: 1-808-879-1607. High season: $58. Low season: $35. Units have kitchen. Pool.

SUNSEEKER RESORT (formerly Maalaea Bay)
551 S. Kihei Rd. Contact: Manager, P.O. Box 276, Kihei, Maui, HI 96753. Phone 1-808-879-1261.

Studio with kitchenette $29; one-bedroom with kitchen $39; two-bedroom with kitchen $50. Extra person $6.

Also special off-season, weekly and monthly rates. Next door to restaurant and tennis. Deposit required with 30-day notice to cancel.

WAILANA SANDS
25 Wailana Place, Kihei, Maui, HI 96753. Phone: 1-808-879-3171 after hours or during day at 1-808-879-2026. One-bedroom apartments with kitchens, queen beds, televisions. High season: $39, low season: $26. 10% monthly discounts. Minimum three-day stay. Deposit required with 30 days notice for refund. NO CREDIT CARDS. Pool.

"MODERATE RANGE"

HALE HUI KAI
2994 S. Kihei Rd., Kihei, Maui, HI 96753. Phone: 1-808-879-1219.

High season: two-bedroom for two $65 - $80. Low season: $55 - $70.

Pool, ocean front location, and laundry facilities. Kitchens.

HALE KAI O KIHEI
1310 Uluniu Rd., Kihei, Maui, HI 96753. Contact: Manager at 1-808-879-2757.

High season: one-bedroom, one bath (2) $350 weekly; two bedroom, one bath (4) $450. Low season: one-bedroom, one bath (2) $250 weekly; two bedroom, one bath (4) $365.

Extra person $10. Four week stay at 5% discount. $75 deposit with 30-day notice of cancellation for full refund. ***Children must be six years or older. NO CREDIT CARDS. Pool, laundry, recreation area.

HONO KAI
Maalaea. Write: Manager, Hono Kai, Wailuku, Maui, HI 96793. Phone: 1-808-244-7012 or 1-800-367-6084.

High season: one-bedroom garden or ocean view $315 - $325 weekly; two bedroom on

WHERE TO STAY – WHAT TO SEE
Kihei/Wailea   Condominiums

water $450 weekly; three-bedroom on water $500 weekly. Low season: one-bedroom garden or ocean view $305 - $315 weekly; two-bedroom ocean front $385 weekly; three-bedroom ocean front $425 weekly.

$100 deposit with 24-hour notice for refund. Minimum five-day stay. Forty-six units located on the beach at Maalaea Bay. Pool and laundry facilities. Kitchens.

HALE KAMAOLE**
2737 S. Kihei Rd., Kihei, Maui, HI 96753. Phone 1-808-879-2698.

High season: one-bedroom, one bath (2) $55; two-bedroom, two bath for (2) $77. Extra person $7. Low season: one-bedroom, one bath $40; two-bedroom, two bath (2).

Extra person $4. 10% discount for 28-day stay or longer. Deposit required to equal two days rental stay per week. Balance due 30 days prior to arrival. Laundry building, two pools, tennis. Some units have washer/dryers. Courtesy phone at office. Maid service only on check out. NO CREDIT CARDS. 188 units in five buildings (two story, no elevator) are across road from very nice Kamaole III beach.

HALE PAU HANA
2480 S. Kihei Rd., Kihei, Maui, HI 96753. Phone: 1-808-879-2715 or 1-800-367-6036.

High season: one-bedroom, one bath for 4 at $75; one-bedroom, two bath for 5 at $75. Low season: discount 24%.

10% monthly discounts. $10 each additional person. Deluxe two-bedroom units—prices available upon request. All units with view. Limited maid service provided. NO CREDIT CARDS. Pool, laundry area, elevator. Near Kamaole II beach.

HALEAKALA SHORES**
2619 S. Kihei Rd. Contact: Manager at 1-808-879-1218.

High season: two bedroom units $85 (sleeps 1-4). $8 extra person charge, seven-day minimum stay. Low season: two-bedroom $45 daily, $280 weekly, extra person $8.

Three-day minimum stay. $100 deposit refundable with 30-day notice. Balance due 30 days prior to arrival. Located across road from very nice public Kamaole III beach. Maid service available upon request. This seventy-six two-bedroom unit complex offers a recreation room, putting green, covered parking, swimming pool, and shuffleboard.

ISLAND SANDS
Contact: Manager, P.O. Box 391, Wailukuk, Maui, HI 96793. Phone 1-808-244-0848.

High season: one-bedroom deluxe (1-2) $49; two-bedroom deluxe (1-2) $67. Low season: deduct $4 per night.

Extra person charge $5. Weekly rates available. Three-day minimum stay required and two-day deposit required within 20 days of confirmation. Refund upon notice 15 days prior to arrival. No charge for children 12 and under. Located oceanfront at Maalaea. Complex offers pool, BBQ, and elevators.

KAMAOLE BEACH ROYALE
2385 S. Kihei Rd. Contact: Manager, P.O. Box 370, Kihei, Maui, HI 96753. Phone: 1-808-879-3131.

High season: one-bedroom (2) $55; two-bedroom (2) $65; two-bedroom deluxe (2) $70; three-bedroom (2) $75. Low season: deduct $15 per night.

WHERE TO STAY – WHAT TO SEE
Condominiums   Kihei/Wailea

Monthly discounts available. Four-day minimum stay requirement. $200 deposit required with balance due on arrival. Forty-five day notice for deposit refund and a $25 service charge is deducted. NO CREDIT CARDS. Sixty-four units in a single seven story building. Located across from Kamaole I beach. Complex has recreation area, laundry room, pool, and roof garden. Elevator. Full kitchens.

KAMAOLE NALU
2450 S. Kihei Rd. Contact: Manager, P.O. Box 157, Kihei, Maui, HI 96753. Phone: 1-808-879-1006.

High season: ocean view $75; ocean front $85 double occupancy. Extra persons $15.

Low season: ocean view $55; ocean front $65 double occupancy. Extra persons $12. Three-day minimum stay. NO CREDIT CARDS. Deposits $200 during high season, $100 during low season with $25 cancellation fee charged. Monthly discounts available. Thirty-six units in a single six story building on beach front, all units offering ocean view. All units are two-bedroom, two bath with large lanai. Kitchens offer dishwashers and all units have washer/dryers. Weekly maid service provided during high season. Pool.

KANA'I A NALU
Hauli Street in Maalaea. Contact: Shelton Rentals, RR 1, Box 388, Wailuku, Maui, HI 96793. Phone: 1-808-244-3911.

High season: ocean view $70; ocean front $80. Low season: ocean view $60; ocean front $70. $7.50 extra person charged. Monthly 10% discount. Minimum five-day stay. $150 deposit with 30-day notice for refund. Make checks payable to Shelton Rentals. Ninety two-bedroom units in four buildings with elevators. Kitchens and washer/dryers in every unit. Pool.

KIHEI AKAHI
Piilani Hwy. Contact: Condo Rentals Hawaii at 1-808-879-2778 or 1-800-367-5242.

High season: studio (2) $50; one-bedroom (2) $60; two-bedroom (4) $82; townhouse (4) $87. Low season: studio $41; one-bedroom $45; two-bedroom $61; townhouse $70.

$5 extra person charge. $100 deposit. Five-day minimum stay. 240 units across from Kamehameha Park II.

KIHEI ALII KAI
2387 S. Kihei Rd., Kihei, Maui, HI 96753. Contact: Manager. Phone: 1-808-879-6880.

High season: one-bedroom, one bath (2) $55; two-bedroom, two bath (4) $77. Low season: one-bedroom, one bath (2) $40; two-bedroom, two bath (4) $56.

Extra person $5 per day. $100 deposit with 30-day notice for refund. Minimum three-day stay. Full payment 30 days prior to arrival. NO CREDIT CARDS. Located across road from beach. All units have washer/dryers, kitchens. Complex features Jacuzzi, sauna, pool, two tennis courts, two BBQ areas, and shuffleboard.

KIHEI BEACH RESORT
36 S. Kihei Rd., Kihei, Maui, HI 96753. Contact: Manager. Phone: 1-800-367-6034.

High season:
one-bedroom $ 72   double occupancy (maximum 4 people)
two-bedroom $107   "   "   " 6 "

WHERE TO STAY – WHAT TO SEE
Kihei/Wailea   Condominiums

Low season:
one-bedroom $ 55   double occupancy (maximum 4 people)
two-bedroom $ 83   "   "   " 6   "

Extra person $8. Weekly and monthly discounts available. Three-day deposit required with 72-hour notice of cancellation during low season and 30-day notice during high season. Balance must be prepaid in full. NO CREDIT CARDS. Fifty-four units are beach front with ocean view. Units have color television, PHONES, kitchens with dishwasher. Resort offers pool, central air conditioning, recreation area, elevator, maid service.

KIHEI RESORT
Kaonolulu Street. Phone: 1-808-879-7441.

High season: one-bedroom (2) $60; two-bedroom (2) $70. Low season: one-bedroom (2) $45; two-bedroom (2) $55.

$4 extra person charge. Deposit $50 per person with refund upon 30 days notice of cancellation. Complex has 64 units, pool, and Jacuzzi.

KIHEI SANDS
115 N. Kihei Rd., Kihei, Maui, HI 96753. Phone: 1-808-879-2624. Contact: Manager.

High season:
  one-bedroom (1-4) $50 and up (double occupancy)
  two-bedroom (1-4) $65 and up   "   "
Low season:
  one-bedroom (1-4) $35 and up   "   "
  two-bedroom (1-4) $50 and up   "   "

Extra person $6 charge with special monthly rates. Minimum three-day stay. $100 deposit with 14-day refund notice. Thirty ocean front units, all with view. Laundry area and pool.

KIHEI SURFSIDE
Contact: Maui Beachfront Rentals, 2936 S. Kihei Rd., Kihei, Maui, HI 96753. Phone: 1-808-879-1488.

High season: one-bedroom, one and one-half bath for two $70. Low season: $47.

Beach front, pool, recreation area. $6 additional person charge. 3 night minimum, maid service every fourth day. 3 day deposit to hold reservation.

KOA LAGOON
800 S. Kihei Rd., Kihei, Maui, HI 96753. Phone: 1-808-879-3002. Contact: Manager.

High season:
one-bedroom, one bath $70 (2 maximum 4) $10 extra person two-bedroom, two bath $85 (2) $100 (3-4) $10 extra person
Low season:
one-bedroom, one bath $50 (2, maximum 4) $7.50 extra person two-bedroom, two bath $60 (2) $70 (3-4) $7.50 extra person

10% monthly discsount. $100 deposit within 10 days, full payment 30 days prior to arrival. Sixty-day cancellation notice. Fourteen-day minimum stay during Christmas holiday. $25 charge for less than five-day stay. Forty-two units have bar and ice-maker, color

Condominiums

WHERE TO STAY – WHAT TO SEE
Kihei/Wailea

television, tub and shower, washer/dryer, pool. Owner operated and managed.

KOA RESORT
811 S. Kihei Rd., Kihei, Maui, HI 96753. Phone: 1-808-879-7879 or from Los Angelos area phone 1-213-461-2717. Toll free California only 1-800-252-0078. Toll free U. S. 1-800-421-0683.

High season:
one-bedroom $65; two-bedroom $85-95; three-bedroom $130-160

Low season:
one-bedroom $45; two-bedroom $55-65; three-bedroom $ 75-120

$100 deposit within 14 days of reservation. Thirty-day notice for refund. NO CREDIT CARDS. Fifty-four units located on spacious five and one-half acre grounds. Two five-story buildings across road from beach. Two tennis courts, pool, spa, Jacuzzi, putting green. Units have kitchen and washer/dryers.

LAULE'A **
980 S Kihei Rd, Kihei, Maui HI 96753. 1-808-879-5247

Low season: 1 bedroom partial ocean view $60; 1 beroom ocean view $67; 2 bedroom partial ocean $74; 2 bedroom ocean view $81; 3 bedroom partial ocean $110. High season: not yet announced.

Gary Boardman is manager of these units completed in 1984. Tastefully decorated in mauves and blues and complete with washer, dryer, microwave, phones and maid service every other day. Only one building has an elevator to the upper floors. Fronting these condos is a public park with 4 tennis courts and a beach that is rather corally. On site are a nice pool area, separate mens and womens saunas, wet bar area, hot tub, BBQ'S.

LAULOA
Hauohi Street. Contact: Manager, RR 1, Box 383, Maalaea, Maui, HI 96793. Phone 1-808-247-5675,

Two-bedroom, two bath units accommodate up to six persons.

High season:
    $75 for 6 nights or less; $65 7-29 nights; $45 30+ nights

Low season:
    $65 for 6 nights or less; $55 7-29 nights; $35 30+ nights

Extra persons charged $5. $100 deposit with 30 days notice for cancellation. Three-night minimum stay. Maid service extra charge. NO CREDIT CARDS. Forty-seven 1,100 square foot units offer washer/dryers, kitchens, and dishwashers. Ocean front and ocean view units as well as pool.

LEINAALA
998 S Kihei Rd, Kihei Maui 96753. Contact: Oihana Property Management: toll free 1-800-367-5234 or locally 1-808-879-2235. High season: 1 bedroom (2) $55; 2 bedroom (4) $65; Low season: 1 bedroom (2) 45; 2 bedroom (4) $55. $100 deposit with 10 day notice for refund. $7.50 additional person. Pool, tennis courts, all ocean view. NO CREDIT CARDS.

WHERE TO STAY – WHAT TO SEE
Kihei/Wailea   Condominiums

LUANA KAI*
940 S. Kihei Rd. Contact: Hawaiian Island Resorts at 1-800-367-7042.

	High season:	Low season:
one-bedroom garden (1-2)	$ 65	$ 50
two-bedroom garden (1-4)	85	65
three-bedroom garden (1-6)	125	100
one-bedroom ocean front (1-2)	75	60
two-bedroom ocean front (1-4)	95	75

Extra person $6, no charge children under age two. Two night deposit required with one week notification for refund. Three-night minimum stay. Towel service mid-week, linen service weekly. These nice, newer units are adjacent to the State Beach Reserve and public tennis courts. The grounds around the 113 units are nicely landscaped and include a putting green, BBQ area, pool, sauna, Jacuzzi. All units have kitchens and washer/dryers. In Canada for reservations call Ellan Vardy and Associates at 1-800-268-9507.

MAALAEA BANYANS
Hauoli St., Maalaea. Phone: 1-808-242-5668. Contact: Manager, RR 1, Box 384, Wailuku, Maui, HI 96793.

High season:
one-bedroom, one bath (1-2, max. 4) $55
two-bedroom, two bath (4, max. 6)   75

Low season:
one-bedroom, one bath (1-2, max. 4) $45
two-bedroom, two bath (4, max. 6)   60

Minimum seven-day stay required. Extra person charge $7.50. Near the Maalaea boat harbor, beachside with pool area, Jacuzzi, BBQ.

MAALAEA KAI
Contact: Manager, RR 1, Box 380, Maalaea, Wailuku, HI 96793. Phone: 1-808-244-4845.

High season:
one-bedroom $55; two-bedroom $75; over 2 persons $6 additional each person.

Low season:
one-bedroom $40; two-bedroom $55; over 2 persons $6 additional each person.

Three-night minimum stay. Deposit of three nights stay with a thirty-day notice of cancellation for full refund. NO CREDIT CARDS. Seventy units are oceanfront, all with view. Complex has laundry facilities, pool, putting green, BBQ, and elevator to upper levels.

MAKANI A KAI
Contact: Manager, RR 1, Box 400, Wailuku, Maui, HI 96793. Phone: 1-808-244-5627 or 1-800-367-6084.

	High season:	Low season:
ocean front one-bedroom	$375 weekly	$325
ocean front two-bedroom	$525 weekly	$425
ocean view two-bedroom	$475 weekly	$400

WHERE TO STAY — WHAT TO SEE
Condominiums   Kihei/Wailea

Twenty-four units in three buildings, beach front at Maalaea. Monthly rates at 10% discount. $100 deposit refundable with 24-hour notice of cancellation. Air conditioned units have dishwashers and complex offers pool and laundry facilities.

MANA KAI
2960 S. Kihei Rd. Contact: Mana Kai, P.O. Box 1808, Fort Collins, CO 80522. Phone: 1-800-525-2025.

	High season:	Low season:
hotel unit (2 persons)	$ 35	$ 34
one-bedroom (4)	95	85
two-bedroom, two bath (4)	120	110

Eight story building houses 92 units on a nice beach. Complimentary car with all except hotel units. 10% discount for thirty days or longer stay. One night deposit required. Complex has laundry facilities on each floor, a pool, and a restaurant off the lobby. They offer the Pritikin Better Health Program which is a one-week program. Their restaurant serves Pritikin meals as well as general meals. (See "Restaurants, Kihei".) The hotel units are just a studio-type room with an adjoining bath. The one-bedroom units have a kitchen. The two-bedroom unit is actually the hotel unit and the one-bedroom combined, with each having separate entry doors.

MAUI PARKSHORE
2653 S. Kihei Rd., Kihei, Maui, HI 96753. Contact: Manager at 1-808-879-1600.

	High season:	Low season:	
one-bedroom (1-4)	$45	$35	$5 extra person
two-bedroom deluxe	65	55	7.50 "
two-bedroom standard	60	45	5 "

NO CREDIT CARDS. Units offer dishwashers, washer/dryers, full kitchens, color television. Pool, sauna, and elevator. Payment in full upon arrival. $100 deposit with 30-day notice for cancellation. 10% monthly discount.

MAUI VISTA
2191 S. Kihei Rd. Contact: Maui Beachfront Rentals at 1-800-367-5232 or 1-808-879-5455.

	High season:	Low season:
one-bedroom (2 persons)	$50	$40
two-bedroom (1-4)	65	55

$7.50 per person extra charge. Some units have air conditioning, some have washer/dryers. All have kitchens with dishwashers. The two-bedroom units are on the fourth floor and are townhouse-style. Nice, newer complex across road from beach. Some ocean view units. Six tennis courts, two pools. We had some problem with sound carrying from neighboring unit.

WHERE TO STAY – WHAT TO SEE
Kihei/Wailea   Condominiums

MENEHUNE SHORES
760 Kihei Rd. Phone 1-808-879-1508. Contact: Gladys Williams, rental agent, P.O. Box 556, Kihei, Maui, HI 96753, phone: 1-808-879-5828.

	High season:	Low season:
one-bedroom, one bath (2)	$55	$40
two-bedroom, two bath (2)	67	55
two-bedroom, two bath (4)	75	55
three-bedroom, two bath (4)	85	75
" " " " (6)	100	85

Extra person $7.50 per night. $100 deposit with $25 cancellation charge unless 30-day notice is given. Dishwashers and some units with washer/dryers. Recreation room and roof gardens. Also available through Kihei Kona Rentals, P.O. Box 618, Kihei, Maui, HI 96753, phone: 1-808-879-3428.

ROYAL MAUIAN
2430 S. Kihei Rd. Phone: 1-808-879-1263, from California call 1-800-252-0076. Contact: Manager, P.O. Box 869, Kihei, Maui, HI 96753.

	High season:	Low season:
one-bedroom, one bath	$ 75	$52 ocean front
two-bedroom, two bath	90	62 ocean front
three-bedroom, two bath	125	90 ocean front
two-bedroom, two bath	70	46 side wing
two-bedroom, two bath	60	42 mtn. view

107 units in a six story building. Five-night minimum stay with 30 days cancellation notification required. 10% monthly discount during high season and 15% monthly discount during low season. Deposit $200 during high season $100 during low season. $25 cancellation charge. Maid service every five days. Private phones in rooms. Air conditioning, elevator, rooftop sundeck, pool, washer/dryers, dishwashers. NO CREDIT CARDS.

SHORES OF MAUI
2075 S. Kihei Rd., Kihei, Maui, HI 96753. Phone: 1-808-879-9140. Contact: Manager.

	High season:	Low season:
one-bedroom (2)	$55 daily/$330 weekly	$40/$240
two-bedroom (4)	$70 daily/$420 weekly	$55/$330

Deposit $100 during low season, one week deposit during high season. 75% of deposit refundable with minimum 30-day cancellation notice. Full payment 30 days prior to arrival. NO CREDIT CARDS. Three-day minimum stay. $7 extra person charge with children under age two free. (Christmas holiday one-week minimum stay.) Monthly rates 25% off. Fifty-unit complex offers pool, BBQ, tennis courts, spa and condo-car packages are available.

WHERE TO STAY – WHAT TO SEE

Condominiums   Kihei/Wailea

SUGAR BEACH
145 N. Kihei Rd. Contact: Maui Beachfront Rentals, 1993 S. Kihei Rd., Kihei, Maui, HI 96753. Phone: 1-800-367-5232.

	High season:	Low season:
one-bedroom ocean front	$75	$60
one-bedroom garden	65	50

Extra person charge $7.50 per night. 215 units in several six story buildings. Elevators. Some units offer washer/dryers, all have kitchens. Pool, Jacuzzi, putting green, air conditioning, gas BBQ grill. Sandwich shop and quick shop market on location. Very nice long, white sand beach.

WAIOHULI BEACH HALE
Contact: Maui Beachfront Rentals, 1993 S. Kihei Rd., Kihei, Maui, HI 96753. Phone: 1-808-879-5455 or 1-800-367-5232.

	High season:	Low season:
one-bedroom unit (2)	$50	$40

$5 extra person per night charged. Fifty-three units in four two-story buildings beachfront at Kihei. Olympic-size lap pool, BBQ area, shuffleboard, near shopping center. NO ELEVATOR.

"DELUXE RANGE"

MAALAEA SURF   800 - 423 - 7953
Contact: Manager, 31 N. Kihei Rd., Kihei, Maui, HI 96753. Phone: 1-808-879-1267.

High season: one-bedroom, one bath units for up to 4 people $96, double occupancy. Two-bedroom, two bath for up to 6 people $148 double occupancy. Low season: 25% less.

Extra person $8. Deposit: one-bedroom $170; two-bedroom $260. Sixty-days notice for cancellation. NO CREDIT CARDS. Fifty-nine units in eight two-story buildings ocean front at Maalaea. Pool and tennis courts.

MAUI BEACHFRONT RESORT (formerly Lipoa)   No Ans.
Uluniu Rd. Located at end of Lipoa St. Contact: Maui Beachfront Rentals at 1-808-879-5455 or 1-800-367-5232.

	High season:	Low season:
two-bedroom standard	$75	$65
two-bedroom deluxe	85	75

$7.50 extra person charged. Eight two-bedroom units in a single two-story building. Large lawn area fronting units. Lanais on upper level. Beach here is well protected. No elevator. Units have washer/dryers, microwaves, and dishwashers. Complex has swimming pool and Jacuzzi.

WHERE TO STAY – WHAT TO SEE
Kihei/Wailea   Condominiums

MAUI HILL
2881 S. Kihei Rd. Contact: Oihana Property Management, 2145 Wells, Wailuku, Maui, HI 96793. Phone: 1-800-367-5234, or 1-808-879-7751.

	High season:	Low season:
one-bedroom	$ 92	$ 74
two-bedroom	105	85
three-bedroom	129	115

These new units have a Spanish flair and are located on a hill across the road from the beach. 140 units are housed in 12 buildings. VERY spacious and only a short walk to beach. Lavishly furnished, units include washer/dryers, air conditioning, microwaves, dishwashers. Pool, and tennis available. Very near Wailea. This would be a great place for a big family allowing lots of room to move around. Some units with good ocean view.

MAUI LU RESORT
575 S. Kihei Rd., Kihei, Maui, HI 96753. Mainland: 1-800-367-5244; Hawaii: 1-800-592-3351; Canada: 1-800-879-5808.

One and two-bedroom cottages for up to three persons at $68.

Additional person $8. Full kitchens, ceiling fans, but no air conditioning. Regular hotel units have air conditioning, small refrigerator, and hot water maker and run $50 standard; $60 superior; and $65 deluxe. 150 units on large grounds with pool shaped like island of Maui.

MAUI SUNSET   *No N/A*
Contact: Manager: 1-808-879-1971.

One-bedroom units $62; two-bedroom, two bath units $84; three-bedroom, three bath units $116.

$7 extra person charge. 225 units in two buildings, located on beach that appeared corally upon our inspection. Complex has pool, sandbox, wading pool, pitch and putt golf green, sauna, and rooftop observation deck. Units are air conditioned with full kitchens including trash compactor.

"LUXURY RANGE"

POLO BEACH CLUB
20 Makena Rd., Wailea, Maui, HI 96753. Phone 1-808-879-8847. Contact: Reservations at the resort.

	High season:	Low season:
ocean front unit (maximum 6)	$180	$130
ocean view unit (maximum 6)	130	100

10% weekly discount. 25% monthly discount. The newest in the Wailea area, this resort is located on the beach front. A single eight-story building with 71 apartments. Underground parking, pool, Jacuzzi. Very secluded area, although this end of the island is under development.

W. List

WHERE TO STAY – WHAT TO SEE

Condominiums   Kihei/Wailea

WAILEA LUXURY CONDOMINIUMS   No

3750 Wailea Alanui. Contact: Canada and Hawaii call collect 1-808-879-1595 or Mainland call toll free 1-800-367-5246. These units are separated into three villages. Two on the ocean front side and one a bit farther away near the tennis center and golf course of Wailea.

EKOLU VILLAGE (golf course area)

one-bedroom with one or two bath $110
two-bedroom with two bath   140

EKAHI VILLAGE

studio (2) $ 70 - 85
one-bedroom with one or two bath (2)   90 - 120
two-bedroom with two bath (4)   175

ELUA VILLAGE

one-bedroom with one or two bath (2) $115 - $170
two-bedroom with two bath (4)   195 - 275
three-bedroom with two/three bath (6)   300 - 375

These price ranges reflect location in complex to the ocean. Children under 16 free in parent's room. Additional $10 per night per person. Four-night minimum. Three-night deposit required. 25% discount for stays 30 days or longer. NO CREDIT CARDS. Deposit forfeited if cancellation is made within 30 days prior to arrival and they are unable to re-rent. Very plush units. The Elua Village is located on Ulua Beach, one of the nicest in the area and, if you choose these condos, we'd recommend these units. These units are also available by calling Gerry Howell at 1-808-879-4726. The savings is substantial. She offers 1 bedroom low season $85-$110, 2 bedroom $120-$245.

Call back → 1-800-231-0611

WHERE TO STAY – WHAT TO SEE
Upcountry and Onward to Haleakala

Pukalani is the gateway to upcountry Maui. This is where you will find the last gas stations before Haleakala. There are also several places to enjoy a hearty meal either enroute up or back. (See Upcountry restaurants)

Haleakala means "house of the sun" and is the largest dormant volcano in the world. The most direct route is to follow Hwy. 37 from Kahului then left onto #377 above Pukalani and then left again onto Hwy. 379 for the last 10 miles. While only about 40 miles from Kahului, the last part of the trip is very slow, with numerous switchbacks. Two hours should be allowed to traverse this course. Sunrise at the crater is a popular and memorable experience, but plan your departure accordingly. Many visitors have missed this spectacular event by only minutes. The Maui News, the free local publication, prints daily sunrise and sunset times. The park offers a recording of weather and viewing conditions and can be reached by calling 877-5124. The ranger's number is 572-7749. Be sure you have packed a sweater as the summit temperature can be 30 degrees colder than the coast and snow is a winter possibility. May to October offers prime viewing with mid-morning generally the clearest viewing time year around. However, fog can cause very limited visability and a call to that recorded number may save you a trip.

At the park headquarters, you can obtain hiking and camping information and permits. Day hike permits are not required, however, they do request you complete a registration form that can be found at the trail heads and deposit it in the box provided. The first stop beyond the headquarters is Kalahakui Overlook. Here you can see the rare silversword which takes up to 20 years to mature, then blooms once in July or August, only to wither and die in the fall. Keep your eye out for the many animals which inhabit the volcano. Wild pig, goats, as well as the Nenei goose are among the local residents. Hunting is permitted on a limited basis (seasonal) in the crater. Check with the ranger for information.

At an elevation of 9,745 feet is the visitors' center which provides an assortment of information on the crater. It is open daily from about 9 a.m. to 4 p.m. (hours may vary due to government cutbacks). The ranger gives an hourly talk which is well worth the wait. A short distance by trail will find you at the Puu Ulaula outlook. This glassed-in vantage point is the best for sunrise and is the highest point on Maui. The view on a good day, is nothing short of awesome. The crater is seven miles long, two miles wide, and 8,000 feet deep. A closer look is available by foot or horseback (see Chapter VII, on horseback tours). There is also a relatively new tour begun by Cruiser Bob's. They bring you up the mountain in a van and then you cruise down on a bike (see Chapter VII, for more information).

The park service maintains 30 miles of well-marked trails, three cabins and two camp sites. The closest cabin is about seven miles away from the observatory.

WHERE TO STAY – WHAT TO SEE
Upcountry and Onward to Haleakala

Arrangements for these cabins need to be made several months in advance and selection is made about 30 days prior to dates requested by a lottery-type drawing.

For more information, write Superintendent, Haleakala National Park, P.O. Box 537, Makawao, Maui, HI 96768.

Short walks might include the three-fourth mile Halemauu Trail to the crater rim, one-tenth mile to Leleiwi Overlook, or two-tenth mile on the White Hill Trail to the top of White Hill. Caution, the thin air and steep inclines may be especially tiring.

Science City can be seen beyond the visitor's center, but it is not open to the public. It houses a solar and lunar observatory, operated by the University of Hawaii, television relay stations, and a Department of Defense satellite station.

If time allows, there is more of upcountry to be seen.

The Kula area offers rich volcanic soil and commercial farmers harvest a variety of fruits and vegetables. Grapes, apples, pineapples, lettuce, artichokes, tomatoes and, of course, Maui onions are only a few. It can be reached by retracking Hwy. 378 down to the Upper Kula Road where you turn left. The protea, a recent immigrant from South Africa, has created a profitable business. The Botanical Gardens offers closehand views with admission charged, adults $2.50, children 50 cents, and hours between 9 a.m. and 4 p.m. Phone: 878-1715. Wine making is making a reappearance after an absence of nearly 40 years. The Tedische Vineyards are a 30,000 acre ranch that made its debut in 1974. The tasting room is located at the Ulupalakua Ranch (not at the vineyards themselves) and provide samples of their pineapple wine. Late 1983 brought a harvest of their first crop of Carnelian grapes which produced a premium champagne in 1984. Phone: 879-6058.

On the way down you may choose to go by way of Makawao, the colorful "cowboy" town and then down to Paia. Both have several good restaurants. (See Upcountry Restaurants in chapter 5.) Unfortunately, the Ulapalakua Road down to Wailea has been closed due to a dispute between the Ranch and the county.

WHERE TO SHOP

The town of Makawao offers a western flavor with a scattering of shops down its main street.

The Pukalani Shopping Center is a new mall with a grocery store and small shops.

PAIA—ALONG THE ROAD TO HANA AND UPCOUNTRY, TOO!

A little beyond Wailuku, and along the highway which leads to Hana, is the

WHERE TO STAY – WHAT TO SEE
Upcountry and Onward to Haleakala

small town of Paia. The name Paia, translated means "noisy", however, the origin of this name is unclear. This quaint town is reminiscent of the early sugar cane era when Henry Baldwin located his first sugar plantation in this area. The wooden buildings are now filled with antique and other gift shops to attract the passing tourist. (See Chapter 5 for more eatery information.)

UPCOUNTRY

Accommodations are limited in upcountry. Five and one-half miles past Pukalani is the Kula Lodge and just beyond, the Silversword Inn. Both offer five rustic bungalows with rates running $40 - $50. Write Kula Lodge, RR 1, Box 475, Kula, Maui, HI 96790 for room rates (phone: 1-808-878-1535). Some rooms have lanais and offer have fireplaces. The Silversword Inn can be contacted by calling 1-808-878-1232. Both sites offer restaurants.

WHERE TO STAY – WHAT TO SEE
The Road to Hana

HANA

Anyone who endures the three-hour (at least) drive to Hana deserves to sport the "I survived the Road to Hana" tee-shirts which are sold locally. While it may be true that it is easy to fall in love with Hana, getting there is quite a different story. The drive to Hana is not for everyone, although many guide books claim otherwise. It is not for people who are prone to motion sickness, those who don't like alot of scenery, those who are in a hurry to get somewhere or those who don't love long drives. However, it is a trip filled with waterfalls, lush tropical jungles, (which flourish with the 340 inch average annual rainfall) and a chance to get a taste of old Hawaii. The maps are deceiving and it appears you could make the 53-mile trip with 617 curves and 56 miniature bridges much more quickly. However, the road is narrow and even with recent repaving, most cars travel in the middle of the road, making each turn a harrowing experience.

The Hana Hwy. was originally built with pick and shovel, which may account for its narrowness. When it was completed in 1927, it provided the first link between Hana and Kahului. There can also be delays on the road of up to two hours if the road is being worked on. In days gone by when heavy rains caused washouts, it is said that people would literally climb the mud barracades and swap cars, then resume their journey. Despite all this, 300-500 people traverse this road daily and it is the supply route for all deliveries to Hana and the small settlements along the way.

Now, if we haven't dissuaded you and you still want to see spectacular undeveloped scenery, plan to spend the whole day (or even a stop overnight in Hana), get a very early start, take a picnic lunch and a warm sweater. We also might recommend that if you drive, select a car with automatic transmission (or else be prepared for constant shifting). Another choice is to try one of the small van tours which go to Hana and leave the driving to them. These vans will take you around the other side of the island, a road not recommended for rental cars. (The tour guide will also be able to point out the sights of interest along the way that are easy to miss!) The last alternative is to fly into Hana's small airport, however, a car can only be rented through one of the local hotels.

WHAT TO SEE

About 20 miles out is Twin Falls. Look for a small roadside trail marker by the Hoolawa Bridge. This area offers a nice swimming hole. Mosquitos can be prolific. Pack your bug spray. There are no safe beaches along this route for swimming, so for a cool dip, take advantage of one of the swimming holes provided along the way.

Waikamoi Ridge—a picnic area and nature trail.

Puohkamoa Falls—This is the sort of half-way point.

WHERE TO STAY – WHAT TO SEE
The Road to Hana

Kaumahina State Park—overlooks the Honomanu Gulch and Peninsula.

Keanae and Wailua—this agricultural area has an abundance of taro fields, also the Miracle Church is located in Wailua. It has a bit of interesting background. It was built of crushed coral and named for the fact that at the time of construction, they had no building material. Then a huge storm hit the beach depositing a load of coral, thus providing the means for building the church.

The YMCA's Camp Keanae—offers overnight accomodations for men & women (housed separately). The rate is $5 a night. Arrival is requested between 4 & 6 pm. Bring your own food & sleeping bag. For more information phone the camp at 1-808-248-8355.

Puaa Kaa St. Park—14 miles before Hana has two waterfalls and pools that are roadside. This is a favorite stop for a picnic lunch. The waterfall and large pool have combined with this lush tropical locale to make you feel sure a menehune must be lurking nearby. There are new restrooms located here.

Keanae Valley Lookout—located just past Wailua on the roadside, look for a turnoff. Park and follow the tunnel of huge tree roots that lead you up the steps to the Lookout. The trek up is worth the excellent view.

With little effort a sharp observor can spot the open ditches and dams along the roadside. These are the Spreckles Ditches built over 100 years ago to supply water for the young sugar cane industry. These ditches continue to provide the island with its supply of water.

Finally, Waianapanapa (WHY A NAHPA NAHPA) State Park is about four miles before Hana, and offers a black sand beach (not safe for swimming), a number of caves, a blowhole, and a lot of old Hawaiian legends. Camping is allowed and there are rustic cabins available for rent (see the Hana Accommodations section).

The last curve of the road will put you at Hana's Gardenland. This is a place well worth the stop. It's free to browse and they thoughtfully provide picnic tables and a restroom. The plants sold here include the rare and beautiful. All available for shipping anywhere. A dozen anthuriums go for only $9.95 (shipping about $5 extra), which beats any other prices we found on the island. If you don't venture to Hana, you can send for their catalog: Hana Gardenland, P.O. Box 248, Hana, Maui, HI 96713-0248, and include 50 cents or call 1-808-248-8975.

Now, back in the car for a drive into downtown Hana, but don't blink, or you might miss it.

Hana Bay has been the site for many events in Maui history. In early days, it was a retreat for Hawaiian royalty as well as being an important military point from which Maui warriors attacked the island of Hawaii and then were in turn attacked. This is also the birthplace of Ka'ahumanu (1768) Kamehameha the Great's favorite wife.

The Black Sand beach at
The Seven Sacred Pools

WHERE TO STAY – WHAT TO SEE
HANA

The climate on this end of Maui is cooler and wetter, creating an ideal environment for agricultural development. The Ka'eleku Sugar Company established itself in Hana in 1860. Cattle, also a prominant industry during the 20th century, continues today. You can still view the paniolos (Hawaiian cowboys) work at nearby Hana Ranch and purchase fresh Maui beef at the Hana Ranch store on Tuesdays.

Some Hana local information:

St. Mary's Church, Saturday Mass 6 p.m., Sunday 8 a.m., or Puuiki Mass at 9:30 a.m. Wanaluna Protestant Church (1832) Services Sunday 10 a.m.

Hana Ranch Store hours: 7:30 a.m. to 5 p.m. Monday through Saturday, 8 a.m. to 4 p.m. on Sunday.

Hasegawa General Store open: 7:30 a.m. - 6 p.m. Monday through Saturday, sometimes on Sunday.

Hana Medical Center: Monday, Tuesday, Wednesday, and Friday 8 a.m. - 5 p.m., Saturday 9 a.m. - 11 a.m. No doctors on Thursday.

Bank of Hawaii: Monday through Thursday 3 - 4:30 p.m. and Friday 3 - 6 p.m.

Library: Monday through Friday 2 - 4 p.m.

Post Office: 8 a.m. - 4:30 p.m. Monday through Friday.

WHAT TO SEE AND WHERE TO SHOP

Hana has little to offer in the way of shopping, however, the Hasegawa General Store offers a little bit of everything. You may even run into one of the celebrities who come to the area for vacation.

Proceeding through the city and past fields of grazing world-famous Maui beef, still on the hoof, you re-enter the tropical wonders once more. Numerous waterfalls cascade along the roadside. About ten curvy miles beyond Hana and you will arrive at one of the reasons for this trip, the Ohe'o Gulch, more popularly called the Seven Sacred Pools. The blue-grey lava flow here has created incredible pools beneath magnificent waterfalls. The water then flows over a small black sand beach and into the ocean. The pools are safe for swimming, so pack your suit, however, swimming off the black sand beach is very dangerous and many drownings and near drownings have occurred here. The bluff above the beach offers a magnificent view of the ocean and cliffs, so have your camera ready. This area is also of historical significance and signs warn visitors not to remove any rocks.

Two miles further on is the Charles Lindbergh grave, located in the small cemetary of the 1850 Kipahulu Hawaiian Church. This is the sight he himself chose only a year prior to his death in 1974, after living in the area for a number of years.

WHERE TO STAY – WHAT TO SEE
HANA

It is possible to travel the back road from Hana thru Upcountry and back to Kahului. Many van tours now travel this route on the very narrow and rutted road (and you thought the Hana road was bad!). Four wheel drive vehicles are recommended and car rental agencies post warnings that travel is not advised on this route for standard cars and rental agenies are not responsible for damage done to cars . This road has an additional hazard. Flash floods, which are most likely November to March, can send walls of water down the mountain, quickly washing out the bridges and/or overflowing the road.

This side of Maui is very arrid and a strong contrast to the lush growth found on the Keanae side.

There are a few stops you might choose from along this course. The Kaupo General Store has been operating for years and offers grocery items.

Take note of the many rock walls. This area supported a very large native Hawaiian population and these walls served as boundaries as well as retaining walls for livestock, primarily pigs. The walls are centuries old and unfortunately have suffered from vandalism by visitors. Cattle are now the principle area residents.

As you enter Upcountry and civilization once more, look for the Tedische Winery. Located at the Ulupalakua Ranch it offers tasting daily from 9 - 4. They began in 1974 and produced only a pineapple wine until 1983 when they harvested their first grapes and now also offer a champagne.

The Botanical Gardens feature a close up look at the unusual protea flowers. Admission is charged.

ACCOMMODATIONS

"BARGAIN, BARGAIN, BARGAIN RANGE"

WAIANAPANAPA STATE PARK
P.O. Box 1049, Wailuku, Maui, HI 96753. Phone: 1-808-244-4354. This is one of the cheapest place to stay on all of Maui unless you can stay with friends or relatives for free!! The State Park Department offers cabins that sleep up to six people. The units have electric lights and hot water, showers and toilet facilities. The kitchen is equipped with a range, but no oven, and a refrigerator. Bedding is provided and clean linens and towels are refreshed every three days. No pets are allowed and bring your own soap! A five-day maximum stay is the rule and guests are required to clean their units before departure, leaving soiled linens. A 50% deposit is required for reservations and they are booked way ahead. A pro-rated list of rates will be sent to you by the Park Department on request, and it being quite lengthy, we will give you a few sample prices:

1 adult-$10/day; 2 adults-$14/day; 1 adult, 1 child-$10.50/day; 2 adults, 2 children-$18/day; 2 adults, 4 children-$20/day; 4 adults-$24/day; and 6 adults-$30/day.

WHERE TO STAY – WHAT TO SEE
HANA

YMCA CAMP KEANAE, at Keanae runs $2 a night. Bring your own sleeping bag. Phone 1-808-248-8355. Separate facilities for men and women.

"MODERATE RANGE"

HANA KAI RESORT APARTMENTS
P.O. Box 38, Hana, Maui, HI 96713. Deluxe ocean front units on Hana Bay, fully furnished including kitchens. Maid service is daily and there are laundry facilities available. Hana Kai would also be glad to arrange a rental car for you while in the area.

Deluxe studio (1-3) single $50, double $53, each extra $6
Deluxe 1-bdrm.(1-4) single $60, double $63, each extra $6

HEAVENLY HANA INN
P.O. Box 146, Hana, Maui, HI 96713. Phone: 1-808-248-8442. Four modern units in a single Japanese-style Inn. Each unit has a two-bedroom bath and lanai arrangement that sleeps two to six people. The Little Blossom Dining Room is open for breakfast from 7-9 a.m. and dinner from 6-8 p.m. A single or double unit room is $50 plus tax, for three persons $58, and for four $68. Each additional person is $6.50.

HANA BAYVIEW
P.O. Box 318, Hana, Maui, HI 96713, c/o Stan and Suzanne Collins. Phone: 1-808-248-7727. This is a three-bedroom vacation home, with carport, sundeck, and yard. $55 for the first two with $7 per person extra charge. A stay of three nights earns a 15% discount and weekly discount of 25%. A 50% advance deposit is required.

"DELUXE RANGE"

KAUIKI CABIN
P.O. Box 318 Hana, Maui, HI 96713, c/o Stan and Suzanne Collins. Phone: 1-808-248-7727. Located in a residential area of Hana, this cabin can sleep up to 10. Fully furnished with kitchen and outdoor BBQ. One bath inside, and an additional shower outdoors amid the lush gardens. Stan and Suzanne also offer a beachfront home for $85 a night and a duplex for $45 with a kitchen. Write them for more information.

HOTEL HANA MAUI
One of the most secluded Maui resorts and a Hana landmark. Built by Paul Fagan, a cattle rancher, the use of this facility was originally limited to his wealthy friends. The then Hotel Hana Ranch was opened for public use in 1947 and renamed Hotel Hana Maui the following year. Write: Hotel Hana, Hana, Maui 96713

Single $130 and up; double $180 and up. Rooms are American Plan and include meals.

The 60-room hotel resembles a small neighborhood with the single story units scattered about the grounds. Numerous hotel activities are offered and a wonderful stable features cookouts and other excursions for the horse fancier. Three miles away is Haoma Beach with private facilities for hotel guests. An outdoor pool is located on the hotel grounds. They also offer a dining room as well as a coffee shop.

RESTAURANTS

INTRODUCTION

This section was the hardest for us to compile, yet the most enjoyable to investigate! We have included the majority of restaurants in the Kihei/Wailea, and Kapalua to Lahaina areas, while covering only some of the best bargains on the Kahului and Wailuku side. Needless to say, we haven't been able to eat every meal served at every restaurant, but we have talked to numerous people to get some varied opinions. We have listed the restaurants in what we hope is the easiest format to follow in order to help you make your choice. The restaurants in each of our six key island areas have been divided into four categories based on price, and then listed alphabetically in those price ranges. We have taken the average meal for a single person at that restaurant, usually dinner, and excluding tax, alcoholic beverages and desserts, listed them at "BARGAIN RANGE" $5 and under, "INEXPENSIVE RANGE" $5 to $10,"MODERATE RANGE" $10 to $15, and "EXPENSIVE" are those $15 and above. We hope that the sample offerings from their menus will also be helpful to you. We have indicated our personal favorites by *'s (the more the better!). A favorite meal out is fresh island fish that has been properly prepared. To help you make a selection from these fish with their unusual Hawaiian names, we have included a section "A Word or Two about Fish". This section gives a brief description of the most popular varieties and is included in the General Information section, Chapter 3. The prices listed were accurate at time of publication, but we cannot be responsible for any price increases. An important post-script here is the rapidity with which the island restaurants open, close and change names. Subsequent editions of this guide will update these changes. Enjoy your meal, and remember those muu-muus are great for covering up all those calories!!

RESTAURANT INDEX

Type of Food	See Page #		See Page #
BRUNCH		CHINESE	
Eight Bells	100	Golden Palace	96
Kapalua Dining Room	110	Hong Kong	116
Lanai Terrace	119	Ma's Dim Sum	97
Makani Coffee Shop	114	Maui Beach Hotel (Buffet)	90
Moana Terrace	103	Ming Court in Kaanapali	97
Raffles	119	Ming Yuen in Kahului	90
Swan Court	106	Orient Express	109
Restaurant of the Maui Moon	109	Stephanie's	89

85

RESTAURANTS

CONTINENTAL
Bay Club	110
Coconut Grove	95
Discovery Room	104
The Garden at Kapalua Resort	110
Kapalua Grill and Bar	109
La Perouse	118
Longhi's	102
Peacock	105
Plantation Veranda	110
Quee Queq	105
Raffles	119
Swan Court	106

DESSERTS
Bakery	93
Kapalua Grill and Bar	109
Lahaina Provision Company	102
Longhi's	102
Marco's	103
Yami Yogurt	94

FRENCH
Chez Paul	104
Gerard's	105
La Bretagne	105
Robaire's	120

FAMILY DINING
Annie's on the Beach	99
Apple Annie's	91
Bettino's	99
Black Rock	100
Chris's Smokehouse	95
Christine's	95
Chucks	115
Col Sanders	95
Cross Roads	122
Dillon's	124
Doreen's Country Inn	122
Hale Kope	116
Hat's	89
International House of Pancakes	114
Kaanapali Beach Hotel Restaurant	96
Kimo's	101

FAMILY DINING (cont'd)
Leilani's	102
Moana Terrace	103
Naokee's	97
Ocean House	97
Ocean Terrace	117
Royal Ocean Terrace	98
Rusty Harpoon	98
Sailmaker	115
Vi's	90

HAWAIIAN
Aloha Cafe	89
Maui Palms	90
Pukalani Country Club	123
Tiki Terrace	104
*Also see Luaus	

ITALIAN
Alex's Hold in the Wall	99
Ambrosia	115
Dollie's	108
Gates of Italy	101
Gospare's	114
Mama's Pizza	97
Marco's	103
Monaco	110
Pizza Hut	98
Ricco's	98
Spatts II	104

INTERNATIONAL
Palm Court	118

JAPANESE
Archie's	90
Fujiya's	89
Fujiyama	95
Nikko's	105
Taiko	104

LUAUS
Hyatt Regency	107
Kaanapali Beach Hotel	107
Kapa Room	107

RESTAURANTS

LUAUS (cont'd)
Kapalua Resort	112
Maui Lu	121
Royal Lahaina	107
Sheraton Hotel *Supposed to be good*	107
Stouffers Resort	121

MEXICAN
Chico's Cantina-Opening soon at Kaanapali	
LaFamilia at Kaanapali	102
La Familia at Kihei	117
Polli's in Makawao	122
Polli's on the Beach	114
Tortilla Flats	99

POLYNESIAN
Don the Beachcomber	100
Jessie's	116
Tiki Terrace	104

SALAD BARS
Chuck's	115
Erik's On The Beach	101
Fairway Restaurant	115
H.S. Bounty	101
Kihei Prime Rib	116
Ocean House	97
Outrigger	117
Royal Ocean Terrace	98

SANDWICHES AND BURGERS
Amilio's Deli	93
Apple Annie's	91
Annie's on the Beach	99
Annie's Sailmaker	115
Azeka's	113
Blackies Bar	93
Bullock's	122
Burger King - Kahului	89
Burger King - Lahaina	93
Cafe Alegro	93
Dairy Queen - Pukalani	122

SANDWICHES AND BURGERS (cont'd)
Ed & Don's	113
Greenthumb's	96
Hamburger Mary's	93
Harpooners Lanai	96
Kau Kau Bar	96
Kihei Natural Foods	114
Kula Lodge	123
Lani's Pancake Cottage	94
Makena Golf Course	114
Makani's Coffee Shop	114
Market Cafe	108
Maui Onion	114
McDonalds - Kihei	113
McDonalds - Lahaina	94
Moose McGillycuddy	97
Organ Grinder	97
Paradise Fruits	113
Pavillion	103
Philadelphia Lou's	113
R.V. Deli	108
Sandwitch	113
Surfside	99
Toda's	89
Togos	94
Tutu's	124
Wetspot	115
Whalers Pub	94
Yami Yogurt	94

SEAFOOD
Ambrosia	115
Blackbeard's	95
Buzz's Wharf	115
Chart House, Kahului	91
Chart House, Lahaina	100
El Crab Catcher	100
Erik's On The Beach	101
Erik's Seafood Grotto	108
Fish Fry	93
H.S. Bounty	101
Harbor Front	101
Island Fish House, Kahului	91

RESTAURANTS

SEAFOOD (cont'd)
- Island Fish House, Kihei 116
- Kahana Keyes 109
- Kihei Seas 117
- Kimo's 101
- Leilani's 102
- Lokelani 105
- Mama's Fish House .... 124 *Supposed to be great*
- Maui Outrigger 117
- Moby Dicks 103
- Ocean House 97
- Skipper's 94
- The Keg 104
- Waterfront 118
- Whale's Tale 99

STEAK/PRIME RIB
- Banyan Inn 95
- Chuck's 115
- Coconut Grove 95
- Eight Bells 100
- Fairway 115
- Kapalua Grill and Bar 109
- Kiawe Broiler 118
- Kihei Prime Rib 116
- Lahaina Provision Company 102
- Makawao Steak House 122
- Naokee's Steak House 97
- Pineapple Hill 109
- Pioneer Inn - South Seas 98
- Royal Kaanapali Golf Course Restaurant 98
- The Keg 104
- Wailea Steak House 118

RESTAURANTS
Kahului/Wailuku

"BARGAIN RANGE"

ALOHA RESTAURANT
LOCATED: Near the Kahului Shopping Center, 127 Puunene Ave., phone 877-6318 *HOURS:* Open seven days a week *PRICE RANGE:* BARGAIN TO INEXPENSIVE *TYPE OF FOOD:* Sandwiches and Hawaiian dishes *SAMPLING:* Sandwiches run $1.10 to $2.50. Dinners run $3.10 to $4.75 *COMMENTS:* The decor is plain and overall this restaurant is fair for service and food, but the prices are dynamite!

BURGER KING
LOCATED: At the Kahului Shopping Center *COMMENTS:* Stop in for a reliable "Whopper".

FUJIYA'S *
LOCATED: 133 Market Cafe, Wailuku, phone 244-0206 *HOURS:* Lunch 11-2, Dinner 2-5:30 *PRICE RANGE:* Bargain *TYPE OF FOOD:* Japanese *SAMPLING:* Yose-Nabe or Sukiyaki $5.00, 3 assorted plates: our choice included marinated chicken, shrimp & vegetable tempura, marinated cabbage, tofu, miso soup, rice, dumplings for $5.00. Sushi is also available. *COMMENTS:* This small cafe offers tasty & ample dishes at very reasonable prices. Their lunch & dinner menus are the same.

HATS (formerly Kawikas)
LOCATED: At the Maui Mall on Kaahumanu Rd. 877-6475 *HOURS:* Daily 8 a.m. to 9 p.m. *PRICE RANGE:* BARGAIN *TYPE OF FOOD:* Everything *SAMPLING:* Hamburgers at $1.55, ham sandwich at $2.10, breaded veal at only $3.10, liver and onions at $2.95 and top that with homemade pastries and desserts *COMMENTS:* Very small with no table service. The menu is large and has a lot of variety. Overall a good stop!

STEPHANIE'S
LOCATED: At the Maui Mall, next to Hat's, phone 871-4142 *HOURS:* Daily for breakfast and lunch *PRICE RANGE:* BARGAIN *TYPE OF FOOD:* Asian and American *SAMPLING:* A buffet bar of Oriental foods allows you to select the dishes you want and you are charged accordingly, i.e.,. any two for $3.50. Also offered are sandwiches and breakfast items.

TODA DRUG STORE
LOCATED: Kahului Shopping Center, phone 877-4550 *HOURS:* Daily, 8:30 a.m. - 4 p.m. *PRICE RANGE:* BARGAIN *TYPE OF FOOD:* Hawaiian, American, eclectic! *SAMPLING:* Hamburgers $1.00, ham sandwiches at $1.35, tomato stuffed with tuna at $1.75 or splurge on their daily special which runs $3.75 and might include beef curry stew, with rice and vegetable (varies daily). *COMMENTS:* You don't find this place crowded with tourists. Located at the back of this drug store you'll find counter seating, local atmosphere and among the best prices on the island for food.

RESTAURANTS
Kahului/Wailuku

"INEXPENSIVE RANGE"

Farrell's, Irma's Bakery and Deli, Harvest House, and Pizza Factory are all additional choices to be found in the Maui Mall (Kahului). The prices are INEXPENSIVE to MODERATE.

ARCHIE'S**
LOCATED: In Wailuku at 1440 Lower Main St., phone 244-9401 HOURS: Monday through Saturday, 10:30 a.m. - 2 p.m., and 5 - 8 p.m. Closed Sundays PRICE RANGE: INEXPENSIVE TYPE OF FOOD: Japanese SAMPLING: Their specialty is (Hama'ko) Teishoku. Don't know what that is? You'll have to stop in and find out. Dinners complete run $4 - $8 COMMENTS: This is a secret that local residents may not want to spread too far! The food is very good and the prices are excellent.

MAUI BEACH HOTEL
LOCATED: On Kahului Bay PRICE RANGE: INEXPENSIVE TO MODERATE TYPE OF FOOD: Varied COMMENTS: This complex has several eating options. 1) Rainbow buffet lunch at Rainbow Dining Room features salad bar with three entrees, rice, potato, bread, and fresh cake; 11:30 a.m. - 2 p.m. daily. $6.00 all you can eat; $5.00 salad bar only. 2) Ten-course Chinese buffet dinner, nightly, except Monday, 5:30 - 8:30 p.m. All you can eat, $9.50; 11 and under, $5.00. Reservations - 877-0051 3) Seafood and prime rib dinner nightly in Rainbow Dining Room (second floor), 6 - 9 p.m., includes salad bar. Reservations - 877-0051.

MAUI PALMS
LOCATED: On Kahului Bay PRICE RANGE: INEXPENSIVE TO MODERATE TYPE OF FOOD: Varied COMMENTS: Choose from the following buffets. 1) Imperial dinner buffet in East-West Dining Room, nightly, except Sunday, 5:30 - 8:30 p.m. Features shrimp tempura, yaki tori, vegetable tempura, Okinawa pork, fish, tako with miso sauce, sushi, and more. $9.50 all you can eat. Reservations - 877-0071. 2) Sunday Hawaiian buffet in East-West Dining Room, 5:30 - 8:30 p.m. Features lomi salmon, Kalua pork, lau lau, squid with coconut milk, pipikaula, tako poki, chicken long rice, haupia poi, and salad bar. All you can eat $9.50; under 11, $5.00 Reservations - 877-0071.

MING YUEN
LOCATED: 162 Alamaha, Kahului, phone 871-7787 HOURS: Lunch daily 11 a.m. - 2 p.m., dinner 5 - 9p.m. PRICE RANGE: INEXPENSIVE TO MODERATE TYPE OF FOOD: Chinese SAMPLING: Cantonese and Szechuan style foods COMMENTS: A little off the beaten track, you'll find this treasure tucked behind Safeway off Kamehameha in the industrial area. Reservations are recommended as this is highly popular. Mastercard and Visa accepted.

VI'S RESTAURANT AND COCKTAIL LOUNGE
LOCATED: Maui Hukilau Hotel in Kahului at Bay. Phone - 877-3311. No reservations accepted HOURS: Breakfast, 7 - 9:45 a.m.; dinner, 6-8:45 p.m. PRICE RANGE: INEXPENSIVE TYPE OF FOOD: Seafood, Polynesian, and steak SAMPLING: Twenty-two complete dinners from $5.50. Forty breakfast selections. Soup and salad bar served with dinner.

RESTAURANTS
Kahului/Wailuku

"MODERATE RANGE"

APPLE ANNIE'S
LOCATED: Kaahumanu Shopping Center on Kaahumanu Ave., Kahului *HOURS:* Daily for breakfast, lunch, and dinner *PRICE RANGE:* MODERATE *TYPE OF FOOD:* Everything *SAMPLING:* Omelets, Mexican, Polynesian, sandwiches, pizza *COMMENTS:* This is one of a chain that is locally owned. This is the place to come if you have a family with a wide variety of tastes. There is something for everyone.

THE CHART HOUSE*
LOCATED: 500 N. Puunene Ave., Kahului, phone 877-2476 *HOURS:* Dinner *PRICE RANGE:* MODERATE *TYPE OF FOOD:* Seafood, beef, and chicken *COMMENTS:* Thought by some to be better than its Lahaina counterpart. You can be sure it will be less crowded on this side of the island. No reservations taken, but a nice ocean view is a consolation.

ISLAND FISH HOUSE (formerly Mr. Hugo's)
LOCATED: Kahului Bldg., 333 Lono Ave., phone 877-7225 *HOURS:* Dinner *PRICE RANGE:* MODERATE *TYPE OF FOOD:* Seafood *COMMENTS:* If this popular haunt of the same name is packed in Kihei, you might try their new location on this side of the island. If they maintain their high quality here, too, it will be a #1 spot.

The Wharf Shopping Center

RESTAURANTS
Lahaina/Kaanapali

"BARGAIN RANGE"

AMILIO'S DELICATESSEN
LOCATED: Lahaina Square (above Lahaina Shopping Center north end of town) Phone 661-8551 HOURS: Daily PRICE RANGE: BARGAIN TYPE OF FOOD: Sandwiches and pizza COMMENTS: Take out or eat in.

THE BAKERY***
LOCATED: 911 Limahana (turn off of Honoapiilani Hwy. by Pizza Hut near Sugar Cane Train depot.) Phone 667-9062. HOURS: Monday through Saturday 7 a.m - 5 p.m., Sunday 7 a.m. - noon PRICE RANGE: BARGAIN TYPE OF FOOD: Pastries, sandwiches, fresh pasta to go. SAMPLING: Whole wheat cream cheese croissants for 85 cents, also ham, or turkey stuffed croissants for $1.00, small sandwiches such as turkey dijon at $1.75. Coffee - 40 cents. Also, huge fresh fruit tortes, fudge, fresh breads, and pasta made here daily. COMMENTS: It's well worth the stop if you are a lover of pastries. The selection is magnificent and tasty, too!

BLACKIE'S BAR
LOCATED: On Hwy. 30 between Lahaina and Kaanapali. Look for the treehouse-type structure with the orange roof. Phone - 667-7979. HOURS: Daily, 10 a.m. - 10 p.m. PRICE RANGE: INEXPENSIVE TO BARGAIN TYPE OF FOOD: Burritos, enchiladas, tacos, nachos, smoked hot dogs, and Louisiana hot links COMMENTS: Jazz on Fridays and Sundays, 5 -8 p.m.

BURGER KING
LOCATED: South end of Lahaina by the Banyan tree HOURS: 6:30 a.m. to 11 p.m. serving breakfast, lunch, and dinner PRICE RANGE: BARGAIN TYPE OF FOOD: Breakfast sandwiches, salad bar at $3.99, and the usual burger delights at prices slightly higher than the mainland COMMENTS: Open air with seating available. Roadside.

CAFE ALEGRO
LOCATED: 991 Limahana Pl., next to Sugar Cane Train depot (turn by Pizza Hut onto Hinau St.). Phone - 667-6743 HOURS: Monday - Saturday, 8 a.m. - 8 p.m. PRICE RANGE: BARGAIN TYPE OF FOOD: Pizza, sandwiches, Mediterranean COMMENTS: Food to go.

FISH FRY*
LOCATED: Lahaina Shopping Center, north end of Lahaina, and at the rear HOURS: Open daily for breakfast, lunch, and dinner PRICE RANGE: BARGAIN TYPE OF FOOD: Besides fish that includes shrimp, scallops, mahi, or cod, they serve up eggs, an assortment of omelets, including Spam and cabbage! SAMPLING: Omelets run $2.35 - $2.95. Plate lunches include Kalua pig at $3.75, roast pork at $3.75, teriyaki at $3.80, and these come with rice or fries, plus coleslaw or macaroni salad. Also, a variety of sandwiches from a 90 cent hamburger to $1.75 for roast pork. COMMENTS: A small seating area inside, but this little place has surprisingly good food and was not busy the times we've been there.

HAMBURGER MARY'S ORGANIC GRILL*
LOCATED: 608 Front St., phone 667-6989. A little off the beaten track, down at the south end of Lahaina across from Kam 3 school HOURS: 7 a.m. - 11 p.m. for breakfast, lunch, and dinner. Cocktails served PRICE RANGE: BARGAIN TO INEXPENSIVE TYPE OF FOOD: Hamburgers and more! SAMPLING: Breakfast served anytime and includes an

RESTAURANTS
Lahaina/Kaanapali

assortment of omelets or two eggs with rice special at $2.25. They have some salads including papaya, avocado, or tomato stuffed with your choice of chicken salad, tuna salad, seafood, cottage cheese, cream cheese, or raw milk cheese at $6.75. They have a large variety of hamburgers, which were the biggest we found on Maui, and run $3.50 for a plain up to $5.50 for a loaded *COMMENT:* Outdoor eating under a kind of canopy covering. Furnishings have seen a better day. You might try splitting a hamburger if you aren't real hungry. They serve them with a knife, as they are too big to get your mouth around.

LANI'S PANCAKE COTTAGE
LOCATED: Wharf Shopping Center, across from the Banyan Tree, 658 Front St., Lahaina, phone 661-0955 *HOURS:* Breakfast and lunch 6:30 a.m. - 3:30 p.m. *PRICE RANGE:* BARGAIN *TYPE OF FOOD:* Breakfast items and sandwiches *SAMPLING:* Pancakes $1.95 - $3.65, omelets $2.95 and up, fish and chips $3.65, burgers and sandwiches $2.95 - $4.50 *COMMENTS:* Very busy during breakfast hours, offering seating indoors on the patio.

MCDONALD'S
LOCATED: Recently moved to a new building, across the street from the old one, located at Lahaina Shopping Center which is on the north end of Lahaina *HOURS:* Open for breakfast, lunch, and dinner *PRICE RANGE:* BARGAIN, slightly higher than Mainland *TYPE OF FOOD:* The usual for McDonald's with a few added items such as Saimin *COMMENTS:* Indoor eating and also a drive-through.

SKIPPER'S
LOCATED: The Wharf Shopping Center, south end of Lahaina, on the first level *HOURS:* Daily *PRICE RANGE:* BARGAIN TO INEXPENSIVE *TYPE OF FOOD:* Seafood *COMMENTS:* Usual fare at Skipper's with slightly higher than Mainland prices.

TOGO'S
LOCATED: 505 Front St., Lahaina, at Lahaina Shores *HOURS:* 9:30 a.m. - 6 p.m. Sunday - Friday; 7:30 a.m. - 3 *PRICE RANGE:* BARGAIN *TYPE OF FOOD:* Sandwiches *SAMPLING:* Twenty-three sandwiches are made in 6, 12, or 24 inch sizes. Sandwiches include veggie with cream cheese, avocado, and sprouts at $3.45, $6.45, or $12.60. BBQ beef with provolone runs $4.15, $7.95, or $15.45. Box lunches available for $5.15 and include sandwich, choice of salad, giant chocolate chip cookie, pickle, and eating utensils. Thirty-five varieties of beer as well as soft drinks are available. *COMMENTS:* Five varieties of bagels. Deli area has desserts such as Swedish cheesecake and baklava.

WHALER'S PUB
LOCATED: 505 Front St., Lahaina, at Lahaina Shores Village, phone 661-3303 *PRICE RANGE:* BARGAIN *TYPE OF FOOD:* Sandwiches, burgers, and patty melts run $3.50 - $4.50 *COMMENTS:* Mostly a place for libations, the menu is very limited.

YAMI YOGURT
LOCATED: At Whaler's Village on the lower level across from the movie theater, phone 661-8843 *PRICE RANGE:* BARGAIN *TYPE OF FOOD:* Salads, sandwiches, and yogurt items. Half a papaya filled with cottage cheese at $2.45. Sandwiches include cheese and egg salad run $2.75 to $3.00 *COMMENTS:* No seating in the restaurant, but a few tables outside.

RESTAURANTS
Lahaina/Kaanapali

"INEXPENSIVE RANGE"

BANYAN INN
LOCATED: 640 Front St., across from Banyan Tree, phone 661-4489 *HOURS:* Dinner, daily *PRICE RANGE:* INEXPENSIVE TO MODERATE *TYPE OF FOOD:* "Homestyle island" *SAMPLING:* Dinners run $9 to $14 and feature steak, prime rib and island cooking. Fresh baked pies and breads are an added treat *COMMENTS:* They have been serving area residents and visitors since 1937 and on weekends offer Hawaiian music.

BLACKBEARD'S
LOCATED: At Wharf Shopping Center, south end of Lahaina, 658 Front St., phone 667-9535 *HOURS:* Lunch 11 a.m. - 4 p.m.; dinner 5 - 10 p.m. *PRICE RANGE:* INEXPENSIVE FOR LUNCH, MODERATE FOR DINNER *TYPE OF FOOD:* Fish, beef, soups, salads, and quiches *SAMPLING:* Hamburgers run $3.95 for an all-American to $5.50 for a gourmet. Luncheon entrees include seafood crepes at $5.25, crab and artichoke omelet at $5.95. Beverages are $1.00. Dinners are slightly higher with steaks running $10.95 for petite top sirloin to a filet mignon at $15.75. Scampi and scallops both run $12.95. Dinners include salad or chowder, rice or potato, and bread *COMMENTS:* Happy hour 5 to 8 p.m. everyday.

CHRIS' SMOKEHOUSE
LOCATED: At Lahaina Square Shopping Center, north end of Lahaina, by Foodland, phone 667-2111 *HOURS:* Lunch 11: 30 a.m. - 2:30 p.m.; dinner 5:30 - 11 p.m. *PRICE RANGE:* INEXPENSIVE *TYPE OF FOOD:* BBQ ribs, steak, fish, and chicken. Also take out

CHRISTINE'S FAMILY RESTAURANT
LOCATED: At Lahaina Square, which is at the north end of Lahaina across from Lahaina Shopping Center, phone 661-4156 *HOURS:* Open 24 hours Wednesday through Saturday; from 6 a.m. - 9:30 p.m. Sunday, Monday, and Tuesday. Serving breakfast (anytime), lunch (11 a.m. - 4:30 p.m.), and dinner (4:30 - closing) *PRICE RANGE:* INEXPENSIVE *TYPE OF FOOD:* "Homestyle" sandwiches, plate lunches *SAMPLING:* Sandwiches are $2-$4.75 ala carte or with salad and fries *COMMENTS:* One of a very few places open 24 hours. Plate lunches run about $4.50 and include chicken, pork roast, or meat loaf. Omelets are $3.25. Ala carte breakfast items are reasonably priced. Breakfast served anytime. Dinners run $5.85 for roast pork or meatloaf to $7.75 for shrimp tempura.

COCONUT GROVE
LOCATED: 1312 Front Street, Lahaina, phone 667-9355 *HOURS:* Breakfast, lunch, and dinner *PRICE RANGE:* INEXPENSIVE TO MODERATE *TYPE OF FOOD:* Continental - seafood - steak

COLONEL SANDER'S CHICKEN
LOCATED: Lahaina Shopping Center, phone 661-3422

FUJIYAMA
LOCATED: Lahaina Shopping Center, phone 667-6207 *HOURS:* Lunch Monday thru Friday 11:00 - 1:30, dinner served 5 p.m. - 9 p.m. *PRICE RANGE:* INEXPENSIVE TO MODERATE *TYPE OF FOOD:* Japanese *SAMPLING:* Combination dinners are served with soup, vegetable salad, rice and tea. They offer teriyaki steak and shrimp tempura or

RESTAURANTS
Lahaina/Kaanapali

sashimi and teriyaki chicken as possible entrees and are priced at $9.50. Special dinners are cooked at your table for two or more and run about $13.50 per person. Choose from sukiyaki or Yakiniku which are accompanied by an appetizer, tsukemono, soup, rice, tea and dessert. Ala carte items are also available. They offer a sushi bar as well as full cocktail service.

GOLDEN PALACE
LOCATED: Lahaina Shopping Center, north end of Lahaina, phone 661-3126 HOURS: Lunch and dinner, 11 a.m. - 9 p.m. Also take out PRICE RANGE: INEXPENSIVE TYPE OF FOOD: Chinese SAMPLING: Entrees are the usual Chinese variety and a few unusual items and run $3 - $4 each with a large bowl of white rice being only 60 cents. Lunch special is $4.25 served 11 a.m. - 2 p.m. and includes sweet and sour pork, chop suey, pot roast pork, shrimp, and steamed rice COMMENTS: We were pleased with the prices and large menu, and didn't mind the linoleum floors and tables, and plastic drinking glasses. We did, however, mind that the food arrived cold. The content of some of the dishes and their preparation left much to be desired during our dinner there. Our service was less than mediocre. Beer, cocktails, and Chinese wine are also available.

GREENTHUMB'S
LOCATED: 839 Front Street in Lahaina, and overlooks the ocean. Phone 667-6126 HOURS: Daily from 10 a.m. to 10 p.m. with orders to go PRICE RANGE: INEXPENSIVE TYPE OF FOOD: Salads, sandwiches, and assorted entrees SAMPLING: Salads include a garden salad at $4.95, a chef salad at $6.95, a Tuna salad at $6.50, a Shrimp salad at $7.95. Sandwiches run $3.95 for avocado and cheese, to their extravaganza with ham, turkey, salami, and cheese at $5.75. COMMENTS: Nice oceanside view and very casual atmosphere. Newer restaurant and very friendly staff.

HARPOONER'S LANAI *
LOCATED: On Front St., Lahaina, wharfside at the Pioneer Inn, phone 661-3636 HOURS: Daily, breakfast from 7 a.m. - 11 a.m. and lunch from 11:30 a.m. PRICE RANGE: INEXPENSIVE TO MODERATE TYPE OF FOOD: Varied SAMPLING: Eggs with ham, links, Portuguese sausage, or bacon for $3.65. Coconut, banana, macadamia nut, or blueberry pancakes at $2.90; French toast $2.90. Lunches might include Portuguese bean soup at $1.95, hamburger $3.55, turkey sandwich $3.35, or mahi burger $4.65 COMMENTS: Our French toast was four half-slices of bread that were thick and custardy. The atmosphere was very rustic and most enjoyable.

KAANAPALI BEACH HOTEL RESTAURANT
LOCATED: Kaanapali Beach Hotel Restaurant, Phone 66l-0011. HOURS: Breakfast from 6:30 a.m.; lunch from 11 a.m., and dinner from 4 p.m. PRICE RANGE: BARGAIN TO INEXPENSIVE TYPE OF FOOD: American COMMENTS: Cafeteria style with $5 dinner specials. A good value.

KAU KAU BAR
LOCATED: Poolside at the Maui Marriott Hotel, Kaanapali HOURS: Breakfast from 7:30 a.m. - 10:30 a.m., lunch and snacks from 10 a.m. - 4 p.m. PRICE RANGE: INEXPENSIVE TO MODERATE TYPE OF FOOD: Breakfast items and hamburgers SAMPLING: Breakfast was a little steep with eggs and toast at $4.75, croissants or other pastry at $1.50. The hamburger at $4.75 was tasty and ample. Kau kau translated from Hawaiian means "eat eat".

RESTAURANTS
Lahaina/Kaanapali

MA'S DIM SUM
LOCATED: Lahaina Square, north end of Lahaina at 840 Wainee, phone 667-9378 *PRICE RANGE:* INEXPENSIVE *TYPE OF FOOD:* Chinese *COMMENTS:* Features "old fashioned Hong Kong style cooking". Take out or catering.

MOOSE MC GILLYCUDDY
LOCATED: 844 Front St., upper level of Mariner's Alley. This small shopping alley is on the north end of town, phone 667-7758 *HOURS:* Breakfast from 7:30 a.m., also lunch and dinner *PRICE RANGE:* INEXPENSIVE *TYPE OF FOOD:* Lots of burgers *SAMPLING:* Early bird breakfast special served 7:30 a.m. - 9 a.m. for $1.99. A moose omelet consists of 12 eggs with two types of cheese, bacon, sausage, mushrooms, sprouts, spinach, and onion for $10.95. Twenty or more burgers are offered including the bareburger, a plain patty with cottage cheese, fruit, and tossed salad, or an Egg McMoose, which is a burger with fried egg and cheese on it, or an Air Burger, which has no meat, no cheese, and no mayo and is a vegetarian burger *COMMENTS:* Early happy hour is 11:30 a.m. - 4 p.m., late happy hour is 4 p.m. - 8 p.m., later happy hour is 8 p.m. on. They also have later evening music on the loud side.

MAMA'S PIZZA
LOCATED: Wharf Shopping Center, 658 Front St., Lahaina, phone 667-2531 *HOURS:* Daily from 11:30 a.m. *PRICE RANGE:* INEXPENSIVE *TYPE OF FOOD:* Pizza and sandwiches

MING COURT
LOCATED: Whaler's Village Shopping Center at Kaanapali, Phone: 667-7781 *HOURS:* Lunch served 11 - 2, Dinner from 5 p.m. *TYPE OF FOOD:* Oriental *SAMPLING:* Cantonese and Szechuan *COMMENTS:* Their menu is similar to their counterpart in Kahului. Mastercard and Visa Accepted.

NAOKEE'S TOO
LOCATED: 1307 Front St., Lahaina, phone 667-7513 *HOURS:* Daily 8am -12:30am *PRICE RANGE:* INEXPENSIVE TO MODERATE B/L/D *TYPE OF FOOD:* Chicken, pork, beef "local food" *COMMENTS:* Plain atmosphere, but good prices Plate lunches run $3.95 for hamburger steak to $6.95 for a one pound N.Y. steak. Included with entree are rice, macaroni, corn & green salad.

OCEANHOUSE
LOCATED: 831 Front St., Lahaina, phone 661-3359 *HOURS:* Cocktails begin at 4 p.m. and early bird dinner special is 5-6 p.m. daily *PRICE RANGE:* INEXPENSIVE TO MODERATE *TYPE OF FOOD:* A little of everything *SAMPLING:* Linguini with white clam sauce, fried chicken, and steamed vegetables with cheese all begin the menu at $6.95. Chicken, BBQ ribs, scampi, and scallops run up to $11.95, with combination plates and king crab legs being in the $13 - $20 range *COMMENTS:* Dining over the water is nice and a benefit here is they do have a children's menu for ages 12 and under. Prices are $4.95 - $6.95 and include bread, butter, vegetable and "starch of the day". Price includes salad bar.

ORGAN GRINDER
LOCATED: 811 Front St., Lahaina, by the seawall, phone 661-4593 *HOURS:* Breakfast, lunch, and dinner *PRICE RANGE:* INEXPENSIVE *TYPE OF FOOD:* Sandwiches and burgers *COMMENTS:* Family-owned and operated with the emphasis on food, not decor. One of the best bargains for a real waterfront view.

RESTAURANTS
Lahaina/Kaanapali

PIZZA HUT
LOCATED: 127 Hinau, Lahaina, phone 661-3696

RICCO'S
LOCATED: Whaler's Village Shopping Center at Kaanapali, lower level, centrally located, phone 661-4433 HOURS: 11 a.m. - 10 p.m. daily PRICE RANGE: INEXPENSIVE TYPE OF FOOD: Sandwiches and pizza SAMPLING: Pizzas are priced by the number for items added: a large cheese plus two items of $9.24. Sandwiches include meatball, roast beef, corned beef, vegetarian, Italian combo, pastrami, turkey, and sausage for $3.59 (mama size) to $3.99 (papa size) COMMENTS: They have a very good assortment of cold beers. They also prepare large "pupu" (hors d'oeuvres platters for about $20.) Pizza available to go.

ROYAL KAANAPALI GOLF COURSE CLUB RESTAURANT
LOCATED: Royal Kaanapali Golf Course, Phone 661-3691 HOURS: Breakfast 6:30 a.m. - 11 a.m.; lunch 11 a.m. - 4 p.m.; dinner 5:30 p.m. - 9:30 p.m. PRICE RANGE: INEXPENSIVE TO MODERATE TYPE OF FOOD: Varied - steak, seafood, and salad bar SAMPLING: Family dinners run about $9 COMMENTS: Lanai or indoor eating. Good breakfasts.

ROYAL OCEAN TERRACE (formerly Crown Room)**
LOCATED: At the Royal Lahaina Hotel, off the lobby, north side of Kaanapali Phone 661-3611 HOURS: Breakfast Monday - Saturday 6 a.m. - 11a.m.; daily breakfast buffet 6:30 a.m. - 10 a.m. Sunday brunch from 9 a.m. - 2 p.m. Lunch Monday - Saturday 11 a.m. - 3 p.m. Dinner daily 6 p.m. - 10 p.m. PRICE RANGE: INEXPENSIVE TO MODERATE TYPE OF FOOD: American and assorted SAMPLING: Sandwiches $5.95 - $7.40. Dinner items include one-half chicken with mushrooms and artichoke hearts for $9.75 or weinerschnitzel at $12.75. Also available are hamburgers at $5.95 COMMENTS: Newly remodeled and very nice, airy restaurant. Their salad bar is terrific! It included 26 items the night we dined and ranged from just lettuce or spinach salad to pasta salad, or excellent new potato salad, shrimp salad, fresh vegetable salad and more. To accompany your green salad, they offer the standard dressings as well as carafes of unusual oils and vinegars to combine for your own, i.e. grape seed oil, walnut oil, raspberry vinegar. The dessert bar tempts you on your arrival and you might want to save room for one of their special ice cream drinks!

THE RUSTY HARPOON
LOCATED: Whaler's Village Shopping Center, Kaanapali, middle of the center and towards the ocean, phone 661-3123 HOURS: Lunch 11 a.m. - 3:30 p.m.; dinner 6 p.m. - 9:30 p.m. PRICE RANGE: INEXPENSIVE TYPE OF FOOD: Lunch sandwiches, dinner is broil-your-own chicken, beef, or mahi SAMPLING: Lunch sandwiches run $4.45 - $5.50. Dinners are limited to five entrees, all of which you cook yourself on their community grill and run $6.75 for a burger to $9.75 for a top sirloin COMMENTS: You save money here by cooking your own. However, the fish is frozen and the all-you-can-eat rice and bean pots were emptied and never refilled on our visit. The green salad which accompanied dinner was warm. They do have evening entertainment from 4p.m. - 6 p.m. and 7 p.m. until closing which is for the younger set, and their Island fresh fruit daiquiries are very popular. Personally, we'd rather pay a little more and have someone else do the cooking.

SOUTH SEAS
LOCATED: At the Pioneer Inn on the south side of Lahaina, harborside, phone 661-3636 HOURS: Open only for dinner PRICE RANGE: INEXPENSIVE TYPE OF FOOD: Seafood,

RESTAURANTS
Lahaina/Kaanapali

beef, and chicken *SAMPLING:* Broil-your-own ground beef for $6.95, chicken for $8.95, or ranch steak for $8.50. Salad bar, baked beans, rolls, or items can be ordered off of the menu *COMMENTS:* Seating here is poolside at the rustic, old Pioneer Inn. Very casual atmosphere and they do offer a children's menu.

SURFSIDE
LOCATED: Maui Surf Hotel, out on their front grounds, Kaanapali, phone 661-4411 *HOURS:* Vary, depending on season and how busy they are, but generally open for breakfast and lunch *PRICE RANGE:* INEXPENSIVE *TYPE OF FOOD:* Varied *SAMPLING:* Sandwiches run $3.25 - $4.95, with ham and cheese at $4.25. Lunch entrees include lasagna at $6.50, fried chicken $5.95, chili and rice $4.95, and fruit boat $6.25 *COMMENTS:* While the prices are inexpensive, you don't get a lot for your money. Not much of a view or anything of excitement on their menu.

TORTILLA FLATS
LOCATED: 658 Front Street, at the Wharf Shopping Center, south end of Lahaina across from the Banyan Tree. You'll find it on the lower level and to the rear of the center, phone 667-9581 *HOURS:* Daily from 11:30 a.m. - 10 p.m., cocktails from 10 a.m. until closing *PRICE RANGE:* INEXPENSIVE *TYPE OF FOOD:* Mexican *SAMPLING:* Huevos rancheros run $5.75, combination dinners are served ala carte or with refried beans, rice, chips, and choice of soup or salad. The dinners run ala carte $6.25 - $7.75, with extra items only a dollar more. Also, some seafood items for those non-Mexican food lovers. *COMMENTS:* They can prepare any item on their menu to go and feature 17 ounce margaritas in strawberry, peach, or pineapple. Who needs food? Visa and Mastercard accepted.

WHALE'S TALE
LOCATED: Across from the Pioneer Inn at 666 Front St., Lahaina, upstairs, phone 661-3676 *HOURS:* Lunch served from 11:30 a.m. - 2:30 p.m.; dinner from 5:30 p.m. Reservations accepted *PRICE RANGE:* INEXPENSIVE TO MODERATE *TYPE OF FOOD:* Seafood and beef *SAMPLING:* Fresh fish, subject to availability and varies. Priced daily. Also, you can find beef short ribs, shrimp tempura, or bouillabaisse along with assorted steaks. Served with rice, vegetable and bread.

"MODERATE RANGE"

APPLE ANNIE'S BEACH HOUSE
LOCATED: Kaanapali near the Maui Surf Hotel, phone 661-3160 *HOURS:* Daily for breakfast, lunch, and dinner *PRICE RANGE:* MODERATE *TYPE OF FOOD:* Varied *SAMPLING:* Omelets, burgers, sandwiches, and seafood. Lunch and dinner menu same.

ALEX'S HOLE IN THE WALL ***
LOCATED: 834 Front St., Lahaina, phone 661-3197 HOURS: Dinner only, 6 p.m. - 10 p.m., daily except Sunday *PRICE RANGE:* MODERATE *TYPE OF FOOD:* Italian *COMMENTS:* Serve pasta, made fresh locally. Visa and Mastercard accepted.

*BETTINO'S***
LOCATED: 505 Front St., Lahaina, phone 661-8810, at the Lahaina Shores Village, a little hard to find, but walk through the complex to the waterfront. This is next door to the Lahaina Shores Hotel *HOURS:* Opens at 7 a.m. for breakfast, lunch, and dinner. Bar opens at 8 a.m. *PRICE RANGE:* INEXPENSIVE TO MODERATE *TYPE OF FOOD:* Everything

RESTAURANTS
Lahaina/Kaanapali

SAMPLING: Try their omelets that offer 30+ choices of ingredients, including macadamia nuts, bananas, zucchini, or clam. Can't decide? Choose the chef's mess omelet that includes all of them for $15. They confided in us that only two people have dared order it! Dinners run $10 - $15 and include chicken dore at $9.95, steamed clams in drawn butter at $9.95, mahi, chicken marsala, or Korean ribs at $10.95. Also, a nice touch are the combination dinners which include a short rib or small top sirloin steak served with your choice of mahi, clams, scampi, shrimp, oysters, scallops, or lobster. Priced from $11.95 - $18.95 *COMMENTS:* This is a little off the tourist track, but well worth the stop. The food is well-prepared and the portions generous. A lot of local residents frequent here. The menu offers an ample assortment of items from which to choose.

THE BLACK ROCK
LOCATED: Poolside at the Sheraton Hotel at Kaanapali, phone 661-0031 *HOURS:* Lunch from 11 a.m. - 3:30 p.m.; dinner from 6p.m. - 9:30 p.m. *PRICE RANGE:* MODERATE *TYPE OF FOOD:* American *SAMPLING:* Salad bar $5.95, honey fried chicken $10.95, prime rib $17.50, light dinner and sandwiches $5 - $9. Children's portions available.

CHART HOUSE
LOCATED: 1450 Front St., Lahaina, phone 661-0937 *HOURS:* Dinner daily 5:30 p.m. - 9:30 p.m. *PRICE RANGE:* MODERATE TO EXPENSIVE *TYPE OF FOOD:* Seafood and beef *COMMENTS:* They don't take reservations and there is usually a wait. You might want to go early, put your name in, and stroll down through Lahaina. They also offer another restaurant in Kahului which has a better view and not such crowds.

DON THE BEACHCOMBER
LOCATED: On the grounds of the Royal Lahaina Resort, Kaanapali, Phone 661-3611 *HOURS:* Nightly for dinner 6 p.m. - 9 p.m. *PRICE RANGE:* MODERATE TO EXPENSIVE *TYPE OF FOOD:* Polynesian, Chinese, and Far Eastern *SAMPLING:* Crispy duck with plum sauce and diced peanuts $8.25, stir-fried shrimp with vegetables $8.95, or Australian lobster fried with black bean sauce $10.95.

EIGHT BELLS**
LOCATED: At the Maui Surf Hotel, Kaanapali. Go through the lobby and to the right, phone 661-4411 *HOURS:* Vary depending on the season. Open generally for breakfast and dinner *PRICE RANGE:* INEXPENSIVE TO MODERATE *TYPE OF FOOD:* Varied *SAMPLING:* Dinners include top sirloin $14.50, catch of the day $13.50, and Hawaiian chicken $12.50. *COMMENTS:* We favor their morning breakfast buffet which has remained at a constant $6.95 for several years. They offer an array of fruit, fresh fruit yogurt, juices, and an assortment of hot items such as eggs, omelets, breakfast meats, and potatoes, that vary daily. Make this your breakfast and lunch!

EL CRAB CATCHER***
LOCATED: Whaler's Village Shopping Center, Kaanapali. It's a little hidden on the ocean side, phone 661-4423 *HOURS:* Dinner *PRICE RANGE:* MODERATE *TYPE OF FOOD:* Seafood their speciality *SAMPLING:* Light suppers include salad and bread and vary from a crab quiche to prime rib sandwich and run $9.95 - $10.95. Other dinners also include a choice of salads - mixed green, caesar for two, hot spinach for two, or daily soup, along with a vegetable and breads. Their fresh fish varies, based on what is available and runs $15.95. Beef dishes run $14.95 - $18.95, and, true to their name, they offer five dinners with crab. *COMMENTS:* This was once an athletic club and the pool remains beachside around which you can dine or enjoy a sunset and cool drink. Some have been known to even take a dip! They do a very good job with their fish preparation. Save room for one

RESTAURANTS
Lahaina/Kaanapali

of their scrumptious desserts. This is a very popular place and reservations are a good idea unless you want an hour or more wait. They also accept Visa, Mastercard, and American Express. Cocktails available.

ERIK'S ON THE BEACH
LOCATED: At the Kaanapali Villas - phone 667-2644 HOURS: 7 a.m. - 11 a.m. for breakfast; 11:30 a.m. - 3 p.m. for lunch; and 5:30 p.m. - 10 p.m. for dinner PRICE RANGE: Inexpensive to Moderate TYPE OF FOOD: Seafood SAMPLING: Breakfast - omelets $4.25 - $4.75 Lunches - hamburger $3.75 Dinners - fish & chips $8.95, petite N.Y. Steak $9.95, Prime Rib $13.95, Lobster $18.95. Dinners served with fried rice or baked potato & salad bar.

GATES OF ITALY (formerly Braissere de Mer)
LOCATED: Kaanapali, they offer free pickup from Kaanapali (Maui Kaanapli Villa) to Kapalua, phone 667-2644 to take advantage of this HOURS: 7 a.m. - 11 a.m. for breakfast; 11 a.m. - 3 p.m. for lunch; and 5:30 p.m. - 10 p.m. for dinner PRICE RANGE: MODERATE TYPE OF FOOD: Italian SAMPLING: Pasta dishes run $5.95 for spaghetti to $7.95 for tortellini. An assortment of veal dishes will set you back $12.95 - $14.95. Seafood includes scampi alla provencale or alla grigli (that's sauteed with garlic and capers). They also offer lobster either in a wine and tomato sauce or baked with drawn butter for $18.95 and $17.95. COMMENTS: No personal checks, but Visa, Mastercard, and American Express are accepted.

H. S. BOUNTY
LOCATED: Kaanapali, Whaler's Village Shopping Center, phone 661-0946 HOURS: Breakfast, lunch and dinner are served. Early bird dinner specials are from 5 p.m. - 6:30 p.m. and available nightly. Dinner is served daily from 5 p.m. - 10 p.m. PRICE RANGE: MODERATE TYPE OF FOOD: Seafood, chicken, and beef SAMPLING: Dinners include salad bar, rice, and bread. Children's portions available on most items at a reduced rate- -just ask. Fish and chips, made with mahi, run $8.75. Teriyaki steak is $12.95. Fisherman's deep fried combo is also $12.95. Bouillabaisse is $14.50 and steaks run $14.95 and up COMMENTS: No reservations taken here. Cocktails served.

HARBOR FRONT*
LOCATED: Wharf Shopping Center, across from Banyan Tree and tucked away on the top level, phone 667-7822 HOURS: Lunch 11:30 - 2 p.m.; dinner 5 p.m. - 10 p.m. PRICE RANGE: MODERATE TYPE OF FOOD: Chicken, fish, and beef SAMPLING: Fish and chips for lunch at $5.90 or seafood combo at $8.95. Dinners include fried chicken at $8.95, however, most other entrees run $10.95 - $16.95 COMMENTS: No harbor view here, and the eating is inside. Their fish is fresh and meals appear to be nicely prepared. This is their second location, having been ousted previously by condo development.

KIMO'S *
LOCATED: 845 Front St., Lahaina, phone 661-4811 HOURS: Lunch and dinner served daily PRICE RANGE: INEXPENSIVE LUNCHES, MODERATE DINNERS TYPE OF FOOD: Seafood their specialty, also beef and chicken dishes SAMPLING: Their fresh fish varies daily as does its price. Baked scallops run $9.95, shrimp Tahitian $11.95. Top sirloin is $9.95 and mahi or Kalua pork run $8.95. Keiki dinners or for less hungry adults include hamburgers and chicken sandwich at $5.50 - $5.95 COMMENTS: Opinions vary greatly about Kimo's. Some really like it and others really don't. They don't accept reservations, so we plan on a wait, put in our name, have the hostess give us a time frame, and just enjoy prowling the Lahaina shops. They have a water front location and if you're really

RESTAURANTS
Lahaina/Kaanapali

lucky, you'll get a table with a view. Our experience has been very good service and nicely prepared fresh fish, however, they do run out of fresh fish sometimes quite early! They also have a bar on the lower level that offers a young crowd and a water front view for sunset.

LAHAINA PROVISION ***
LOCATED: 200 Nohea Kai Dr. at the Hyatt Regency Hotel, phone 667-7474 HOURS: Lunch from 11:30 a.m. - 3 p.m. and dinner from 6 p.m. - 11 p.m. The lounge is open from 11:30 a.m. - 11:30 p.m. PRICE RANGE: MODERATE TO EXPENSIVE TYPE OF FOOD: Seafood and beef SAMPLING: Luncheon hamburger is $5.75, liver is $8.50, or fresh fish is $9.50. Dinners run $14.50 for chicken with Maui onions to $18.00 for a NY steak COMMENTS: This restaurant is cleverly perched above the pool and on the edge of one of the Hyatt's waterfalls. This place may be a favorite if you're a chocolate lover. They have a CHOCOHOLIC BAR that features rich ice cream with an incredible choice of terrific temptations to top it with. If you have dinner, it's an additional $3.00, but you can come later for dessert only and indulge for $3.50. Reservations are recommended and major credit cards are accepted.

LA FAMILIA
LOCATED: At Kaanapali, 2290 Kaanapali Parkwy, phone 667-7902. Amidst the golf course, but well marked. Enter Kaanapali from the south side for easiest access HOURS: 7 a.m. - 10:30 p.m. daily PRICE RANGE: MODERATE TYPE OF FOOD: Mexican and assorted other selections SAMPLING: Breakfasts run $3.25 to $4.95. Dinner selections include a spinach quiche at $6.50, soup and salad at $5.95, burritos at $6.95, or tostada supreme at $7.50 COMMENTS: They recently moved from their Kahului restaurant, which was extremely popular, to branches at Kaanapali and Kihei. Only Kaanapali is now serving breakfast. They note that they endeavor to use pure organic food whenever possible. Some say it was better in their old location, however, they're generally packed nightly, so they must be doing something right.

LEILANI'S***
LOCATED: Whaler's Village Shopping Center, toward the beach, phone 661-4495 HOURS: Dinner from 5 p.m. PRICE RANGE: MODERATE TYPE OF FOOD: Seafood, pork, beef, and chicken SAMPLING: Early bird dinner specials run $8.50 and are served 5 p.m. - 6:30 p.m. offering you a choice of BBQ half-chicken, steak, mahi or teriyaki brochette, and a choice of seafood chowder, Portuguese bean soup, or salad. Their regular menu selections include Azeka's ribs at $10.95, pork ribs at the same price, and fresh fish at $15.95 COMMENTS: Just look what three million dollars will do! This was a Chuck's restaurant until the owners, who also operate Kimo's and the Kapalua Bar and Grill, renovated it into a much nicer open air restaurant with a bar on the lower beach level. They have also enlarged it a great deal. The early bird specials are a wonderful bargain and may not continue once this restaurant gets established. They also offer a limited children's menu, and some luscious desserts. They don't take reservations or personal checks, but do honor major credit cards.

LONGHI'S**
LOCATED: 888 Front St., Lahaina, phone 667-2288 HOURS: 7:30 a.m. - 10 p.m.; dessert served until 11p.m. PRICE RANGE: MODERATE TO EXPENSIVE TYPE OF FOOD: Varied SAMPLING: Menu given orally by waiter. They are famous for their desserts; good breakfasts, too. A possible choice might include zucchini frittatta, shrimp Longhi, prawns amaretto COMMENTS: They have become a near legend in Lahaina and have recently

_____ *RESTAURANTS*
Lahaina/Kaanapali

done a little remodeling. It is easy to get carried away here, order too much, and get surprised with a hefty check! They offer capuccino and a nice wine selection.

*MARCO'S***
LOCATED: Mariner's Alley, 844 Front St., Lahaina. This small shopping area is on the north end of Lahaina, near the emerald store. The restaurant is in the back corner, phone 661-8877 HOURS: Daily from 9 a.m. for a light breakfast, 11a.m. and on for lunch, and 5 p. m. on for dinner PRICE RANGE: MODERATE TYPE OF FOOD: Italian SAMPLING: Their breakfasts consist mostly of pastries and coffee. Dinners might include an Italian salad made with rice, chicken, mushrooms, olives (Italian ones!), and onion. It looked great for $4.50. Dinners generally run $5 - $10 with a small pasta for $5.25, or three types of calzones for $6. Their five-course dinner varies nightly COMMENTS: This inside and patio eatery is small, quaint, and clean. It opened in September of 1983 and is a branch of Mazzi's restaurants, which have become very popular in Oregon. The staff here was very personable and the Italian ice creams and ices were divine. Stop in just for a dish of this cooling delight--it's a step up from regular ice cream.

*MOANA TERRACE***
LOCATED: Lower level of the Maui Marriott Hotel, Kaanapali, phone 667-1200 HOURS: 6:30 a.m. - 11 p.m. PRICE RANGE: MODERATE TYPE OF FOOD: Varied SAMPLING: Monday through Saturday their breakfast buffet runs $8.75 and they also offer items off of the menu. Sunday brunch is 10 a.m. - 2 p.m. and includes champagne at $13.95. Lunch is 11 a.m. - 2:30 p.m. with sandwiches and salads. From 5 p.m. - 6:30 p.m. they offer a very popular early bird dinner special which includes a choice of fish of the day, teriyaki beef, or chicken for $7.95. Hot entrees are served from 5 p.m. - 10 p.m. with dinner available from 6 p.m. - 9:30 p.m. During their dinner they also offer a choice of their buffet for $11.95 for adults and $7.95 for children under 12. A light dining menu is offered from 5 p.m. - 6:30 p.m. and 10 p.m. - 11 p.m. COMMENTS: This restaurant gets the award for the most menus. The poor hostess has at least eight menus depending on the day of the week and the time of the day! Their breakfast buffet at $8.95 looks great for a hearty eater and offers fresh fruits and juices, eggs cooked to your order, and Belgian waffles. On the menu they have macadamia pancakes or a strawberry waffle at $5.50 that are quite tasty. Their early bird dinner special is very popular, so plan on getting there early. Major credit cards accepted. Dinner reservations might be a good idea.

MOBY DICK'S
LOCATED: Grounds of Royal Lahaina Resort at Kaanapali, phone 661-3611 HOURS: Dinner nightly 6 p.m. - 9:30 p.m. PRICE RANGE: MODERATE TO EXPENSIVE TYPE OF FOOD: Seafood and steak SAMPLING: Dinners served with "colorburst" salad and rice. Salads and soups are extra at $1.95 - $3.25, garden vegetables or baked potato are $2.50. Entrees - filet of sole Lanai $10.95, (sauteed in butter and topped with shrimp, pineapple, and green onions), chicken teriyaki $11.95, sauteed delmonico shrimp $13.95, t-bone $16.95

PAVILLION
LOCATED: 200 Nohea Kai Dr., Kaanapali, lower level of the Hyatt Regency Hotel, phone 667-7474 HOURS: Lunch daily from 11:30 a.m. - 6 p.m.; dinner from 6 p.m. - 11 p.m. PRICE RANGE: MODERATE TO EXPENSIVE TYPE OF FOOD: Varied SAMPLING: Luncheon offerings include a tuna salad sandwich at $4.75, and pita bread sandwich at $6.75. Dinners run $11.50 - $16.50 COMMENTS: This is near the pool of the Hyatt. They offer the lunch menu for dinner also, which is nice for the less hearty eater. A children's

RESTAURANTS
Lahaina/Kaanapali

selection includes a peanut butter, jelly, and banana sandwich or grilled cheese for $3.25, or pizza dish at $5.25.

SPATS II
LOCATED: 200 Nohea Kai Dr., Kaanapali, Hyatt Regency Hotel. Go through the lobby, turn right, and go down a set of stairs. Phone 667-7474 *HOURS:* Dinner only *PRICE RANGE:* MODERATE TO EXPENSIVE *TYPE OF FOOD:* Italian their specialty *SAMPLING:* Petti di Pollo Milanese at $13.50, Scaloppini al Marsale at $17, and generally the menu runs about $14 - $19. They are served with a fresh vegetable and potato *COMMENTS:* Reservations recommended and a little dressier atmosphere.

THE KEG (Formerly The Blue Max)
LOCATED: 730 Front St., Lahaina, Phone: 661-3137 *HOURS:* Dinner from 5 p.m. *PRICE RANGE:* MODERATE *TYPE OF FOOD:* Steak and Seafood *SAMPLING:* Dinners run $8 to $19

TAI KOH (formerly Paniola Steak House)
LOCATED: Kaanapali Villas, phone 667-6234 *HOURS:* Nightly 4 pm - 2 am *PRICE RANGE:* MODERATE TO EXPENSIVE *TYPE OF FOOD:* Japanese *SAMPLING:* Butterfish $9.95, Sukiyaki $14.95, Combination dinners $12.95. *COMMENTS:* Sunset Specials offered 5-6:30 for $8.95. The entree varies nightly but includes soup or salad, rice tea & ice cream.

TIKI TERRACE
LOCATED: Kaanapali Beach Hotel, phone 661-1011 *HOURS:* Breakfast 7 a.m. - 11 a.m.; dinner 6 p.m. - 9:30 p.m.; brunch served Sundays *PRICE RANGE:* MODERATE *TYPE OF FOOD:* American, Polynesian *SAMPLING:* Breakfast - varieties of pancakes run $3.25 - $3.95, omelets at $5.95. Dinners include rice, vegetable, roll, and featured is a mini luau for two, or BBQ chicken at $8.95, prime rib at $10.95. Sunday brunch is $10.95 and includes champagne.

"EXPENSIVE RANGE"

CHEZ PAUL**
LOCATED: Five miles south of Lahaina at Olowalu, phone 661-3843 *HOURS:* Dinner 5:30 p.m. - 10:30 p.m. *PRICE RANGE:* EXPENSIVE *TYPE OF FOOD:* French *SAMPLING:* Dinners run about $20 and the menu includes veal, fish, duck, and beef in French sauces, pate, escargot, shrimp, and some very special desserts *COMMENTS:* This small rstaurant has maintained its popularity even though it's tricky to find and has changed ownership. (The original owner used to make change out of his pocket.) The decor is slightly art deco, small, and romantic. The food and service are generally excellent. The wine list is expensive and ordering by the glass might be a good idea. Reservations are recommended strongly and Visa and Mastercard are accepted.

DISCOVERY ROOM
LOCATED: At the Sheraton Hotel, atop the picturesque black rock, phone 661-0031 *HOURS:* Breakfast 6:30 a.m. - 9:30 a.m.; dinner daily *PRICE RANGE:* EXPENSIVE *TYPE OF FOOD:* Continental and American *SAMPLING:* They offer two dinner menus which rotate, one is Tuesday, Wednesday, Friday, and Sunday. The other is Monday, Thursday, and Saturday. They have similar prices, just different preparations of the same foods. A pork meal will run $19.75, chicken dinner at $19.50. This does include an appetizer, soup

RESTAURANTS
Lahaina/Kaanapali

or salad, and coffee or tea COMMENTS: Entertainment is offered at their 8:30 dinner show or at a 9:30 cocktail show. Add $2 entry fee and a two-drink minimum to the cocktail showing.

GERARD'S
LOCATED: In Lahaina on Lahainaluna Street. This is a major street which intersects with Front Street near the center of Lahaina. Phone 661-8939 HOURS: Lunch from 11 a.m. and dinner served Monday through Saturday from 6 p.m. PRICE RANGE: EXPENSIVE TYPE OF FOOD: French SAMPLING: Vary daily, but might include - roast beef au jus, duckling ala orange, braised leg of lamb, pepper steak, fresh chicken breast sauteed in raspberry vinegar sauce, or steak tartare. Desserts are made fresh daily COMMENTS: This is reminiscent of an open air cafe in France. The owner is also the chef!

QUEE QUEQ
LOCATED: Maui Surf Hotel, Kaanapali. Go through the lobby and to the right. It is out near the beach. Phone 661-4411 HOURS: Dinner only PRICE RANGE: EXPENSIVE TYPE OF FOOD: Varied SAMPLING: Entrees run $12.95 - $14.50 and are ala carte. Salads run an extra $2.50 - $4, rice is $1.75, and baked potato $1.95. Dinner selections are broad and include scampi ala creme, veal chasseur, lemon chicken, and abolone with oyster sauce. COMMENTS: A little on the expensive side, but there is an added attraction of music from the adjoining cocktail lounge—the kind for slow dancing.

LA BRETAGNE RESTAURANT FRANCAIS***
LOCATED: 562C Front St., Lahaina, phone 661-8966 HOURS: Dinner only PRICE RANGE: EXPENSIVE TYPE OF FOOD: French SAMPLING: Entrees run $17-$19 & include salad, vegetable, french bread and coffee. COMMENTS: This house was once the home of Sheriff Kaluakini, a lawman during Lahaina's heyday. A little tricky to find off Front Street. Reservations are highly recommended. Visa and Mastercard accepted, and while dress is casual, shorts aren't advised.

LOKELANI
LOCATED: 100 Nohea Kai Drive, at the Maui Marriott Hotel, Kaanapali, lower level, phone 667-1200 HOURS: Dinner served 6 p.m. - 10 p.m. PRICE RANGE: EXPENSIVE TYPE OF FOOD: Seafood SAMPLING: Small sirloin at $14 up to a seafood sampler at $20. Also, stuffed scampi, sauteed fresh fish, scallops, or crab legs join the menu. Dinners include salad, vegetable, and rolls. A garden atmosphere, with an air of an earlier Lahaina town. Reservations recommended. Major credit cards accepted.

NIKKO'S JAPANESE STEAK HOUSE
LOCATED: 100 Nohea Kai Drive at the Maui Marriott Hotel, Kaanapali, phone 667-1200 HOURS: Dinner only PRICE RANGE: EXPENSIVE TYPE OF FOOD: Japanese SAMPLING: Chicken $15.50, steak or shrimp at $20. Dinner includes an appetizer, Japanese broth and Oriental salad. COMMENTS: Reservations recommended. Major credit cards accepted. Part of the price is the "show". The chef works at your table and is adept at knife throwing and other dazzling cooking techniques.

PEACOCK RESTAURANT**
LOCATED: 2550 Kehaa Drive, Kaanapali, just above the major Kaanapali hotels on the golf course. Phone 667-6847 HOURS: Lunch and dinner PRICE RANGE: EXPENSIVE TYPE OF FOOD: Continental, Polynesian SAMPLING: Dinners generally run $15 - $22 and include a vegetable, and potato, rice, or pasta. Salads for two run $3.75 for the Peacock salad, or $4.25 for hot spinach. Also available is a dinner salad at $2.50. Entrees include

RESTAURANTS
Lahaina/Kaanapali

scallops in a white wine, shallot, and mushroom sauce for $13.95, pork mango - thinly sliced pork in a mango and brandy sauce - for $12.50, broiled lamb chops at $18.50, or veal oscar at $17.75 COMMENTS: The decor here is tastefully done with open air Oriental motif. The service and food are both good and reservations are recommended. Attire can be casual or dressy. Major credit cards are accepted.

SWAN COURT**
LOCATED: Hyatt Regency Hotel, Kaanapali. Going through lobby, turn to the left and down the stairs or elevator, phone 667-7474 HOURS: Open for breakfast and dinner. Brunch is 6:30 a.m. - 11 a.m. PRICE RANGE: MODERATE TO EXPENSIVE TYPE OF FOOD: Continental SAMPLING: Their brunch runs $9 and includes fresh-squeezed orange juice, crepes, macadamia pancakes with a variety of toppings, cereals, yogurt, fresh fruits, and a good choice of hot breakfast foods. The menu items run $6 - $9 with juice or fruit alone being $3, so the buffet is the best value. Dinners are ala carte $15 - $22, salads $4 - $5, and soups $3.25 - $5.50 COMMENTS: You will pay a little more here, but the atmosphere and the view of the Swan Court are worth it for a special treat! Reservations, especially for dinner, are advised. Major credit cards accepted.

LUAUS

SHERATON MAUI HOTEL
They feature Chief Faa, the fire knife dancer, and the price runs $30 for adults and $18 for children. They recreate Polynesian history which might be a little too involved for some children. The price includes rum punch, a shell lei, and a buffet dinner. This luau is only Tuesday, Thursday, and Sunday nights and begins at 5:30 p.m. Phone 667-9564 for reservations.

KAPA ROOM
This luau is nightly except for Tuesdays at the Maui Surf Hotel. The buffet and show run $21.50 and the food includes prime rib, pork, chicken, salads, and desserts. The decor is attractive and they also depict the early beginnings of Maui. Dress can be casual or fancy. Reservations are recommended. Visa and Mastercard are accepted. Phone 661-4411 for reservations.

THE ROYAL LAHAINA
Offers a sunset view with cocktails at their open bar, a Polynesian buffet on Kaanapali Beach which includes Kalua pig, poi, and mahi mahi followed by a Polynesian review. Nightly except Monday beginning at 5:30 p.m. This luau runs $27 for adults and $17 for children under 12. Phone 661-3611 for reservations.

KAANAPALI BEACH HOTEL
Offers dinner show featuring Hawaiian entertainer Nephi Hanneman. The show called "Nephi-Man Alive" is featured Tuesdays thru Saturdays. The prime rib dinner, show, tax, tip and two drinks runs $31 for adults, $19 for children under 12.

HYATT REGENCY
Presents Drums of the Pacific outdoors as both a dinner and cocktail show Monday through Saturday. The dinner show begins at 5:30 p.m. and includes mai tais, soup, salad, and a choice of fish, steak, or chicken. The price for adults is $32. The cocktail show begins at 7:45 p.m. and runs $18.

RESTAURANTS
Kapalua/Napili/Kahana

"BAR ONLY"

KAPALUA BAY RESORT—LOBBY BAR ****
Early evenings here provide a fabulous sunset in an elegant setting. Pupus served are complimentary and vary, however, on one occasion we had a variety of fresh imported cheeses and small shishkabobs to cook ourselves over a small BBQ. The tropical drinks run $4 - $6 with some being the size of small fishbowls. We've never had any trouble getting a table here. A guitarist playing in the background is a nice touch, too!

"BARGAIN"

MARKET CAFE
LOCATED: Kapalua Bay Hotel Shops 669-4888 HOURS: Daily for breakfast, and lunch and dinner. Open 7am to 9pm PRICE RANGE: BARGAIN TO INEXPENSIVE TYPE OF FOOD: Pastries, continental SAMPLING: Sandwiches $5-$7. Try their eggs benedict at $5.25, tropical pancakes at $4.50, and some yummy pastries. Beer & wines. Coffee $.95, Fruit juice. COMMENTS: This small restaurant is part of a market that carries some unusual imported foods.

R. V. DELI
LOCATED: Roadside by Slaughterhouse Beach HOURS: Daily, most afternoons PRICE RANGE: BARGAIN TYPE OF FOOD: Burgers, hot dogs, ice cream, and drinks COMMENTS: Peter L. Dyck, Sr. has found this alternative use for his "recreational vehicle", thereby the name R. V. He can be found in this same spot most days and has an interesting saga about how he traveled the United States and ended up selling burgers on Maui.

"INEXPENSIVE"'"

DOLLIE'S
LOCATED: 4310 Honoapiilani Hwy., phone 667-2623 HOURS: Breakfast, lunch, and dinner PRICE RANGE: INEXPENSIVE TYPE OF FOOD: Pizzas, sandwiches COMMENTS: Items delivered and food to go! It is located five miles north of Kaanapali at Kahana Manor.

"MODERATE"

ERIK'S SEAFOOD GROTTO
LOCATED: 4242 Lower Honoapiilani Hwy. on the second floor of the Kahana Villa Condo, phone 669-4806 HOURS: Dinner daily 5:30 p.m. - 10 p.m. PRICE RANGE: INEXPENSIVE TO MODERATE TYPE OF FOOD: Seafood with limited beef and one chicken selection SAMPLING: Dinners include chowder or salad, potatoes or rice, and bread. Mainland fish including trout at $10.95 and salmon are served up as well as fresh island fish. Shellfish meals include lobster thermidore at $15.95, crab imperial at $12.95, and the lone single chicken entree is served sauteed at $10.95. Desserts are very limited and include only a choice of ice cream or sherbets. COMMENTS: The best value is their early

RESTAURANTS
Kapalua/Napili/Kahana

bird dinner special from 5:30 p.m. - 6:30 p.m. The meal offered varies daily. Visa, Mastercard, and American Express are all honored.

KAHANA KEYES
LOCATED: At the Royal Kahana at Kahana Beach, phone 669-8071 (they provide courtesy pickup in Kaanapali area). *HOURS:* Lunch 10:00 - 2:00 and dinner 5:30 - 10:00 *PRICE RANGE:* INEXPENSIVE TO MODERATE *TYPE OF FOOD:* Seafood and steak *SAMPLING:* Seafood Curry at $10.50, Pacific Prawns at $15.95, Chicken Haleakala at $8.95, Top Sirloin at $10.95 or Rack of lamb for $14.95. *COMMENTS:* They offer an early bird dinner special served daily from 5:30 - 7:00 which varies daily for $8.95. This special includes salad bar, rice, potatoes or pasta. They offer a number of items in children's portions at $6.95. They offer good salad bar.

KAPALUA GRILL AND BAR **
LOCATED: 200 Kapalua Drive, just across the road from the Kapalua Resort and a short drive up Kapalua Drive, phone 669-5653 *HOURS:* Lunch Monday through Saturday 11:30 a.m. - 3 p.m.; dinner 5:30 p.m. - 10 p.m. *PRICE RANGE:* MODERATE *TYPE OF FOOD:* Seafood, assorted others *SAMPLING:* Lunches include burgers at $4.50 up to $6.50, hot sandwiches $3.95 - $7.90. The dinner menu offers seafood, veal and chicken dishes which run the $9.95 to $12.95 range. Their wine list is very good with choices ranging from $8.25 to $12 a bottle *COMMENTS:* This is a sister facility to Leilani's and Kimo's. Its menu is a little more gourmet in its selections. The rust and green motif is very nicely carried out with a golf course and ocean view that only adds to the pluses of this restaurant. It's a popular restaurant, so you might want to call ahead. Visa and Mastercard are accepted.

ORIENT EXPRESS
LOCATED: At Napili Shores Resort, one mile before Kapalua, phone 669-8077 *HOURS:* Dinner Tuesday through Sunday, 5 p.m. - 10 p.m., closed Monday *PRICE RANGE:* INEXPENSIVE TO MODERATE *TYPE OF FOOD:* Thai Chinese cuisine *SAMPLING:* Red curried beef at $6.35, garlic shrimp at $6.55, stuffed chicken wing at $6.95, or sweet and sour vegetables at $5.50 *COMMENTS:* This very unusual menu offers some taste treats you may not have tried. Early bird specials from 5 p.m. - 7p.m. Take out available.

PINEAPPLE HILL
LOCATED: Up past Napili to Kapalua, turn right after passing the entrance to the Kapalua Hotel. You'll then travel up a road lined with enormous Norfolk pines. Phone 661-0964 or 669-6129 *HOURS:* Dinner 5:30 p.m. - 10 p.m. with cocktails beginning at 4:30 p.m. *PRICE RANGE:* MODERATE *TYPE OF FOOD:* Continental *SAMPLING:* Dinners include salad, rolls, rice, or potatoes. Ten dinners from which to choose include Pineapple Hill chicken at $8.95, New York steak at $14.95, and teriyaki steak at $12.95. The wine list is also a little sparse with only 20 wines *COMMENTS:* This was once the home of a plantation manager, and has been converted into a restaurant with one of the loftiest settings for sunset viewing. Cocktails can be enjoyed out on the front lawn while watching the sun descending. The interior decor is not nearly so elegant. Visa, Mastercard, and American Express are all accepted.

RESTAURANT OF THE MAUI MOON
LOCATED: At Napili Kai Beach Club on their beachfront. This is about 10 miles north of Lahaina. Phone 669-6271 *HOURS:* Breakfast, lunch, and dinner *PRICE RANGE:* MODERATE TO EXPENSIVE *TYPE OF FOOD:* Varied *SAMPLING:* Breakfast offers their "different" buffet for $7.00. This includes a table from which to choose fruit, juices, and other cold items with the cooked items coming straight from the kitchen. Lunch includes

RESTAURANTS
Kapalua/Napili/Kahana

sandwiches that run $2.75 to $3.95 with a hot dog priced at a hefty $3.50. Dinners are priced $14.95 to $19.95 and include veal and seafood. The salad bar alone will cost you $9.95, but is extensive, even including soup. Hawaiian music performed Monday, Wednesday, Saturday, and sometimes Thursday nights 8:30 p.m. - 10:30 p.m.

"EXPENSIVE"

THE BAY CLUB ****
LOCATED: At Kapalua near the entrance to the resort, phone 669-8008 after 5 p.m., 669-5656 before 5 p.m. HOURS: Lunch 11:30 a.m. - 2 p.m.; dinner 5:30 p.m. - 9:30 p.m.; pupus served 3 p.m. - 5 p.m. *PRICE RANGE:* EXPENSIVE *TYPE OF FOOD:* Continental/French *SAMPLING:* Lunch choices include a baron of beef on a bun for $6.00 or how about the more exotic choice of a papaya stuffed with diced Cantonese chicken and served with chutney finger sandwiches, also priced at $6.00. Dinners include a salad and vegetable. Their fresh fish is cooked six different ways, with one choice sauteed with avocado and crab claws. Capon is another dinner entree which is cooked in beer batter and served with hot guava sauce. The dinners generally run between $18 and $22. *COMMENTS:* Set on a promontory, this restaurant not only offers a magnificent panoramic ocean view, but it also has a pool around which you can enjoy cocktails and pupus. One of the few restaurants to still have a dress code on Maui. Shoes and shirt are required for lunch and jackets and shoes for dinner. A pianist serenades you through dinner adding a romantic touch. Reservations are strongly recommended and your major charge cards are accepted.

KAPALUA RESORT DINING ROOM (The Garden) ****
LOCATED: At the Kapalua Bay Resort Hotel, phone 669-5656 HOURS: Breafast 7 - 10 a.m., luncheon buffets and dinner nightly *PRICE RANGE:* EXPENSIVE *TYPE OF FOOD:* Continental *SAMPLING:* Crayfish and chicken brochette with cantaloupe and papaya at $18.00, Linguine and scampi with tomatoes, saffron and cream. Dinners served ala carte. A large selection of salads run $2.50 to $9.00. Soups are an additional $2.50. Their dinner menu is on a two week rotation, so there is always something new and different to try. *COMMENTS:* Enjoy continental dining in this semi-open tropical setting. Excellent food and service make this a pleasant dining experience. Also offered by the resort is the very popular Mayfair lunch buffet. It runs $14.50 and is served Monday - Saturday from 12 noon - 2:30 p.m. and Sunday from 11:30 a.m. - 2:30 p.m. Previously just called "the dining room", it is now referred to as "The Garden". They feature a cruvinet which allows you to enjoy a single glass of a fine wine. An expresso machine is also a recent addition. Jackets are not required, but are recommended.

MONACO **
LOCATED: At the Napili Shores Resort, 5315 Honoapiilani Hwy., phone 669-8077 *HOURS:* Dinner from 6 p.m., late supper 10 p.m. until midnight *PRICE RANGE:* MODERATE TO EXPENSIVE *TYPE OF FOOD:* French provencial and northern Italian *SAMPLING:* Veal dishes, steaks, fish, duck, and pasta *COMMENTS:* Reservations are recommended at this plush Italian eatery. Dine on Victorian chairs of velvet while viewing the bubbling courtyard fountain.

PLANTATION VERANDA ****
LOCATED Kapalua Bay Resort, 500 Bay Drive, Phone 669-5656. *HOURS:* Dinner only, days and hours open vary seasonally, call for current hours. *PRICE RANGE:* EXPENSIVE

RESTAURANTS
Kapalua/Napili/Kahana

TYPE OF FOOD: Continental *SAMPLING:* Dinners ala carte. Filet of Beef Bengal with cream, ginger and fresh parsley $20, or try noisettes of spring lamb with marsala and chantrelles. *COMMENTS:* This formal setting offers elegance in dining. Their cruvinet offers you fine wine by the glass. An expresso machine is a pleasant addition as well. Jackets are requested attire and reservations are advised.

LUAUS
Kapalua/Napili/Kahana

LUAUS

Every Tuesday night at the Kapalua Bay Resort Hotel is a luau. Cocktails begin at 6 p.m. The buffet features Hawaiian food and begins at 7 p.m. Buddy Fo begins his Hawaiian show at 8 p.m. The price is $30 for adults, plus tax and gratuity, children 11 and under are $17.50. Reservations can be made by calling 669-5656.

RESTAURANTS
Kihei/Wailea

"BARGAIN RANGE"

AZEKA'S SNACK SHOP **
LOCATED: Azeka's Place shopping center on South Kihei Rd. *HOURS:* 9:30 a.m. - 4 p.m., Monday through Saturday *PRICE RANGE:* BARGAIN *TYPE OF FOOD:* Burgers and plate lunches *SAMPLING:* Teriyaki beef plate at $3.50, burgers for 90 cents, and coffee 25 cents. Turkey or tunafish sandwiches. *COMMENTS:* The old Azeka's market lost out to a bulldozer in the summer of 84 to be replaced with a new market and snack bar towards the rear of the new parking lot. The snack shop has improved its appearance 200% and maintained the incredibly low prices on its lunch foods. The teriyaki burger wasn't a burger but marinated beef and tasty for $1.70. The hamburger at $.90 (deluxe $1.10) was great too!

ED & DON'S
LOCATED: Wailea Shopping Center *HOURS:* Daily *PRICE RANGE:* BARGAIN *TYPE OF FOOD:* Sandwiches and ice cream *SAMPLING:* Sandwiches are widely assorted and run $2.50 to $3.50, beverages are 50 cents. Cones are $1.00, and other fountain treats are available.

MC DONALD'S
LOCATED: 1900 area of South Kihei Rd. at the Kihei Shopping Center *HOURS:* Breakfast, lunch, and dinner. Breakfast served only from 6 a.m. - 10 a.m. *PRICE RANGE:* BARGAIN *TYPE OF FOOD:* Fast *SAMPLING:* There are a few unusual island items added to the menu. For breakfast, you can choose Portuguese sausage with rice for $1.74 and chase it down with chilled guava juice *COMMENTS:* You can't escape the Golden Arches even here on Maui. Indoor seating is available here in a limited number of bright blue flowered booths. The prices generally are just slightly higher than mainland prices.

*PARADISE FRUIT**
LOCATED: 1913 South Kihei Rd., phone 879-1723 *HOURS:* 24 hours *PRICE RANGE:* BARGAIN *TYPE OF FOOD:* "Healthy oriented" sandwiches, salads, and smoothies *SAMPLING:* Veggie sandwich runs $2.60, turkey sandwich $3.10, salads priced $3 - $4. Smoothies and yogurt shakes are $1.50 - $2.00 *COMMENTS:* This is an open air fruit and vegetable market that also sells some sundry items. Tucked in the back is their walk up snack bar, which is primarily take out, as we didn't see any seating around. Their yogurt shakes were delicious!

PHILADELPHIA LOU'S
LOCATED: Azeka Shopping Center, in the back area *HOURS:* 7 a.m. - 11 p.m. weekdays, until midnight on weekends *PRICE RANGE:* BARGAIN *TYPE OF FOOD:* Fast food and sandwiches *SAMPLING:* Their breakfast menu is limited. Three eggs, hashbrowns (the pre-cooked little patty type), and rice, bagel, or toast run $2.75. Lunch items include a bagel with lox and cream cheese for $4.50, or for a hungrier appetite, try their 18-inch ham, roast beef, or turkey hoagie for $7.50 *COMMENTS:* Four booths are available for indoor eating, although with the popular video games in the rear, it was a little noisy. Box lunches are available as is an all-natural Maui-made ice cream at $1.00 a scoop. No credit cards taken.

THE SANDWITCH
LOCATED: 145 North Kihei Rd., in front of Sugar Beach Condominiums, phone 879-3262

RESTAURANTS
Kihei/Wailea

HOURS: Lunch daily PRICE RANGE: BARGAIN TYPE OF FOOD: Sandwiches SAMPLING: Large variety of sandwiches prices $3.50 - $4.50 and available to go or to eat there.

"INEXPENSIVE RANGE"

GOSPARE'S PLACE
LOCATED: 1993 South Kihei Rd., in the Island Surf Bldg., phone 879-8881 HOURS: PRICE RANGE: INEXPENSIVE TYPE OF FOOD: Pizza

INTERNATIONAL HOUSE OF PANCAKES
LOCATED: Azeka's Place shopping center on South Kihei Rd. HOURS: Sunday - Thursday 6 a.m. - midnight, Friday and Saturday 6 a.m. - 2 a.m. PRICE RANGE: INEXPENSIVE TYPE OF FOOD: Breakfast, lunch, and dinner choices are all served anytime SAMPLING: Omelets $3.25 - $4.95, waffles $2.95 - $3.95, sandwiches include grilled cheese at $3.95, or a steak sandwich at $5.95. Dinners run $4.95 - $6.75 and include soup or salad, roll and butter COMMENTS: A children's menu is available. Very crowded on weekends.

KIHEI NATURAL FOODS
LOCATED: Azeka's Place shopping center, in the health food store HOURS: Daily PRICE RANGE: INEXPENSIVE TYPE OF FOOD: Smoothies, fresh juices, salads, and sandwiches.

MAKANI'S COFFEE SHOP
LOCATED: Intercontinental Hotel at Wailea. Go to the right from the front lobby. Phone 879-1922 HOURS: Breakfast 6 a.m. - 11 a.m., breakfast buffet daily 6 a.m. - 10 a.m. ($9.75), lunch served 11 a.m. - 4 p.m., dinner 4 p.m. - midnight PRICE RANGE: INEXPENSIVE TYPE OF FOOD: American SAMPLING: Lunch offers soups, salads, and a variety of burgers in the $5 - $6 range. Dinner offerings include saimin noodles at $5.75 and shrimp curry at $9.95 COMMENTS: A children's menu available. This casual setting offers a pool and ocean view. Visa and Mastercard accepted.

MAKENA GOLF COURSE RESTAURANT
LOCATED: Makena Golf Course, just beyond Wailea, phone 879-1154 HOURS: Opens 9:30 a.m. for take out, 11 a.m. - 4 p.m. for meals with indoor seating, cocktails until 5 p.m. PRICE RANGE: INEXPENSIVE TYPE OF FOOD: Salads and sandwiches SAMPLING: Salads (seafood, fruit, and green $4 - $6), BLT $3.95, burger $4.95, coffee 85 cents COMMENTS: Opened in 1981 and furnished in a tan and green theme, this open air restaurant features a golf and ocean view. Visa and Mastercard accepted.

MAUI ONION
LOCATED: 3550 Wailea Alanui, Wailea, phone 879-4900. Find it poolside at Stouffer's Wailea Beach Resort HOURS: Daily for lunch and early dinner PRICE RANGE: INEXPENSIVE TYPE OF FOOD: Sandwiches SAMPLING: Burgers and sandwiches are priced $5 - $6, Maui onion rings are scrumptiously priced at $2.75, coffee is $1.25. Haagen Das ice cream is also featured. Visa, Mastercard, and American Express honored.

POLLI'S ON THE OCEAN
LOCATED: 101 S. Kihei Rd., Kealia Village. Phone 879-5275 HOURS: 11 a.m. - midnight PRICE RANGE: INEXPENSIVE TYPE OF FOOD: Vegetarian Mexican COMMENTS: A deck over the beach offers outdoor dining and cocktails. This is a new location for Polli's,(the other is in Makawao) and their menu is expanded. Items priced $3.25 - $6.50 Major credit cards accepted.

RESTAURANTS
Kihei/Wailea

SET POINT not currently operating

WET SPOT
LOCATED: Intercontinental Hotel, Wailea, by their central pool, phone 879-1922 HOURS: Lunch and early dinner PRICE RANGE: INEXPENSIVE TYPE OF FOOD: American SAMPLING: A limited number of entrees are priced $6 - $9 and include steak, chicken or mahi mahi. Salads run $6 - $7 and sandwiches $5 -$6.

"MODERATE RANGE"

AMBROSIA
LOCATED: Wailea Shopping Center, in the center portion of the mall, phone 879-6667 HOURS: Lunch 11 a.m. - 4 p.m, happy hour 3 p.m. - 6 p.m., and dinner 5:30 p.m. - 9:30 p.m. PRICE RANGE: INEXPENSIVE TYPE OF FOOD: Seafood and Italian SAMPLING: Lunches include fresh mahi mahi at $6.95, lasagna at $4.95, sanwiches run about $5.00. Early bird dinner specials require you to vacate your table by 7 p.m., but entitles you to mahi mahi or BBQ chicken for $7.95. Dinners include a large assortment of fish served 10 ways and then you choose either a broiling or sauteing method of cooking. Meals run $13 - $15 and include veal dishes and Italian items.

ANNIE'S SAILMAKER
LOCATED: Azeka's Place shopping center, on South Kihei Rd. Phone 879-4446 HOURS: For breakfast, lunch, and dinner PRICE RANGE: INEXPENSIVE TO MODERATE TYPE OF FOOD: Everything COMMENTS: They have a broad menu, as do all the Apple Annie's on the island. The decor here is nautical. Entertainment in their loft type area is nightly with ID required and an admission charged.

BUZZ'S WHARF*
LOCATED: Maalaea Wharf area, phone 244-5426 or 661-0964 HOURS: Dinner only PRICE RANGE: MODERATE TYPE OF FOOD: Seafood specialty SAMPLING: Pacific oysters $9.95, Shrimp tempura $12.95, Fresh fish $15.95

CHUCK'S
LOCATED: Kihei Town Center, 1900 area of South Kihei Rd., phone 879-4488 HOURS: Lunch 11:30 a.m. - 2:30 p.m., Monday through Friday, dinner nightly 5:30 p.m.- 10 p.m. PRICE RANGE: INEXPENSIVE TO MODERATE TYPE OF FOOD: Beef, seafood SAMPLING: Lunch items include cold, beef, ham, or turkey for $3.75, or hot BLT, cheeseburger, or French dip which run $3 - $4.50. Dinners include a nice salad bar (ala carte it's $6.95), fresh fish for $12.95, teriyaki at $10.95, or prime rib, their 10 ounce cut, at $12.95. Early bird dinners are 5:30 p.m. - 6:30 p.m. and for $7.95 include salad bar, rice, beverage, and your choice of mahi or chicken COMMENTS: No reservations, but call ahead and they will let you know what kind of wait there is. Also, their early bird special may not be offered during peak tourist season. Children's menu has dinners $5 to $8. Happy hour 11:30 a.m. - 5 p.m. A salad bar is served from 11:30 a.m. - 10 p.m. and check their daily plate lunch which runs about $3.50.

FAIRWAY
LOCATED: Wailea Golf Course Clubhouse. Look for the sign on South Kihei Rd. near Stouffer's Resort. Phone 879-4060 or 879-3861 HOURS: 6:30 a.m. - 11 a.m. for breakfast; 11 a.m. - 4 p.m. for lunch; and 5:30 p.m. - 9:30 p.m. for dinner PRICE RANGE: MODERATE TO EXPENSIVE DINNERS TYPE OF FOOD: Varied SAMPLING: Breakfast

RESTAURANTS
Kihei/Wailea

selections include pancakes at $3.25, hashbrowns,and eggs for $3.50. Omelets run $5. Lunch offers turkey sandwich at $4.25, burger at $4.75, turkey clubhouse at $4.75, or pineapple salad at $5.50.. Dinners are priced between $12.95 and $23.75 and include a salad bar. Entrees to choose from include beef, seafood, and chicken COMMENTS: This restaurant is open-air with outdoor seating available. It offers a nice view of the course. Cocktails are available from the adjoining bar, the Waterhole. Their ice cream drinks are richly refreshing anytime of day. Here is an idea to tempt your palate: Fairway Grasshopper - creme de menthe, creme de cocoa, ice cream all blended and topped with chocolate mint liquer and chocolate sprinkles. Wailea Almond Joy - Amaretto, Kahlua, ice cream blended and topped with whipped cream and almond slices. Brandy Alexander - brandy, ice cream, and creme de cocoa blended and sprinkled with nutmeg. These wonderful concoctions run $4-ish. Dinner reservations are suggested and major credit cards honored.

HALE KOPE COFFEE SHOP
LOCATED: MAUI LU RESORT, 575 South Kehei Rd, 879-5858 HOURS: Breakfast 7am - 10 am PRICE RANGE: Inexpensive

HONG KONG
LOCATED: 760 South Kihei Rd. in the Menehune Shores Condominiums, phone 879-2883 HOURS: Lunch and dinner PRICE RANGE: MODERATE TYPE OF FOOD: Seafood, Oriental SAMPLING: Individual dishes from $5 include Szechwan style cooking COMMENTS: Vinyl table cloths and patched carpeting were uninspiring. Our experience was very small portions of food and on the greasy side. Entertainment 7 nights a week, 9 p.m. - 1 a.m. Visa and Mastercard okay.

"MODERATE"

*ISLAND FISH HOUSE****
LOCATED: 1945 South Kihei Rd., phone 879-7771 HOURS: Dinner, 5:30 p.m. PRICE RANGE: MODERATE TO EXPENSIVE TYPE OF FOOD: Seafood SAMPLING: Complete dinners include chicken teriyaki at $9.95, scallops at $13.95, shrimp polynesian at $15.95, and their daily fresh fish which is offered cooked six different ways. COMMENTS: The fish is consistantly excellent and we give it our award for the best fresh island fish. The service is very good and the wine list offers numerous choices. Reservations are a must here, and you may want to try their new Kahului location.

JESSIE'S LONGHOUSE
LOCATED: Maui Lu Resort, 575 South Kihei Rd., phone 879-5858 HOURS: Lunch served from noon, Dinner 6 - 9 p.m. Tuesday, Saturday and Sunday. Luau on Monday and Wednesday Luau Mon. and Wed. 12 - 6 PRICE RANGE: MODERATE TYPE OF FOOD: Polynesian, beef, and seafood SAMPLING: Almond chicken at $11.95, seafood curry at $13.95, and steak and fish at $16.95 COMMENTS: Dinner is served from 6 p.m. with their Hawaiian Revue at 8 p.m., dancing following. Tuesday - Saturday. Reservations required.

*KIHEI PRIME RIB HOUSE**
LOCATED: 2511 South Kihei Rd., in the Nani Kai Village, phone 879-1954 HOURS: Dinner from 5 p.m. - 10 p.m. PRICE RANGE: MODERATE TYPE OF FOOD: Beef is their specialty. Also seafood and chicken SAMPLING: Ribs at $11.95, polynesian chicken at $8.95, prime rib in varied cuts from $12.95 - $16.95, salad bar only $7.95, lobster and prime rib $13.95. BEST BUY!!! Early bird dinner special of chicken or rib at $7.95

RESTAURANTS
Kihei/Wailea

COMMENTS: Dinners include a salad bar or Caesar salad or red snapper chowder and is served either with fettuccini noodles or rice. Homemade bread also accompanies your meal. Their salad bar was very good, and the choices included the sweet Maui onions. Our beef was good, however, our lobster was a little flavorless. The high-beamed ceilings with the hanging plants offer a nice effect for the gorgeous wood carvings done by Bruce Turnbull and paintings by a German artist, Sigrid. They offer piano entertainment nightly.

KIHEI SEAS
LOCATED: 2439 S. Kihei Rd., by Kam II Park, and located upstairs at the Rainbow Mall. Phone 879-5600 HOURS: Breakfast 7 a.m. - 11 a.m.; lunch 11:30 a.m. - 2:30 p.m.; and dinner from 5 p.m. on PRICE RANGE: MODERATE TYPE OF FOOD: Seafood their specialty SAMPLING: Breakfast - pancakes $1.95,ham and eggs at $3.95, omelets $2.95 - $4.50; lunch - burgers $3.50, French dips $3.85; dinners include NY steak at $12.95, teriyaki chicken at $9.95, shellfish platter at $16.95. Dinners include salad bar, rice, and roll. COMMENTS: Opened in the summer of 1983, and hopefully will continue to maintain the high quality they established when they opened.

LA FAMILIA
LOCATED: 2511 South Kihei Rd., at Kai Nani Village, phone 879-8824 HOURS: Cocktails begin at 4 p.m. PRICE RANGE: MODERATE TYPE OF FOOD: Mexican SAMPLING: Tostado $7.50, and the usual Mexican entries priced $4 - $8. Also available are fish, burgers, and quiche for the non-Mexican palates. COMMENTS: 99 cent margaritas from 4 p.m. - 6 p.m. have been bringing in the crowds. How long they will continue this special we couldn't say. La Familia was very popular in Kahului before opening a branch here and in Kaanapali and closing their original restaurant. Maui frequenters expressed the fact that they preferred the original location for atmosphere and food. La Familia advertises that they use organic foods whenever possible.

OCEAN TERRACE
LOCATED: 2960 South Kihei Rd., Mana Kai Hotel, phone 879-2607 HOURS: Breakfast 6:30 a.m. - 11 a.m.; lunch 11:30 a.m. - 2 p.m.; dinner from 6:30 p.m. Happy hour 3 p.m. - 6 p.m. PRICE RANGE: MODERATE TYPE OF FOOD: Seafood, chicken, and beef. "Healthy Pritikin" menu is also served SAMPLING: Breakfast - three-egg omelets from $5.45 and macadamia nut pancakes at $3.95. Lunch offerings include a daily soup and sandwich special at $4.25, chef salad at $4.95. Dinners include fresh fish at $10.95, wok prepared Oriental specials nightly from $9.50. Dinners come with salad bar, homemade soup, bread, rice, or potato and coffee. COMMENTS: Pritikin Better Health Cuisine is also featured here for breakfast, lunch, and dinner. These low cholesterol meals have no added salts or fats. Examples are granola, fresh fruit, and skim milk at $4.75, turkey and vegetable pita with fresh fruit at $4.50. Oriental wok special dinners served with brown rice at $8.95. You can also choose to stay here at the Mana Kai Hotel for their week-long Pritikin Better Health Program.

MAUI OUTRIGGER
LOCATED: 2980 South Kihei Rd., phone 879-1581 HOURS: Lunch 11 a.m. - 3 p.m.; happy hour 3 p.m. - 5 p.m.; dinner 5 p.m. - 9:30 p.m. PRICE RANGE: MODERATE TYPE OF FOOD: Seafood, chicken, beef, and pasta SAMPLING: Linguine marinara at $10.50, NY steak at $13.95, prime rib at $13.95, or honey-dipped chicken at $10.50. Some menu items available in children's portions. Dinners include salad bar and rice pilaf COMMENTS: This restaurant is literally ON the beach. We would recommend it for cocktails and a nice sunset. Visa and Mastercard accepted.

RESTAURANTS
Kihei/Wailea

PALM COURT
LOCATED: 3550 Wailea Alanui at Stouffer's Wailea Resort. Enter through lobby and down one flight. Phone 879-4900 HOURS: Nightly dinners PRICE RANGE: MODERATE, All dinners $15.50, BUFFET STYLE TYPE OF FOOD: International buffet varies nightly SAMPLING: Sunday features Oriental dishes such as Peking duck, sesame pork, and fresh fish. Mondays they offer German cuisine such as beef rouladen. Tuesday is Italian night when dishes such as osso buco are served. Wednesday travel to Great Britain, at least in spirit, and sample prime rib, with Yorkshire pudding. Thursdays they feature French cooking with chicken Wellington and scallops mornay to name a few. Friday is dinner with the Hawaiian touch, Kalua pig or mahi mahi are among the samplings. Saturday is Swiss, with stuffed breasts of veal or ballotine of chicken on the buffet table. Also, salads and various other accompanying dishes complete the nightly buffet. COMMENTS: This open-air dining hall is festively decorated in reds and greens, offering evening breezes and an ocean view. Reservations are accepted only for a group of 10 or more. Aloha attire acceptable. Visa, Mastercard, American Express, and Diners are all honored.

WAILEA STEAK HOUSE
LOCATED: 100 Wailea Ike Drive, Wailea, phone 879-2875. Easy to find sign near the Hotel Intercontinental indicates turn-off HOURS: Dinner from 5:30 p.m. PRICE RANGE: MODERATE TYPE OF FOOD: Fish and beef SAMPLING: Top sirloin steak at $12, salad bar only $8, breast of chicken $11, and scampi $16 COMMENTS: Located on the 15th fairway of Wailea's Blue Golf Course, there is some outdoor seating available. The wine list is limited, but they offer a nice salad bar which is always a nice addition to dinner. No reservations for a group of less than six, however, we had no trouble getting seated and the hostess said that generally there is no problem if you arrive by 7 p.m. A nice cocktail lounge is adjoining which offers very good sunset viewing.

WATERFRONT*
LOCATED: At the Milowai Condo at Maalaea, about a 10-minute drive from the Kihei area and 20 minutes from Kaanapali. Phone 244-9028 HOURS: Dinner 7 days a week from 5:30 p.m. - 10 p.m. Cocktails from 5 p.m. PRICE RANGE: MODERATE TO EXPENSIVE TYPE OF FOOD: Seafood specialty SAMPLING: Seafood crepes at $10.95, NY pepper steak at $15.95, fresh fish of the day $15.95, whole fresh fish (baked with ginger and oyster sauce for two) at $16.50, and veal oscar $16.95 COMMENTS: Their fresh mahi mahi was nicely prepared. Advance reservations are requested.

"EXPENSIVE"

KIAWE BROILER*
LOCATED: Maui Intercontinental Hotel in Wailea, phone 879-1922. Finding the hotel is the easy part, finding this restaurant through their maze of hallways was a little trickier. Watch for the signs HOURS: Lunch 11 a.m. - 4 p.m.; dinner 6 p.m. - 10 p.m. PRICE RANGE: MODERATE TO EXPENSIVE TYPE OF FOOD: Specialty is their Kiawe charcoal broiled dishes SAMPLING: Salad bar alone $7.25, Kiawe grilled steaks $15 - $20, veal cutlet runs $17.25, cornish hen or ribs at $13.25. COMMENTS: Informal rattan decor is featured and Visa, Mastercard, American Express are accepted.

LA PEROUSE ****
LOCATED: Maui Interconintal Hotel in Wailea, phone 879-1922 HOURS: Dinner only, from 5:30 p.m. PRICE RANGE: EXPENSIVE!!! TYPE OF FOOD: Continental SAMPLING:

RESTAURANTS
Kihei/Wailea

Start with a bowl of Callaloo soup for $5.25. This is a very rich soup made of crab meat, taro, and coconut milk. Their breadfruit vichyssoise is a novelty at $3.25. A house green salad will run $4.75. Dinners are accompanied by a vegetable and include fresh fish at $18.50, whole chicken at $17.50, and rack of lamb at $21.50 (both the chicken and lamb require an extra 45-minute preparation time) COMMENTS: The decor here is awesome. The huge iron gate, which is the entry, is formidable, with the interior an Oriental theme. The heavy Koa wood which lines the dining area is elegant, but must have required the demise of an entire forest. They do have a dress code here which requires men to wear shirts with collars. Sandals and shorts are not acceptable. We noticed most men here, however, did don a shirt and tie. The service is very good and we found the Callaloo soup richly wonderful. The house green salad was more an edible picture, being artistically arranged to include sprouts, Maui onions, cherry tomato, red cabbage, lettuce, cucumber, and mushrooms. A complimentary appetizer of fried brie arrived while we selected a wine. They have two lists, with one featuring wines from their private cellar. Prices were a little steep, with the least expensive ones running about $20. They did offer their house wine by the glass, and we found it pleasant both in taste and in price ($2.50). While the entrees are ala carte, they were served with a small amount of rice and the plate was garnished with a cauliflower and broccoli flowerette which had been lightly steamed. The dessert cart (3.50 each) has selections which vary daily. Our choice was Gran Marnier souffle which came warm from the kitchen and was more than enough for two at $5.00. An after-dinner sweet and a complimentary cigar were offered at meal's end. Background music accompanies your meal as well. Reservations are a must. Major credit cards accepted.

LANAI TERRACE *
LOCATED: Maui Intercontinental Hotel, Wailea, to the left from the front lobby. Phone 879-1922 *HOURS:* Sunday brunch only, from 9 a.m. - 1 p.m. *PRICE RANGE:* EXPENSIVE, the buffet is currently priced at $15.50 *TYPE OF FOOD:* Varied *COMMENTS:* Tables laden with a wonderful assortment of lunch and breakfast dishes, fresh fruits, and don't forget to save room for at least two trips to the dessert table. Reservations are a really good idea. Major credit cards accepted.

RAFFLE'S ****
LOCATED: 3550 Wailea Alanui at Stouffer's Wailea Resort, phone 879-4900. Enter through lobby and down one flight *HOURS:* Sunday brunch 9 a.m. - 2 p.m.; dinner 6:30 p.m. - 10:30 p.m. *PRICE RANGE:* EXPENSIVE *TYPE OF FOOD:* Continental *SAMPLING:* Brunch includes champagne, fresh fruits, petite lamb chops, Oriental dishes, chicken, and fish. You might try gravlaks, a salmon marinated in dill and anise with mustard sauce. Also, a salad bar, eggs benedict, omelets made to your request. Pastries and desserts to delight any sweet tooth. Currently $19.50. Dinners include Rack of Washington State Lamb at $22, lobster at $25, island prawns au whiskey at $19.50, mahi, ono, or opakapaka (as available) at $18.50. The wine list includes Italian, French, California and Washington State, Australian, and German choices. Blue Nun is about the least expensive at $11, with most running between $18 and $25. *COMMENTS:* Raffle's bears an Oriental theme, in keeping with its Singapore origin. Sir Thomas Stamford Raffles (1781 - 1826) was the British Founder of the city where the Raffles Hotel has become a legend. The service here was the best that we encountered anywhere. The buffet, while pricey, is a terrific splurge. The dessert bar was constantly being replenished and each new offering looked better than the last. The chocolate mousse merited a second serving and the chocolate rum cake was rich and moist. Aloha wear is acceptable—an extra large muu-muu

RESTAURANTS
Kihei/Wailea

might not be a bad idea! We enjoyed Tony Van Steen's piano entertainment.

ROBAIRE'S ***
LOCATED: 61 South Kihei Rd., Kihei, phone 879-2707 HOURS: Tuesday through Saturday, dinners served 6 p.m. - 10 p.m. *PRICE RANGE:* EXPENSIVE *TYPE OF FOOD:* French *SAMPLING:* NY steak $18.95, cordon bleu $12.50, rack of lamb $16.75, and duckling ala orange $16.25 *COMMENTS:* This smallish restaurant emphasizes food, not decor and reservations are a must for their limited seating. They were offering a special where every item on the menu could be had for the same price of $12. You might call and hope they are offering a similar deal! Visa, Mastercard, and American Express accepted.

LUAUS

MAUI LU offers luaus Monday, Wednesday, and Friday in their Luau Gardens at 575 South Kihei Rd., beginning at 5 p.m. for one hour of cocktails followed by a buffet dinner and then a Polynesian show. The $28 charge covers tax and tip. Phone 879-5858 for reservations.

The Aloha Mele luncheon is also offered at the MAUI LU resort each Thursday. Cocktails begin at 11 a.m. with lunch and entertainment following until 1:30 p.m. Reservations can be made by calling 879-5858. Priced at $12.50 including tax and tip.

STOUFFER'S WAILEA RESORT offers a Tuesday night luau which begins at 6 p.m. Their Hawaiian feast is followed by a review. The $29.50 charge includes tax and tip for adults. Children 12 and under are charged $15.50. Phone 879-4900 for information or reservations.

RESTAURANTS
Upcountry

MAKAWAO:

MAKAWAO STEAK HOUSE
LOCATED: 3612 Baldwin, Makawao, phone 575-8711 *HOURS:* Daily for dinner except Monday *PRICE RANGE:* MODERATE *TYPE OF FOOD:* Steaks, fresh fish, salad bar, and freshly baked breads *SAMPLING:* Chicken Zoie $11.95 (Breast stuffed with creamed spinach) 3 types of steaks, sirloin, N.Y., or Teriyaki, all of Maui beef $10.75 - $12.95. Fresh fish. Dinners include salad bar. *COMMENTS:* Cocktails & wine list. Opens at 5pm with early bird special 5-6:30. We enjoyed fresh Muu, a mild white fish.

POLLI'S
LOCATED: 1202 Makawao Ave., Makawao, phone 572-7808 *HOURS:* Daily dinners, lunch served Tuesday - Saturday *PRICE RANGE:* INEXPENSIVE *TYPE OF FOOD:* Vegetarian Mexican *COMMENTS:* This small Mexican restaurant is also open for Sunday brunch!

PUKALANI AREA:

BULLOCK'S OF HAWAII
LOCATED: Just past Pukalani Shopping Center on the right side going up the mountain *HOURS:* Breakfast, lunch, and dinner *PRICE RANGE:* BARGAIN *TYPE OF FOOD:* Fast *SAMPLING:* An avocado sandwich at $1.65, a moonburger runs $3.25 (it was lunchtime here when the first astronaut walked on the moon), or a guava shake at $2.25. Breakfasts include two eggs, bacon, and toast for $2.25. The lunch and dinner menus are the same. *COMMENTS:* This stop doesn't feature extensive decor (not any decor for that matter), and has the novelty of your food being cooked, served, and your bill rung up all by the same person (or at least on our visit). The food is served on paper plates. Visa and Mastercard accepted with a $10 minimum.

CROSS ROADS RESTAURANT
LOCATED: Pukalani Shopping Center (formerly Apple Annie's) phone 572-9525 *HOURS:* Daily 11am - 10pm for lunch and dinner *PRICE RANGE:* Inexpensive to Moderate *TYPE OF FOOD:* Seafood sandwiches and omelets $2.75 to $4.10. Complete or ala carte dinners. 8 oz N.Y. steak $10.95, ala carte $9.45. Seafood platter $8.75, ala carte $7.45. Full bar and wine list. Children's menu available.

DAIRY QUEEN
LOCATED: Pukalani Shopping Center *HOURS:* Mostly lunch *PRICE RANGE:* BARGAIN TO INEXPENSIVE *TYPE OF FOOD:* Burgers

DOREEN'S COUNTRY INN
LOCATED: One block above Pukalani Shopping Center, phone 572-7877 *HOURS:* Daily 7 a.m. - 10 p.m. *PRICE RANGE:* INEXPENSIVE TO MODERATE *TYPE OF FOOD:* American, Polynesian, beef, and seafood *SAMPLING:* Breakfast for $4.25 includes bacon, eggs, and pancakes, or a chili sunrise omelet runs $3.75. Lunch includes a Hawaiian plate for $6.95, a seafood platter for $5.25, or a hamburger for $2.50. Saimin and won ton are $2.75, or try their dinner featuring fried chicken at $5.99, T-bone at $9.95, or shrimp

RESTAURANTS
Upcountry

tempura at $8.50 COMMENTS: Four ceiling fans cool a dozen booths that have tables donned with red vinyl checked table cloths, and a small water glass with a fresh flower or two is added. This family-run restaurant has an unusual assortment of wall decor, including trophies of mountain sheep, deer, and a goat from Molokai. Our waitress was Doreen's charming 13 year old daughter. Their menu is very broad and we found our lunch portions to be generous. Visa and Mastercard are accepted. Take-out food orders are available.

KULA LODGE*
LOCATED: About five miles past Pukalani on Haleakala Hwy., phone 878-1535 HOURS: Breakfast 7 a.m. - 11 a.m.; lunch 11 a.m. - 2:30 p.m.; dinner 5:30 p.m. - 9 p.m. Dinner is served Wednesday through Saturday and reservations are recommended PRICE RANGE: INEXPENSIVE TO MODERATE TYPE OF FOOD: American SAMPLING: Breakfast selections include a three-egg omelet at $3.95, or French toast at $2.85. Lunches include a reuben sandwich at $6, a hamburger at $4.75, and salads which range from $4.50 - $6.75 COMMENTS: A nice added benefit here is the fireplace, a warming delight after a cold trip to the mountain top, a panoramic view, and cocktails.

PUKALANI TERRACE COUNTRY CLUB
LOCATED: Turn right just before the shopping center at Pukalani and continue down until the road ends. 3600 Pukalani Rd., phone 572-1325 HOURS: Open daily with Sunday brunch PRICE RANGE: INEXPENSIVE TO MODERATE TYPE OF FOOD: Hawaiian is their specialty SAMPLING: A Kalua Pig Hawaiian plate runs $6.95, tripe stew is $6.25, and the more conventional hamburgers run $3.75 - $5.25 COMMENTS: A nice view of the Island from here. You might consider a stop on the way down for a drink and a nice sunset.

SILVERSWORD INN
LOCATED: About five miles past Pukalani and across the road from Kula Lodge HOURS: We were unable to get information as they were closed for remodeling.

RESTAURANTS
Hana/Paia

HANA:

This quiet town offers a limited choice of eateries.

TUTU'S at Hana Bay offers the most reasonably priced meals in the area with sandwiches and the like served from 8:30 a.m. - 4 p.m.

The HOTEL HANA MAUI offers a dining room which is open for lunch and dinner. They also have a coffee shop that is open daily. The coffee shop is self serve. Continental breakfast runs $3.00. Lunch is a buffet. For $4.75 choose the salad bar with selections such as green salad or macaroni salad. $5.50 entitles you to make your own sandwich with package type lunch meats. $6.50 is sandwich, salad, and hot dish. Drinks $.80, $.90. Beer and cocktails.

The HASEGAWA GENERAL STORE is open daily and has food items as well as a little bit of everything else!!

PAIA:

There are two restaurants in the Paia area that are our favorites and would be a pleasant stop on your way to Hana or Haleakala.

DILLON'S
LOCATED: Downtown Paia, 89 Hana Hwy., phone 579-9113 HOURS: Breakfast, lunch, and dinner PRICE RANGE: INEXPENSIVE TO MODERATE TYPE OF FOOD: Varied COMMENTS: We enjoyed a hearty breakfast. Generous portions and some unusual items such as Kahlua pancakes.

MAMA'S FISH HOUSE ***
LOCATED: Hwy. 36 just past Paia (hard to spot turnoff), phone 579-9672 HOURS: Dinner only PRICE RANGE: EXPENSIVE TYPE OF FOOD: Seafood COMMENTS: A little steep price wise, but all the fish is fresh. Reservations suggested.

SUNSETS AND NIGHTLIFE

Here are a few suggestions as to what to do when and after the sun goes down on Maui. These locations usually offer entertainment, however, call to see what they are offering and which night as it varies. Also check the Bulletin Board publication or This Week which list current late night happenings.

SUNSET WATCHING SUGGESTIONS

On the front lawn of the Pineapple Hill Restaurant near Kapalua.

From the lobby bar of the Kapalua Bay Resort with their wonderful pu-pus.

At the Kapalua Grill and Bar

On the promentory of the Bay Club at Kapalua

Atop Black Rock in the Sheraton's Discovery Room

At the Hyatt Regency's Lahaina Provision Company

Enroute down from Haleakala you can't beat the Pukalani Country Club

The Maui Outrigger provides your sunset view from surfside.

The Wailea Steak House offers a nice cocktail lounge for sunset viewing.

Located at the Wailea Golf Course is the Fairway. Not only can you enjoy a fabulous sunset, but indulge in one of their ice cream drinks with a punch.

Enjoy the lobby bar at Stouffer's Wailea Resort for an evening sunset.

LAHAINA AREA NIGHTSPOTS

Bettino's, phone 661-8810

Barkentine Bar - nightly dancing at the Kaanapali Sheraton, phone 661-0031

Blackbeards - early and late night entertainment, phone 667-9535

Blackies Boatyard - Friday and Saturdays 5 p.m. - 8 p.m., phone 667-7979

Discovery Room - fancy atmosphere and prices at the Sheraton, 8:30 dinner show and 9:30 cocktail show (cover charge). phone 661-0031

El Crab Catcher - nightly entertainment, phone 661-4423

Hyatt Regency - dancing at Spatts II evenings, phone 661-7474

Kahana Keyes - nightly entertainment, featuring live music by popular Maui bands, dancing from 7:30 p.m.,phone 669-8071

Kaanapali Beach Hotel - times vary for their nightly entertainment, phone 661-1011

La Familia - Wednesday thru Saturday nights at Kaanapali, phone 667-7902

SUNSETS AND NIGHTLIFE

Longhi's - phone 667-2288 for their current happenings

Maui Marriott - evening entertainment at their lively Banana Moon (catch a bikini contest!) or the more sedate dancing at their lobby bar.

Moose McGillycuddy's - nightly entertainment of live bands in a casual atmosphere 9 p.m. - 1 a.m., phone 667-7758

Peacock - Tuesday thru Saturdays at 8 p.m., phone 667-6847

The Pioneer Inn - A Lahaina hot spot with varying entertainment

Rusty Harpoon - located at Whaler's Village they feature early evening live music

KIHEI AREA NIGHTSPOTS

Inu Inu - nightly entertainment, except Monday, at the Hotel Intercontinental in Wailea

Kihei Outrigger - phone 879-1581

Kihei Seas - nightly musical entertainment on an organ, phone 879-5000

Lost Horizon - nightly dancing at Stouffer's Wailea Resort

BEACHES AND BEACH ACTIVITIES

INTRODUCTION

Maui's beaches range from small to long, white sand to black sand or rock, and from well developed to (at least for a little longer) remote and unspoiled. We have outlined the prime beaches in the hope it will give you the opportunity to explore beyond your hotel beachfront.

Most of the major resorts are located on prime beach property. All of Maui's major beaches are publicly owned and have right-of-way access, however, the access is sometimes tricky to find and parking may be a problem!

Organization of this chapter will be the division of beaches into seven areas: Makena, Wailea, Kihei, Maalaea to Lahaina, Lahaina and Kaanapali, Kahana-Napili-Kapalua and beyond, and the Wailuku/Kahului area. We include locations, access to the beach, facilities available, type of beach, and appropriate beach and water activities.

Parking areas are provided at most major developed beaches, but are generally limited to 30 cars or less, making an early arrival at the more popular beaches a good idea. In the undeveloped areas you will have to wedge along the roadsides. It is vital that you leave nothing of importance in your car, as theft, especially at some of the remoter locations, is very high.

At the larger developed beaches, a variety of facilities are provided. Many have convenient rinse-off showers, drinking water, restrooms, and picnic areas. A few have children's play or swim areas. The beaches near the major resorts often have rental equipment available for snorkeling, sailing, body surfing, and even underwater cameras. These beaches are generally clean and nicely maintained. Above Kapalua and below Wailea, where the beaches are generally undeveloped, expect to find no signs to mark the location, no facilities, and less cleanliness.

Additional information on beaches, and good scuba and snorkeling locations, can be found in the following publications. The Maui Beach Press, a free and handy guide found around the Island that covers the general location and facilities of the major beaches. Beaches of Maui County, by John Clark, can be found in bookstores on the Island and is a comprehensive guide to all the Island's beaches and includes much historical information. Snorkeling and Dive Maui, by Lou Zitnik, can be found in dive shops or bookstores and covers 10 favorite snorkel and dive locations. 50 Locations for Scuba and Snorkeling on the Island of Maui, by Chuck Thorne, tells it all in its title.

Our favorite beaches have been indicated by *'s.

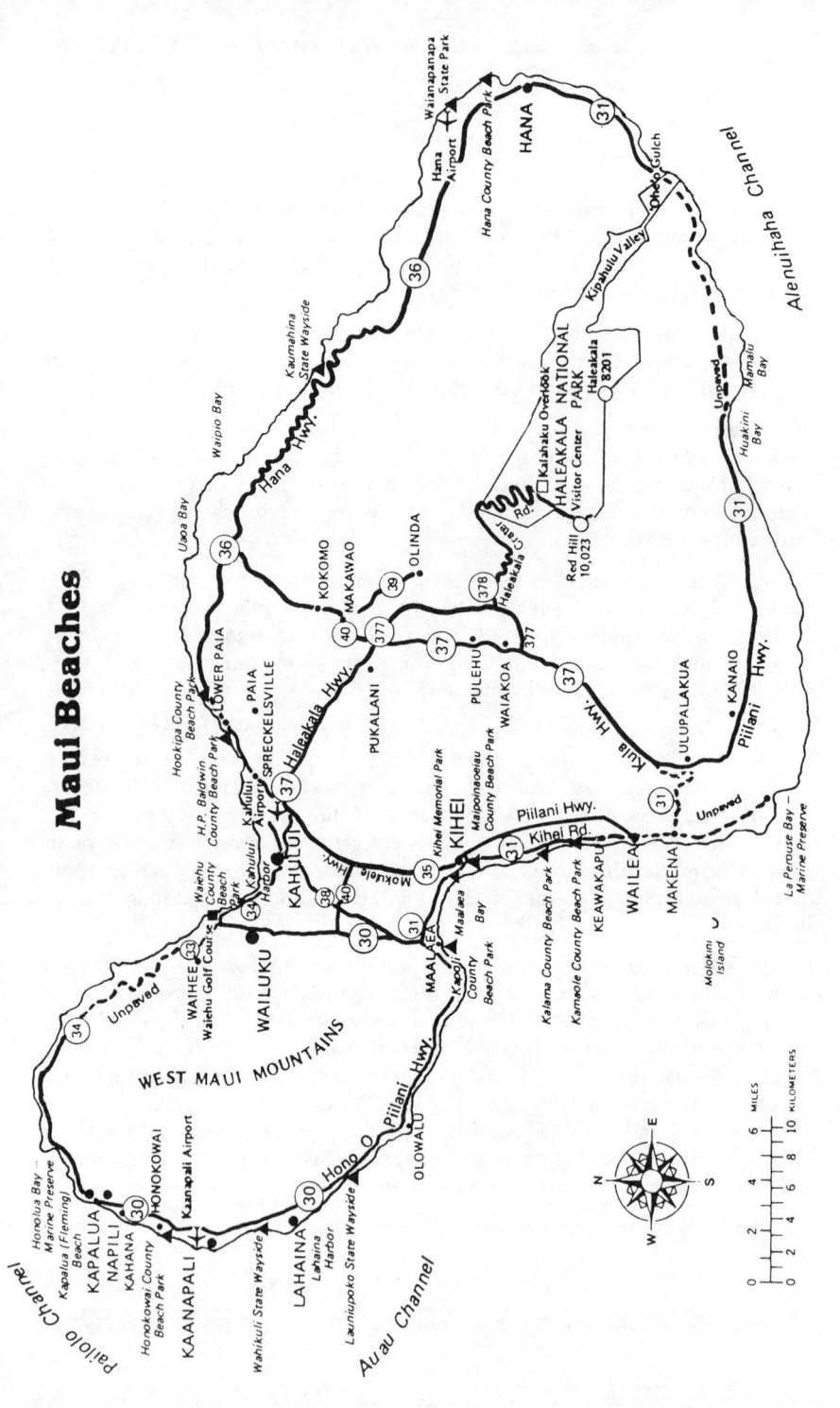

BEACHES AND BEACH ACTIVITIES
Makena Area

MAKENA BEACHES

This area includes the beaches south of Polo Beach and the Polo Bay Condos, to La Perose Bay. (Past this point, you either hike or need to have a four-wheel drive.) The Makena Beaches are undeveloped and relatively unspoiled, for a while longer at least, and not always easy to find as there are no signs, and some beaches are not visible from the road. There are absolutely no facilities at any of these beaches and parking is where you can find it. The nearest grocery is at the Wailea Shopping Center, however, food is available at the Makena Golf Course Restaurant. There is a turn-off to the golf course about 1.7 miles past Polo Beach. There is a pay phone at the old church about 1.9 miles past Polo Beach, or at the Makena Golf Course or Polo Beach Condos.

All entrances to beaches are located by mileage, to the nearest tenth, from the Polo Beach Condos, where development stops and unpaved road begins. This area is changing, with road work and resort development in progress. Although development has begun, much more is desired by various developers. However, local opposition to further beach development in this area has managed, so far, to keep this in check.

We hope our directions with exact mileage will help you find these sometimes hard-to-find and lovely beaches.

PALAUEA BEACH
ACCESS: .75 miles from Polo Beach. Park at Po'olenalena Beach and walk 100 feet back toward Polo Beach over a small hill and you'll see it. FACILITIES: None. TYPE OF BEACH: Nice, white sand beach, gentle onshore slope, somewhat recessed providing fair protection. ACTIVITIES: Swimming, bodysurfing.

PO'OLENALENA BEACH
ACCESS: .7 miles from Polo Beach. Cut back from new road under construction. Beach is visible from road, park under trees off road. FACILITIES: None. BEACH: Wide, white sand beach with gentle slope. ACTIVITIES: Good swimming.

CHANG'S BEACH
ACCESS: Small section of beach between two small rocky points at south end of Po'olenalena Beach.

MALUAKA BEACH
ACCESS: Not visible from road and no convenient public access.

FIVE GRAVES
ACCESS: 1.35 miles from Polo Beach are two turn-offs from the main road. This is the site of five 19th century graves. There is no beach, however, this is a scuba and snorkeling site. Entry is over the rocks and is definitely not for beginning snorkelers.

BEACHES AND BEACH ACTIVITES
Makena Area

NOTE: UPCOUNTRY ROAD
ACCESS: 1.4 miles from Polo Beach. Currently closed in dispute over maintenance.

NOTE: MAKENA GOLF COURSE AND RESTAURANT
ACCESS: 1.7 miles from Polo Beach to turn off, clearly marked.

NOTE: OLD CHURCH
ACCESS: 1.9 miles from Polo Beach to roadside payphone.

PAPIPI BEACH
ACCESS: 1.5 miles from Polo Beach. This beach is right along the road. FACILITIES: Nice new parking area for approximately 20 cars No other facilities. BEACH: Small (75 feet), sandy crescent of beach, well protected, gentle slope, calm. Beach unappealing because of its nearness to the road. ACTIVITIES: Area looks more attractive for fishing.

PAPAKUEWA
ACCESS: 1.65 miles from Polo Beach along side of road. Limited roadside parking. FACILITIES: None. BEACH: Small, rockstrewn, sandy beach. ACTIVITIES: Not too attractive unless you're a fisherman. Possible snorkeling around rocks to left of beach.

ONEULI BEACH (Black Sand Beach)
ACCESS: 2.75 miles from Polo Beach to a very rutted dirt road turn-off. It's 3/10 mile to the beach. Go slow and carefully. FACILITIES: None. BEACH: Coarse black sand beach with entire length of beach lined by exposed reef. ACTIVITIES: Sunbathing, but water activities precarious due to reef at water's edge. Note—be careful of broken glass in soft sand above beach. The south end of beach ends at Pu'u Ola, (Miller Hill) the cinder cone.

ONELOA BEACH (Makena Beach, Big Makena Beach)
ACCESS: 2.9 miles from Polo Beach to first dirt road entrance for north end of beach. 3/10 mile from turn-off to beach and parking area, with room for about 20 cars. 3.25 miles to parking area at southern end of beach. Parking and beach visible from road. There are two mid-beach dirt entrance roads from main road. FACILITIES: None. Emergencies—1.2 miles back to Makena Golf Course turn-off, 1 mile back to pay phone at church. BEACH: 3/5 mile long, wide, white sand beach. 360 foot cinder cone Pu'u Olai at north end of beach. Beach has quick, sharp drop-off and rough shore break. ACTIVITIES: Swimming, not good for children. Body surfing is sometimes good. Snorkeling around rocky point at cinder cone is only fair to poor with not much to see, and not for beginners due to the usually strong north to south current.

PU'U OLAI BEACH (Makena Beach, Little Makena Beach, "Nude Beach")
ACCESS: 2.9 miles from Polo Beach, take first Oneloa Beach entrance and park at Oneloa Beach. From there, you hike over the cinder cone. FACILITIES: None. BEACH: Flat, white sand beach, with a shallow sandy bottom, semi-

BEACHES AND BEACH ACTIVITIES
Makena Area

protected by shallow cove. *ACTIVITIES:* Swimming good, usually gentle shore break. Bodysurfing sometimes. Snorkeling around point on left. Watch for strong currents. The main activity here, although illegal, is nude sunbathing.

AHIHI-KINAU (NATURAL RESERVE AREA)
ACCESS: 4.2 miles from Polo Beach, right along side road. Reserve indicated by sign. Parking is very limited along side of road. *FACILITIES:* None. 2.55 miles back to Makena Golf Course Restaurant. 2.35 miles back to church pay phone. *BEACH:* There is a small 6 foot wide sandy beach along side the remnants of an old concrete boat ramp, located in cove so it is well protected. Very shallow beach which turns to rocks about 6 feet out. Watch out for urchins in the very shallow water as you are entering and exiting. *ACTIVITIES:* Excellent snorkeling on calm days. Remember, this is a reserve—look, but don't harm or take.

LA PEROUSE BAY
ACCESS: 6.0 miles from Polo Beach. From Ahihi-Kinau you travel over fairly rough road carved through a lava flow. *FACILITIES:* None. *BEACH:* You either hike or use a 4-wheel drive to go the 1.7 miles from roads end at La Perouse Bay to the Kanaio beaches. If you hike, wear good hiking shoes, you'll be walking over stretches of sharp lava rock. There are a series of small beaches, actually only pockets of sand of various compositions, with fairly deep offshore waters and strong currents. There is one black sand beach which is fairly nice. Also in this area there is good shell collecting among the big rocks.

BEACHES AND BEACH ACTIVITES
Wailea Area

WAILEA BEACHES

This area generally has small, lovely, white sand beaches which have marked public access. Parking is off street and restrooms as well as rinse-off showers are provided.

POLO BEACH
ACCESS: In front of new Polo Beach Resort Condominiums, public access sign is easy to spot. FACILITIES: Parking for 40 cars in paved parking area. Showers and restrooms. BEACH: Beaches are a short walk on a paved sidewalk and down a short flight of stairs. There are actually two beaches separated by large rocks. The north beach is about 400 feet long and the south beach about 200 feet long. The beaches slope steeply offshore and are not well protected, causing a rough shore break. The beach is dotted with large rocks. ACTIVITIES: Swimming and snorkeling are poor to fair.

WAILEA BEACH
ACCESS: Marked public access 1/2 mile south of Intercontinental Resort. Paved road down to nicely landscaped parking area providing room for about 40 cars. FACILITIES: Restrooms and outside rinse-off showers. Rental sailboats and windsurfing boards are available. BEACH: Beautiful wide crescent of gently sloping white sand. Gentle offshore slope. ACTIVITIES: Good swimming. Snorkeling is fair to left (south) around rocks with moderate currents, not much coral or many fish.

ULUA BEACH**
ACCESS: Marked public access, sign "Ulua/Mokapu Beaches" located near Stouffer's Wailea Resort. FACILITIES: Small paved parking area with a short walk to beach. Showers and restrooms. Rental equipment a short walk away at the Wailea Ocean Activities Center. BEACHES: Beautiful white sand beach fronting Elua Resort complex. Ulua and Mokapu Beaches are separated by a narrow point of rocks. Area around beaches is nicely landscaped because of the resorts. The beach is semi-protected and has a sandy offshore bottom. ACTIVITIES: Swimming is good. Excellent snorkeling in morning around lava flow between beaches. Popular scuba diving area. Come early to get a parking space!

MOKAPU BEACH
ACCESS: Marked public access (Ulua/Mokapu Beach) is near Stouffer's Wailea Resort. FACILITIES: Small parking area, restrooms and showers. Rental equipment at Nearby Wailea Resort Activities Center at Stouffer's. BEACH: White sand. ACTIVITIES: Excellent swimming. Snorkeling excellent in morning around rocks which divide the two beaches.

BEACHES AND BEACH ACTIVITIES
Wailea Area

KEAWAKAPU BEACH
ACCESS: A) Paved parking for 50 cars across street from beach, about .2 miles south of Mana Kai Resort. Look for beach access sign on left as you travel south. B) Access to southern end of beach—go straight at left turn off to Wailea, road says "Dead End". Parking for about 30 cars. FACILITIES: A) None. B) None. BEACH: A) Two small crescent shaped white sand beaches separated by small rocky point. B) Beautiful, very gently sloping white sand beach. ACTIVITIES: A) Good swimming—off shore sandy bottom, fair snorkeling around rocks at far north end. B) Swimming good for kids. Snorkeling off rocks on left. Scuba diving—popular dive spot. 400 yards off shore in 80-85 feet of water is an artificial reef of 150 car bodies.

BEACHES AND BEACH ACTIVITES
Kihei Area

KIHEI BEACHES

The Kihei Beaches aren't quite as beautiful as Wailea's Beaches and they don't have the nicely landscaped parking areas, or the large, beautiful resort complexes (this is condo country). They do offer increased facilities such as BBQ pits, picnic tables, drinking water, and grassy play areas. The Kamaole I and III beaches even have lifeguards. The area extends from Wailea to Maalaea Bay and the beaches are listed in that order.

KAMAOLE III
ACCESS: Well-marked Kamaole III Beach sign across from Kamaole Sands Condominiums. FACILITIES: Off-street parking, picnic tables, BBQ's, restrooms, rinse-off showers, drinking water, playground equipment, and a grassy play area. BEACH: 200 yards long, narrow (in winter) white sand beach with some rocky areas, and a few submerged rocks. ACTIVITIES: Swimming - fair, snorkeling - fair around rocks at south end of beach, bodysurfing - sometimes.

KAMAOLE II
ACCESS: Across from Kai Nani shopping and restaurant complex. FACILITIES: On-street parking, restrooms, rinse-off showers, rental equipment. BEACH: White sand beach between two rocky points with sharp drop-off to overhead depths. ACTIVITIES: Swimming - good, bodysurfing - sometimes.

KAMAOLE I
ACCESS: Well-marked sign across from Kamaole Beach Club. FACILITIES: Off-street parking for 30 cars. Picnic tables, restrooms, rinse-off showers, rental equipment, children's swimming area. BEACH: White sand beach (500 yards long). ACTIVITIES: Swimming - good, bodysurfing - good at times. NOTE: Small pocket of sand between rock outcroppings at right end of beach is known as Young's Beach. It is also accessible from Kaiau Street with parking for about 20 cars. Public right-of-way sign at end of Kaiau Street.

KALAMA BEACH PARK
ACCESS: Well-marked 36 acre park. FACILITIES: 12 pavillions, 3 restrooms, showers, picnic tables, BBQ grills, playground apparatus, soccer field, baseball field, tennis courts, volleyball and basketball courts. Lots of grassy park area. BEACH: There is no beach (in winter), only a large bolder breakwater. Good view of southern Maui cinder cone, Molokini, Molokai, and the northern Maui area.

KAWILILIPOA AND WAIMAHAIKAI AREAS
ACCESS: Any of the cross streets off South Kihei Road will take you down toward the beach where public right-of-ways are marked. FACILITIES: Limited parking, usually on street. No facilities. BEACH: The whole shoreline from Kalama Park to Waipulani Street (3-4 miles) is an area of interrupted beaches fronted by residential housing and small condo complexes. Narrow sandy

BEACHES AND BEACH ACTIVITIES
Kihei Area

beaches with lots of coral rubble from the fronting reefs. Snorkeling in mornings on calm days can be good.

KAWILIKI POU
ACCESS: End of Waipulani Street. FACILITIES: Paved off street parking for 30 cars, restrooms, large grassy area, public tennis courts. Fronts Maui Sunset Hotel. BEACH: Tall graceful palms line the shoreline. Narrow sand beaches generally strewn with coral rubble.

KAONOULULU BEACH PARK
ACCESS: Across the street from the Kihei Bay Surf. FACILITIES: Off-road parking for 20 cars, restrooms, drinking water, rinse-off showers, picnic tables, four BBQ grills. BEACH: Very small, well protected by close-in reef.

MAI POINA OE IAU BEACH PARK
ACCESS: On South Kihei Road, fronting Maui Lu Resort. FACILITIES: Paved parking for 8 cars at Pavillion (numerous other areas to park along road). 5 picnic tables, restrooms, showers. BEACH: Very long white sand beach, inshore bottom generally sandy with patches of rock, fronted by shallow reef. ACTIVITIES: Swimming and snorkeling best in morning before early afternoon winds come up. Popular windsurfing area in the afternoon.

MAALAEA BAY BEACH
ACCESS: Public access is from many areas along South Kihei Road. FACILITIES: None. BEACH: A three mile curving stretch of white sand from Maalaea boat harbor to Kihei. The beach is generally backed by low sand dunes. ACTIVITIES: Casual beach activities are best in the morning before the strong mid-morning prevailing winds come up. Due to the length of the beach and the hard-packed sand near the water, this has become a popular place to jog. Windsurfing is popular in the afternoons.

BEACHES AND BEACH ACTIVITES
Maalaea to Lahaina

BEACHES BETWEEN MAALAEA AND LAHAINA

The beaches are in order from Maalaea to Lahaina and are easy to spot from Honoapiilani Highway.

PAPALAUA STATE WAYSIDE PARK
FACILITIES: Picnic tables, BBQ grills, portable restrooms. *BEACH:* Long, narrow beach with shallow, but rocky bottom. *ACTIVITIES:* Swimming - good, mainly for children. Snorkeling - fair.

OLOWALU BEACH
FACILITIES: None. *BEACH:* Narrow beach covered the entire length by Kiawe trees. Offshore is shallow and rocky with patches of sand. *ACTIVITIES:* Swimming - fair, snorkeling - fair in deeper area when water is calm and clear.

AWALUA BEACH
FACILITIES: None. *BEACH:* Sandy inshore bottom with a gentle slope. *ACTIVITIES:* Popular for swimming.

KULANAOKALAI BEACH
FACILITIES: None. *BEACH:* Long, wide, dark detrital sand beach with a gentle offshore slope. *ACTIVITIES:* Popular swimming area, bodysurfing -sometimes.

LAUNIUPOKO STATE WAYSIDE PARK
FACILITIES: Picnic tables, BBQ grills, restrooms, showers, paved parking. *BEACH:* Short, wide sandy beach. *ACTIVITIES:* Large, man-made wading pool with sandy bottom for children.

BEACHES AND BEACH ACTIVITIES
Lahaina and Kaanapali

LAHAINA AND KAANAPALI BEACHES

The Kaanapali Resort is probably one of the best known beach resort areas in the world, and if a beach has to be developed, it might as well be like this.

PUAMANA BEACH PARK
ACCESS: On-street parking near Lahaina Shores complex at south end of Lahaina. Public right-of-way to beach at south end of Lahaina Shores complex. *FACILITIES:* Restrooms and showers at resort. *BEACH:* Narrow sand beach fronting Lahaina Shores complex. The entire beach is fronted by a reef about 30 yards out which protects the beach. The beach is generally sandy offshore with a gentle slope. The water stays fairly shallow out to the reef and contains some interesting coral formations. The area offers fair snorkeling on calm days and in clear water. A good place for beginning snorkelers and children.

WAHIKULI STATE WAYSIDE PARK
ACCESS: There are many paved off-street parking areas between Lahaina and Kaanapali. *FACILITIES:* Many small pavillions with picnic tables, restrooms, showers, and BBQ grills. *BEACH:* Areas of sandy beach sloping gently to deeper areas. *ACTIVITIES:* Good swimming, fair snorkeling. Generally there are one or two rafts renting jetskiis. Popular area because of good swimming and facilities.

HANAKAOO BEACH
ACCESS: The beach fronts the Hyatt Regency Maui, Maui Marriott Resort, Kaanapali Alii,Maui Surf, Whaler's Shopping Center and Condos, Kaanapali Beach Hotel, and Sheraton Maui, and is known as the Kaanapali Beach Resort. Access is through the Kaanapali Resort area. Turn off Honoapiilani Highway at any of the three entrances. This area was not designed with non-guest use in mind and parking is definitely a problem.

A) The Hyatt end of the beach is only a short walk from the large parking area of the Wahikuli State Wayside Park nearest the hotel.

B) Public right-of-way to left of Hyatt lower parking lot where there is parking for 10 cars only.

C) Public right-of-way beach access between the Hyatt and Marriott, but no parking.

D) Public right-of-way between Marriott and Kaanapali Alii with parking for 11 cars only.

E) Public right-of-way between Kaanapali Alii and Maui Surf, but no parking.

F) Public right-of-way between Kaanapali Beach Resort and the Sheraton with parking for 11 cars only.

BEACHES AND BEACH ACTIVITES
Lahaina and Kaanapali

G) There is public parking at the Whaler's Shopping Center, but with beach access only through the complex.

H) A couple of hotels offer paid parking areas (i.e. Marriott).

I) The Maui Surf, Sheraton, and Hyatt have hotel guest parking areas and it is so posted—looks convenient, but do so at your own risk.

J) There is no on-street parking anywhere in the Kaanapali Resort complex.

FACILITIES: The Hyatt, Marriott, Maui Surf, and Sheraton all have convenient facilities from the beach with restrooms, showers, bars, rental equipment, and shops. BEACH: Long, wide, beautiful white sand beach with an abrupt drop-off to deep water. No offshore reef, however, there are areas of offshore coral from the Hyatt to the Maui Surf at times, depending on weather conditions. ACTIVITIES: Good swimming and wave playing, however, there are two or three points along the beach where the waves consistently break fairly hard, and these areas are not a good place for children. In the winter, snorkeling can be fair to good off the Maui Surf Hotel when the coral is exposed underwater. The best snorkeling is at Black Rock, fronting the Sheraton Hotel. The water is almost always clear and fairly calm, with many types of nearly tame fish due to the popularity of hand feeding by snorkelers. Bread and frozen peas seem popular, or you might try packaged dry noodles. The best entrance to the water is from the beach alongside Black Rock. Keep an eye out for people jumping and diving from the rocks above.

KAANAPALI BEACH
ACCESS: This beach begins at the north side of Black Rock and runs for over a mile to the north fronting the Royal Lahaina Resort and the Maui Kaanapali Villas. Turn off Honoapiilani Road (just past Kaanapali Resort) on road marked Kaanapali Airport. There are a few places to park on the side of the road near the public access beach sign. Parking lots nearby are posted for hotel and airport patrons. FACILITIES: Only those available at the nearby hotels. BEACH: Wide (usually) white sand beach with steep drop-off to deep water. It is usually calm and except for the steep drop-off, a good place to swim. Snorkeling around Black Rock is almost always good with excellent visibility.

BEACHES AND BEACH ACTIVITIES
Kahana, Napili, Kapalua, and Beyond

KAHANA, NAPILI AND KAPALUA BEACHES

HONOKOWAI PARK
ACCESS: Turn off the Honoapiilani Hwy. on one of the side streets past the airport and get onto Lower Honoapiilani Hwy. which parallels the beach. The park is across the street from the Honokowai Superette (grocery store). FACILITIES: Paved off-street parking for 30 cars, 11 picnic tables, 5 BBQ pits, restrooms, showers, nice grassy park with shade trees. Grocery store across the street with pay phone outside. BEACH: White sand beach lined by wide shelf of beach rock. Between shelf rock and reef there is a narrow, shallow pool with sandy bottom. ACTIVITIES: Good swimming area for small children. There is a break in the reef at north end of the beach where you can get snorkeling access to the outside reef. Water sport equipment is available for rent at Honokowai Store.

UNMARKED--*north of Honokowai Park* ACCESS: Visible from Lower Honoapiilani Hwy. FACILITIES: Limited roadside parking - no facilities. BEACH: Very small sandy beach.

KAHANA BEACH
ACCESS: Beach fronts the Kahana Beach Resort. FACILITIES: Limited off-road parking at south end of beach access road. BEACH: Narrow white sand beach. Offshore area is shallow with rock and sand, semi-protected by reef. ACTIVITIES: Good swimming, beach may be cool and windy in afternoons.

KEONENUI BEACH
ACCESS: No convenient access. FACILITIES: None. BEACH: Beach mostly cobble strewn lined by retaining wall.

NAPILI BAY
ACCESS: A) A small, easily missed public right-of-way and Napili Beach sign, just past the Napili Shores. Look for Napili Place street. On-street parking at sign for Napili Surf Beach Resort. There is a public beach right-of-way sign (easily missed) showing entrance to beach. Public telephone in parking lot of Napili Surf. B) Second entrance at public beach right-of-way and Napili Sunset, Hale Napili, and Napili Bay signs on Hui street. On-street parking and pay phone at entrance to beach walk. FACILITIES: None, other than at hotels fronting the beach. There is a grocery store just past the second entrance at the Napili Village Hotel. Look for the Napili Grocery Store sign. BEACH: Long, wide crescent of white sand between two rocky points. The offshore slope is moderately steep to overhead depths. Usually very safe for swimming and snorkeling except during winter storms when large waves occasionally come into the bay. At the south end of the beach are a series of shallow sandy tide pools which make an excellent place for children to play.

BEACHES AND BEACH ACTIVITES
Kahana, Napili, Kapalua, and Beyond

KAPALUA BEACH** *(Fleming Beach)*
ACCESS: Just past the Napili Kai Beach Club you will see a public right-of-way sign. FACILITIES: Nice off-street parking area for about 30 cars. Showers and restrooms. Above the beach are the lovely grounds of the Kapalua Bay Resort. BEACH: A beautiful crescent of white sand between two rocky points. The beach has a gentle slope to deeper water, maximum about 15 feet. From the left point, a reef arcs across toward the long right point creating a very sheltered bay, probably the nicest and safest swimming beach on Maui. Shade is provided by numerous coconut trees lining the backshore area. ACTIVITIES: Swimming is almost always excellent with plenty of play area for children and shady places to get out of the sun. Snorkeling is usually excellent with many different kinds of fish and interesting coral. Large coral heads may be found near the right rocky point. REMEMBER, this is a popular beach and parking is limited.

ONELOA BEACH
ACCESS: Public right-of-way sign just past the Kapalua Bay Resort. FACILITIES: Paved off-street parking for 12 - 15 cars only, no other facilities. BEACH: Long, straight white sand beach, shallow sand bar extends to the surfline. The beach is posted with warning sign "No swimming at time of high surf due to dangerous currents". Also, this area tends to get windy and cloudy in the afternoons, especially in the winter months.

D. T. FLEMING BEACH PARK
ACCESS: Clearly marked park with off-street parking on both sides of road. FACILITIES: There are restrooms, showers, picnic tables, and BBQ grills situated on the grassy dunes above the beach. BEACH: A long white sand beach with an offshore sand bar, however, the beach itself is steep. Because of this situation, when swells hit the beach, dangerous water conditions can occur. The beach is posted "Dangerous Swimming".

MOKULEIA BEACH *(Slaughterhouse)*
ACCESS: On Highway 30, past D. T. Fleming Beach Park, look for cars parked along the roadside, and the R. V. Deli. Park your car and hike down one of the steep dirt and rock trails—they are not difficult. FACILITIES: The R. V. Deli is parked here most of the day year around, serving cold drinks, hamburgers, hot dogs, and snacks. He also helps keep the beach and road clean and his presence deters auto vandalism and theft. Other than the deli, there are no facilities. BEACH: White sand beach with gentle slope to deep water, bordered by two rocky points and situated at the foot of steep cliffs. The left middle part of the beach is usually clear of coral and rocks even in winter when the beach is subject to erosion. ACTIVITIES: During the winter, swimming is safe when the ocean is calm or fairly calm. However, when the surf is heavy, dangerous water conditions exist. This is THE bodysurfing spot, especially in winter. The summer is generally much better for swimming. Snorkeling is fair to good, especially around the left rocky point where there is a reef. Okay in winter when the ocean is calm and visibility good, better in summer. NOTE: The beach

BEACHES AND BEACH ACTIVITIES
Kahana, Napili, Kapalua, and Beyond

known as Slaughterhouse because of the once existing slaughterhouse on the cliffs above the beach, not because of what the ocean can do to body surfers in the winter when the big ones are coming in! Remember this is part of the Honolua-Mokuleia Bay Marine Life Conservation District—look, but don't disturb or take.

HONOLUA BAY *
ACCESS: The next bay past Slaughterhouse is Honolua Bay. As you drive down into the bay, watch for a dirt side road on the left. Park here and walk in along the road. FACILITIES: None. BEACH: Irregular patches of sand with an old concrete boat ramp in the middle. ACTIVITIES: Excellent snorkeling in summer, spring, and fall and in winter only on calm days. Enter at the boat ramp and follow the reefs either left or right. Surfing can be excellent here especially in winter when storm generated big waves come in. A good vantage point is the cliffs at the right point of the bay, accessible by car on a short dirt road off the main highway.

BEACHES AND BEACH ACTIVITES
Wailuku/Kahului Area

WAILUKU AND KAHULUI BEACHES

Beaches along this whole side of the island are generally poor for swimming and snorkeling. The weather is generally windy or cloudy in winter and very hot in summer. Due to the weather, type of beaches, and distance from the major tourist areas on the other side of the island, these beaches don't attract many tourists.

WAIHEE BEACH PARK
ACCESS: From Wailuku take Kahekili Highway about three miles to Waihee and turn right onto Halewaiu road, proceed about one-half mile to the Waihee Municipal Golf Course. From there a park access road takes you into the park. FACILITIES: Paved off-street parking, restrooms, showers, and picnic tables. BEACH: This is a long, narrow, brown sand beach strewn with coral rubble from Waihee Reef. This is one of the longest and widest reefs on Maui, and is about one thousand feet wide off the park. The area between the beach and reef is moderately shallow with good areas for swimming and snorkeling when the ocean is calm. Winter surf or storm conditions can produce strong alongshore currents. Do not swim or snorkel at the left end of the beach as there is a large channel through the reef which usually produces a very strong rip current. Area is generally windy.

KANAHA BEACH PARK
ACCESS: Just before reaching the Kahului airport, turn left, then right on reaching Ahahao Street. FACILITIES: The far south area of the park has been landscaped and includes BBQ's, picnic tables, restrooms, and showers. Paved off-street parking is provided. BEACH: Long (about one mile) wide, white sand beach with a shallow offshore bottom composed of sand and rock. Plenty of kiawe trees in the area make footwear essential. ACTIVITIES: The main attraction of the park is its peaceful setting and view, so picnicking and sunbathing are the primary activities. Swimming would appeal mainly to children. Surfing can be good here. If surf is too large for you at Ho'okipa Beach, come here.

H. A. BALDWIN PARK
ACCESS: The park is located about 1.5 miles past Spreckelville on the Hana Highway. FACILITIES: Large off-street parking area, a large pavillion with kitchen facilities, picnic tables, and BBQ's. There are also restrooms, showers, a baseball and a soccer field. BEACH: A long, wide white sand beach with a steep slope to overhead depths. ACTIVITIES: This is a very popular park because of the facilities and the very consistent, although usually smallish, shorebreak, which is good for bodysurfing. Generally, swimming is poor, however, there are two areas where exposed beach rock provide a relatively calm place for children to play.

BEACHES AND BEACH ACTIVITIES
Wailuku/Kahului Area

HOOKIPA BEACH PARK
ACCESS: About two miles past Lower Paia on the Hana Highway. *FACILITIES:* Restrooms, shower, four pavillions with BBQ's and picnic tables, paved off-street parking. *BEACH:* Small, white sand beach fronted by a wide shelf of beach rock. The offshore bottom is a mixture of reef and patches of sand. *ACTIVITIES:* Swimming is not advised. The area is popular for the generally good and at times (during winter) very good surfing. Wind surfing is also very popular here. This is a good place to come and watch both of these water sports.

The Sugar Cane Train

RECREATION AND TOURS
Land Tours

INTRODUCTION

A mild year around climate makes recreation on Maui ideal. A bountiful array of water, land and air tours are offered all around this island. The very popular sports of golf and tennis are featured at a variety of lush locations. Maui's scenic environment can also be appreciated on horseback from several stables. Tips on biking, camping, hiking and running are also featured in this chapter. The final section of this chapter takes a brief look at shopping areas. This is considered recreation by many women!!

LAND TOURS

Cruiser Bob's: Provides a van trip and light breakfast enroute to Haleakala and then a bike for your 3-1/2 hour downhill trek, with a stop for lunch along the way. For $70 this may be the thrill of a lifetime! Phone 579-9574.

Grayline: Provides a variety of tours on a large-size bus. Phone 877-5507.

Holo Holo Tours: A Hana trip for $49 includes continental breakfast and picnic lunch. To Haleakala, various packages depending on meals provided and optional tours of Lahaina $35 - $50. They use small vans. P.O. Box 1591, Lahaina, Maui, HI 96761, phone 661-4858.

Maui Special Tours: Jack Van't Groenewout is your guide to old Hana ($45 full day), central Maui and Upcountry ($35 half day) or Haleakala ($35 half day). His tremendous knowledge of the area makes for an informative & fun trip.

No Kai Oi Scenic Tours: Takes you to Hana, Iao Valley, Haleakala, Lahaina. 531 S. Papa Ave., phone 871-9008.

Personalized Small Group Tours: See Hana for $38.50, Haleakala for $30, or west Maui for $17.50. Tours are provided in small vans. Phone 871-9551.

The Sugar Cane Train: Their main depot is located just outside of Lahaina, turn at the pizza hut sign. They charge adults $4.25 for a one way fare, two way is $6.50. Children 2 - 12 years are charged $2.00 one way and $3.25 round trip. They also have several package options which include the "Orient Express" which is a round trip train ride plus a scenic voyage on the Lin Wa II for $14.00 adults, $7 children. A "Historic Lahaina" excursion includes a train ride plus tour of the Baldwin House and the Carthinagin II for $10 adults and $3.00 children. If you plan on a full day round trip excursion, go early in the day as the return trips can be sold out quickly. Phone 661-0089.

RECREATION AND TOURS
Land Tours - Water Tours

Roberts-Hawaii Tours: 877-5038. Offers one of the largest selection of land tours in their big air conditioned buses. They depart to all scenic areas from Kahului, Kihei/Wailea, and the west Maui hotels. Phone 877-5038 for more information.

Trans Hawaiian Maui: A day trip to Hana departs 7 a.m. and returns about 5:30 p.m. For $40 it does not include lunch. Phone 877-7308.

WATER TOURS

Aikane: This 45' racing catamaran sails from Maalaea Harbor to Molokini. Snorkeling, lunch, beer & wine are all included. Adults $45, children under 12 $30. Sunset cruise with appetizers & cocktails $27.50. Phone 879-8188.

Alihilani Yacht Charters, Lahaina: Aboard the 40' teak and mahogany cutter, the Alilhilani, choose from the following tours: 1/2 day trip to Lanai, $52, 3 hour snorkel sail, $40, full day snorkel, $70, 2 hour sunset sail, $25,

Private charters are also available. The full day sails include lunch as well as snorkeling gear and instruction, underwater cameras (bring own 110 film), prescription face masks, and jackets for fishing or sailing. Phone 661-3047.

Anela Kai: This 40 x 20 catamaran sails to the Lanai reef with 2 - 6 passengers. Free snorkel and fishing gear for half day $40, full day, $70. Lunch or pupus and beverage included. Phone 242-7218.

Captains Nemo's Emporium: Located at 700 Front at Dickenson, Phone 661-5555. Their 58' Catamaran, Seasmoke, was built originally for James Arness and is reputed to be the fastest cat on the island. They leave from Kaanapali to Lanai at 8am for scuba and snorkeling. They offer a continental breakfast enroute and a buffet lunch of fried chicken as you anchor off Turtle Cove. They return at 2pm. $65 for snorkeling, $75 for certified divers, $85 for beginning divers.

Central Pacific Divers: They offer scuba dives. Stop in their shop at 780 Front Street, Lahaina, phone 661-8718. They also have a good selection of snorkel and scuba equipment for rent or sale.

The Coral See: Slip #1, Lahaina Harbor, departs daily in the 65' glass bottom boat. One half day picnic/snorkel tour includes equipment, lunch and open bar for $39 (children, $19.50). Phone 661-8600.

Hawaiian Sailing Adventures: P.O. Box 302, Lahaina, Maui, HI 96761 They offer a four hour sail for $39, or an eight hour sail for $69, on the 46 x 25 Trimax trimaran. Phone 667-7511, Monday through Friday, 8 a.m. - 5 p.m. or 667-6547, Saturday and Sunday, 9 a.m. - 5 p.m.

Jamin Jet Skiis: phone 242-4339. Located across from Suda's Store off Kihei Beach.

RECREATION AND TOURS
Water Tours

Kaanapali Jet Ski: Located in front of Whaler's Village, phone 667-7851.

Kamehameha Catamaran Sails: Slip #67, Lahaina Harbor. A two hour snorkel tour includes equipment and soft drinks for $20 (adults), $15 (children). Three hour afternoon snorkel sail and lunch $30 (adults), $20 (children). Sunset sail includes soft drinks and Maui Chips. Adults $19 and children $13. 15 passenger limit. Phone 661-4522.

Kaulana: offering a variety of options on their 70' catamaran, a sunset dinner cruise is featured four nights a week, adults $32, under 12, $16. A picnic snorkel to Lanai $40 adults, children $20., Sunset cocktail cruise $20 adults, $10 children and more trips available seasonally. Phone 667-2518.

Kiele V: departing the Hyatt is this 55' catamaran. A 10 a.m. - 2 p.m. snorkel sail includes continental breakfast, snorkel equipment, and mini-deli lunch. Adults $45, children under 12 $20. Cocktail sail includes snacks, open bar along with the magnificent Maui sunset for adults $25, and children under 17 $10. Phone 667-7474, ext. 3104.

Lahaina Para Sail: A flight includes a scenic boat ride through the Lahaina Harbor. Contact them at 628 Front Street, Lahaina, or phone 661-4887. Trips by reservation.

Lin Wa Cruises: depart 6 times daily from Lahaina Harbor, Slip #3. Provides a view through the bottom of this Chinese junk. Adults $9.50, children under 12 $4.75. Phone 661-3392.

Mareva: Lahaina Harbor. Only two - six passengers are aboard this 30' sloop to experience sportfishing or snorkeling. One half day snorkel $40, sunset sail $25, full day with lunch $75. Charters available. Phone 667-7013.

Maui Adventures: Lahaina Harbor, Slip #4. This catamaran can provide snorkeling tours complete with guide and equipment. It features a slide for easy water entry. Half day runs $20. Phone 661-3400.

Mea'u: Snorkel, scuba, or sail on the 42' Mea'u. Phone 661-0429 or 669-6683. P.O. Box 11267, Lahaina, Maui, HI 96761. Snorkel $65, beginning scuba $85 (no experience), certified scuba $75.

Maui Sailing Center: WATERSKIING! Departing from Keali Beach Village, it runs $20 per one half hour, or $35 per hour which includes boat and driver. Phone 879-5935, beginning 7 a.m. (weather permitting).

Nancy Emerson Surfing Lessons: taught in gentle surf for the novice. Phone 224-3728.

Pardner: Lahaina Harbor, Slip #28. This 46' ketch provides all day snorkel and sail at $75, one half day $45, or two hour sunset sail at $30. Accommodates 2 - 6 passengers. Phone 661-3448.

Prince Kuhio: Choose between a half day snorkel trip to Molokini for $47.50

RECREATION AND TOURS
Water Tours

adults $30 children, a gourmet dinner cruise featuring Hawaiian music for $35, or a full day trip to Molokini. The Molokai trip departs at 7:30, serves a continental breakfast enroute, a tour of Molokai with lunch at Hotel Molokai and a return trip serving snacks & cocktails. Sails from Maalaea Harbor. 242-4575.

Rainbow Custom Water Sports: Snorkeling, Waterskiing, Spearfishing, sportfishing, whale watching, scuba diving. 4 adults maximum or 2 adults and 3 children. 2 hr minimum $99, $39 each additional hour. Full day charter $333, 1/2 day $177. Phone 1-808-661-3980 or write PO BOX 11662, Lahina, Maui HI 96761

Rayonna Sailing Charters: Lahaina. Two - six passengers can enjoy a daily sail departing Kaanapali at 10:30 a.m. returning at 3 p.m. A picturesque sail to Honolua Bay for snorkeling also includes lunch, gear, and underwater camera, $45. Phone 661-3787.

Scotch Mist: Maui's oldest sailing charter began in 1970 and operates two boats. The Scotch Mist I offers half day snorkel sail for $50, the Scotch Mist II at $40. The Scotch Mist I offers full day trips at $80, Scotch Mist II's full day sail is $85. Champagne sunset on the Scotch Mist I runs $33, II runs $25. Family rates and private charters available. Phone 661-0386.

Sea Sails: Choose from a variety of packages including a 1 1/2 hr. sunset cocktail sail or a 3 hr picnic - snorkel sail. Contact; Lahaina Sea Sport Activity Center at 850 Front Street, 1-808-667-2759.

Seabern Yachts: Rent a 27', 28' or 36' yacht for partial day, full day or week to qualified sailors only. For more information phone 661-8110.

Seabird Cruises: A one day trip to Lanai or Molokai $59. One half day snorkel or dinner sail $32. Sunset cocktail sail $22, whale watch sail $15. Phone 661-3643.

Seaport Cruises: Departing from Maalaea Harbor for a one half day snorkeling trip to Molokini which includes instruction, equipment and lunch. The 53' yacht leaves at 8 a.m. Phone 879-1919.

Suntan Special: A Santa Cruz 50 ocean racer offers half day snorkel sails for $30-$40. Sunset sails for $30. All day sail $85. Private boat charter available at $200 an hour.

Trilogy Excursions: Enjoy a day long trip to Lanai on 40' cutter or 50' ketch rigged trimarams for $85. Includes light breakfast, with lunch cooked on beach at Lanai. Departs about 6:30 a.m. Phone 661-4743.

Unicorn Tours: Depart Lahaina Harbor for trips to Lanai or Molokai. One half day to Lanai $36, one half day to Molokai $56, all day to Molokai or Lanai $80. Evening champagne cruise $20. Phone 879-6333 or 242-5659 after hours.

Wailea Ocean Activities Center: Phone 879-4489. They offer a variety of sport

RECREATION AND TOURS
Water Tours

fishing, partial or full day scuba, snorkeling, whale watching (seasonal), and champagne sunset dinners.

Wailea Kai: departs Maalaea Harbor, $45 for half day snorkel trip to Molokini. Departs 7:45 a.m. and includes gear, instruction, two snorkeling dives, and a deli lunch. Fresh fruit, rolls, and beverage are served upon your morning arrival. (See author's comments which follow) Phone the Wailea Activities center at 879-4489 for reservations or information.

Windjammer Cruises: A day sail to Lanai or sunset dinner cruises are available. Contact 667-6834. A Trip to Lanai

A Trip To Lanai

A trip to the island of Lanai for an all-day snorkel excursion begins early in the morning (bring your camera). For our trip we went on the Trilogy, crewed by three of the Coon family members. Although we did not sight any whales on our trip, the school of dolphins sighted must have been near 300, and it was an awesome experience.

After a two-hour motoring trip, we anchored at Manele Harbor and walked the three-to-four block distance to the beach. A spacious white sand beach offered restrooms and a rinse-off shower. The snorkeling, we feel, was superior to that even at Molokini. We swam out to what appeared to be a moving black reef and were overwhelmed to see a mass of silvery-white fish swimming in a school of what looked like a million. Be forewarned, that barracuda and shark sometimes lurk around the edges of these schools. The beginning snorkelers were carefully instructed in a tide pool before entering the ocean. Although many on our cruise were senior citizens, they all did splendidly and commented that they only wish they'd gone snorkeling before!

After an hour or more of snorkeling we walked back to the harbor where a table, beautifully set (no paper plates here!) was awaiting us. A green salad tossed with Mrs. Coon's secret dressing began the meal, followed by teriyaki chicken (cooked by the crew), Saimin noodles, peas, and fresh pineapple for dessert.

While dishes were being done, we hopped the bus for a trip to Lanai City (population 2,300), which is the only city on the island. Unless retired, both parents must work to support their families on this island where the cost of living is high. Owned by Castle and Cook, it is one huge pineapple plantation, and almost all are employed in the pineapple industry. Expansion is planned which will result in numerous resort units replacing the new single ten-room hotel. The population is expected to increase upwards to 25,000 people with tourists. We were glad to see the island in its current peaceful form.

Back to the boat for the motor trip home, and then a sail up the south side of

RECREATION AND TOURS
Water Tours

Maui back to the Lahaina Harbor.

We would recommend the Trilogy trip to anyone considering a day trip to Lanai. They were extremely personable and made the outing a very special one.

A Trip To Molokini

Sailing out of the Maalaea Harbor, the boat will take you to the 10,000 year old dormant volcano called Molokini. The one-hour cruise (they don't sail) takes you to the center of the crescent-shaped island, the only remnant of the volcano. In this area, the water depth is 15 - 20 feet and visibility is generally 150 feet with 76 degree water temperature. Once used as a bombing target, shells and bombs (defused) can still be spotted by the observant diver or snorkeler. The land is now a bird sanctuary and the water a marine preserve, allowing for some very good views of coral and an array of fish. Trespassing on the island is prohibited as well as the taking of any marine life. The back side of the island is unsafe for all but the boldest of skin divers, as Molokini drops off to a depth of 300 - 400 feet and provides housing for the more aggressive marine life, such as the hammerhead shark. Within the safety of the crescent, the only dangers are an occasional reef shark, which are more content with the fish than the snorkeler and perhaps a rare jellyfish. We were fortunate enough to catch a glimpse of a reef shark, luckily going away from us!

For our excursion we chose the Wailea Kai. A breakfast of sweet rolls, coffee or juice, and fresh fruit awaited us upon our early morning arrival. The crew on this 65 foot catamaran was lively, well-informed, and entertaining, providing an in-depth explanation of the gear as we cruised to the island.

Once anchored, they offered two dives, and had a member of the crew in the water on a raft to help any snorkelers in distress. They also provided life vests that could be automatically inflated and boogie boards for additional flotation support. One crew member brought in samples of marine life, (want to pet an octopus?), and put on a clever show. The marine life was then carefully returned to their underwater homes.

Lunch consisted of a make-your-own sandwich smorgasbord of beef, turkey, and ham.

A second snorkel dive opportunity offered an option of accompanying a crew member for a reef tour.

Then it was homeward bound with complimentary beer and wine along with a nicely commentated tour of the sights on Maui as we approached.

While charging a bit more than some of their competitors, they boast that they offer two dives, while the others offer only one. They also promise to get you out to the reef ahead of the other boats allowing them the best anchorage for snorkeling. Scuba divers are also invited along for an extra charge. Fishing

RECREATION AND TOURS
Water Tours - Miscellaneous

poles can be rented ($10) to a limited number of passengers to troll enroute to and from Molokini (our fishermen were not successful). Underwater cameras are also available for an extra charge.

The Seabird Cruise also travels to Molokini. They serve morning juice or coffee enroute to the island and tend to carry fewer passengers, thus offering more opportunity to move around the boat. The Seabird gives snorkel instruction upon arrival at Molokini and offers only one dive time, but it is an hour and a half and ample for most snorkelers. The seabird does not offer the fishing or scuba options. They do provide a deli-type (ready-made) sandwich for the trip back to Maui.

The choice is yours, but for beginning or more advanced snorkelers, a trip to Molokini might be a memorable half-day experience. Remember, on any tour, book early!!

MISCELLANEOUS

Fishing

Our best advice to those interested in some deep sea fishing is to visit the Lahaina Wharf in front of the Pioneer Inn. There are stands along the pier with information on various fishing trips offered. It can be a costly trip, running about $350 if you want to charter a boat alone.

Windsurfing

The Maui Sailing Center offers lessons for those interested in learning this fast growing sport. Classes are held on Maalaea Bay, generally from March through December. Contact the Maui Sailing Center, Kealia Beach Village, 101 North Kihei Road, Kihei, Maui, HI 96753, phone 879-5935.

Whale Watching

Maui has become well known for its good vantage points from which to enjoy whale watching. Every year beginning in November and continuing until April, the humpback whales arrive in the warm waters off the Hawaiian Islands for breeding, and their own sort of vacation! The sighting of a whale can be an awesome and memorable experience with the humpbacks, small as whales go, measuring some 40 - 50 feet and weighing in at 30 tons. While viewing from the shoreline is possible, you may want to join a cruise to get a closer view. Many leave from the Maalaea and Lahaina Harbors, however, you may want to

RECREATION AND TOURS
Miscellaneous - Rental Equipment

check into the one sponsored by Pacific Whale Foundation at Azeka's Place, Suite 303, Kihei, phone 879-6530. As they are a research group, they are very well-informed and knowledgeable about the best areas to spot the whales. Greenpeace is located at 628 Front Street in Lahaina, phone 667-2059. This environmental group can provide you with the names of other good whale watching expeditions with a portion of the price going to Greenpeace to help in their efforts to protect the whales. The Carthinagin at the Lahaina Harbor has a chart showing the points where whales have been sighted. You can report your sightings by calling Whale Watch Hotline at 879-6530.

RENTAL EQUIPMENT

Equipment

Snorkel gear can be rented at any of the many dive shops. The rates run in the neighborhood of $5 a day for fins, mask and snorkel. They are also available at the beaches of many of the major hotels, with the prices substantially higher, as much as $20 a day. Equipment is provided on all snorkel cruises.

Two popular areas for the rental of small sailboats in the Kaanapali area are the beach fronting the Hyatt Regency Hotel and also in front of the Kaanapali Hotel. Prices at the Hyatt run $15 an hour for a Laser, Hobie cats either 14' or 16' run $25 to $35 an hour. In the Wailea area boats are available at Wailea Beach.

Equipment for skin diving, snorkeling, and bodyboards can be rented at the following locations and purchased too! If you can, shop around, prices are competitive, but vary.

LAHAINA AREA:

American Dive Maui, 628 Front Street Lahaina, phone 661-4885

Central Pacific Divers, 780 Front Street, Lahaina, phone 661-8718

Hawaiian Reef Divers, 129 Lahainaluna, Lahaina, phone 667-7647

Honokowai Store in Honokowai

KIHEI AREA:

Kihei Sea Sports at Kihei Town Center, phone 879-1919

Maui Dive Shop Azeka's Place Shopping Center, phone 879-3388

Skin Diving Maui, 2411 South Kihei Road, Kihei, phone 879-1502

RECREATION AND TOURS
Rental Equipment - Air Tours

Rental equipment is also available at most major hotels, but the rates are higher. If you have a condo, you will sometimes find snorkeling equipment or bodyboards stowed in a cupboard for the visitors' use. On major beaches, such as Kapalua Bay, Kaanapali, and Wailea, sailboats and other water items are available for rent.

AIR TOURS

Awesome Maui Helicopter Tours: Phone 661-8889. P.O. Box 1775, Lahaina, Maui, HI 96761. $165 for whole island tours $125 for Haleakala tours.

Central Pacific Airlines: P.O. Box 10547, Lahaina, Maui, HI 96761, phone 871-7622 or 242-7894. Leaves Kahului Airport, hotel pickup provided, in a twin-engine Cessna 402. The Hana tour includes four hours on the ground seeing sights such as the general store and the seven sacred pools. A picnic lunch is provided and then a return flight through the Haleakala Crater for $119.50. Their Molokai-Kalaupapa tour is the same price and includes a four-hour ground trip to the historical leper settlement founded by Father Damien. Lunch is provided.

Kenai Air Helicopter: phone 661-4427. The narrated tour begins at Kaanapali airport and first flies over Haleakala Crater then down to the lush village of Hana.

Paragon Air: Aerial tours available around Maui ($95 1/2/ hr) Maui, Lanai & Molokini ($130 1hr 45 min), Hana air & ground tour ($120, 4hr 30 min), Kalaupapa, Maui & Lanai air & ground tour ($155, 6 hrs). Phone 1-808-244-3356. Departs from the Kahului airport.

Papillon Helicoptors: departing from Kapalua. Air tours of the upcountry include spectacular views, champagne breakfast on the slopes of Ulupalakua. Phone 669-4884.

Maui Helicopter Adventures: Phone 879-1601. Based at the Hotel Intercontinental in Wailea. See ancient Hawaiian villages, waterfalls, jungles, and Haleakala offered in their array of tours. P.O. Box 1002, Kihei, Maui, HI 96753. Remote excursion $105, panoramic journey $135, and Maui unlimited $180.

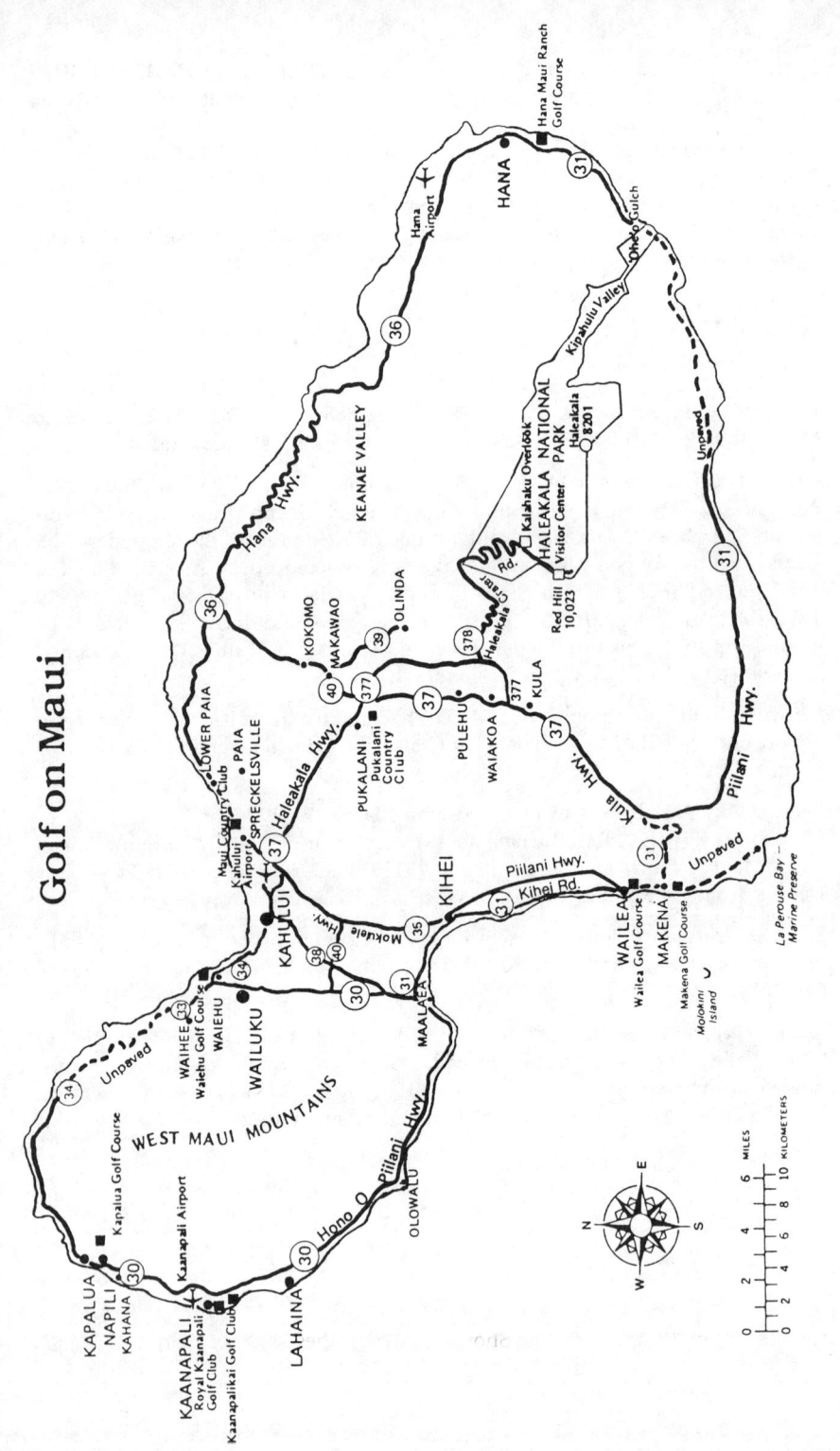

RECREATION AND TOURS
Golf - Tennis

GOLF

Kapalua Bay Golf Club is a public course at Kapalua. Eighteen holes with a par 71 will cost $35 for green fees and $10 for the mandatory cart. The Kapalua Golf Club Villa also offers 18 holes with a par 73 and the price is the same. Phone 669-8044.

Makena Golf Course is down beyond Kihei and Wailea and the newest of courses on the island. Eighteen holes with a par 72 will cost $26 including cart. Phone 879-3344.

Maui Country Club is a private course, with visitors allowed on Mondays only. The front 9 holes have a par 37 and cost $10. The back 9 holes have the same par and price. A cart is $6 for 9 holes. Located in the Paia area, phone 877-0616.

Pukalani Country Club is located in upcountry Maui. It has two 9-hole courses, each having a par 36. Green fees are $4 for 9 holes and $7 for 18. A cart is $6 for 9 holes and is mandatory weekdays between 8:30 a.m. and 3:30 p.m. and all day on weekends and holidays. Phone 572-1314.

Royal Kaanapali North offers 18 holes, with a par 72 and green fees are $27. A golf cart is mandatory and will run $11. Royal Kaanapali South is also par 72 with $27 green fees and a mandatory golf cart at $11. Phone 661-3691.

Waiehu Municipal Golf Course has 18 holes with a par 72. Green fee is priced at $10 weekdays and $15 weekends. A cart is optional at $10. Phone 244-5433.

Wailea Golf Course offers two courses. The Orange Course is 18 holes with a par 72 and costs $30 for green fees with a cart mandatory and priced at $10 per person. The Blue Course is also 18 holes, par 72, with green fees and cart priced the same. Wailea hotel guests can play either course for $15 and island residents play for $18.

TENNIS

Many condos and major hotels offer tennis facilities, however, there are quite a few very well kept public courts. They are, of course, most popular during early morning and early evening hours.

Hana - Hana Ball Park, two lighted courts.

Kahului - Kahului Community Center has two lighted courts.

Kihei - Kalama Park has two lighted courts. Two public courts are also to be found fronting the Maui Pacific Shores, however, these are not lighted.

RECREATION AND TOURS
Tennis

Lahaina - Lahaina Civic Center has two lighted courts and there are four lighted courts at Malu-ulu-olele Park.

Makawao - Eddie Tam Memorial Center has two lighted courts.

Pukalani - Pukalani Community Center has two lighted courts.

Wailuku - Maui Community College has four lighted courts available after school hours. Phone 244-9181. Seven lighted courts are at the Wailuku Community Center and four more courts at the Wailuku War Memorial, which is also lighted.

Some hotels and private courts offer their facilities to the public:

Maui Marriott Resort, Lahaina, phone 667-1200. Guests and non-guests can play on five unlighted courts for $10.

Maui Sunset, in Kihei, phone 879-1971, has two courts which are not lighted, but can be played at no charge.

Maui Surf at Kaanapali, phone 661-4411, charges hotel guests $4 per person and non-guests $5 each to play on their three courts which are not lighted.

Napili Kai Beach Club at Napili Bay, phone 669-6271, has two courts and charges hotel guests $4 singles, non-guests $6. There are no lights on these courts.

Royal Lahaina Hotel, at Kaanapali, has the 2nd largest tennis facility on the island. They have 11 courts, 6 of them lighted and one is a stadium court. $10 for singles and $15 for doubles, after 7 p.m. add $2. Phone 661-3611.

Sheraton Maui Hotel at Kaanapali has three lighted courts. Hotel guests $5 per person per hour, non-guests run $6. Phone 661-0031.

The Kapalua Bay Hotel offers the Tennis Garden. Phone 669-5677 for information and reservations on playing their 10 courts. Hotel guests are free, non-guests are priced at $4. Tennis attire required at all times.

Wailea Tennis Center has fourteen courts, three are lighted. Phone 879-1958. Per court rate per hour runs $8 single, $10 double (add $2 after October 15), night rate $10 single, $15 double (add $2 after October 15). Three grass courts run $18 singles and $24 for doubles. Courts open 7 a.m. - 9 p.m.

The following hotels and condominiums offer tennis facilities restricted to their guests:

Hale Kamaole Condominiums in Kihei, phone 879-2698. The Maui Vista Condominiums, also in Kihei. Hotel Hana in Hana, phone 248-8211. Hyatt Regency Hotel at Kaanapali, phone 667-7474, guests are charged. The Kaanapali Plantation at Kaanapali, phone 661-4446. Kuleana, Mahinahina, Lahaina,

RECREATION AND TOURS
Tennis - Bikes - Camping

phone 669-8080. Maalaea Surf near Kihei at Maalaea, phone 879-1267. The Mahana at Kaanapali, phone 661-8751. Papakea Beach Resort, Kaanapali, phone 669-4848, moderate fee charged. Puamana, Lahaina, Maui, phone 667-2551. Royal Kahana Resort, Kahana, 669-8051. The Whaler, Kaanapali, phone 661-4861. The Kaanapali Alii also has tennis facilities.

BIKES

A & B Moped Rentals - 3511 Honoapiilani Hwy., Honokowai General Store, phone 669-0027. They also have underwater cameras, jet skiis, boogieboards, tours and snorkel or dive gear.

Coast to the Coast: Located at Captain Nemos on 700 Front street or phone Mountain High Bicycle Tours 661-4644. They provide a gourmet breakfast & lunch, plus a specially designed bike for the trip down Haleakala.

Cruiser Bob's - 222 Papalua St., phone 667-7717, at Lahaina TravelLodge. Open daily 9 a.m. - 5:30 p.m. For a real thrill, take their van trip to Haleakala and then brake your way down the mountain. A lunch is provided. $70. They leave about 6:30 a.m. and return about 3:30 p.m. They are also beginning a once-a-week sunrise excursion for the early risers!

Go Go Bikes Hawaii, Inc. - Bikes and moped rentals, free pickup in west Maui area. $5 per hour or $25 per day. Phone 669-6669.

T's Beach Rentals - Kahana. Corrective snorkel lens masks $20. Canvas rafts, surfboards, and beach chairs. Phone 669-6568.

CAMPING

County & state camping permits are required for camping in many of the parks. County permits are available at the Maui War Memorial in Wailuku, phone 244-5514. State permits are issued 8am -noon & 1-4:15 pm Monday through Friday at the State Office Building, Department of Land and Natural Resources, 54 High st, Wailuku, phone 244-4354.

Haleakala National Park permits are issued at the park headquarters for tent camping on a first come basis on the day you plan to stay, beginning at 7:30am until 4pm daily. The reservations for Haleakala cabins are set up at a monthly lottery. Send requests to Haleakala National Park, PO BOX 369, Makawao, Maui, Hi 96768. phone 572-9177 or 572-9306.

Wainapanapa State Park near Hana. Tent camping, 12 cabins. More information on this location can be found under the Where to Stay - Hana Chapter.

RECREATION AND TOURS
Camping - Hiking - Running

Kaumahina State Wayside, Hana. Tent camping.

Hosmer Grove, Haleakala National Park. Tent camping. No permit required.

Oheo Gulch, Haleakala National Park, Hana. Tent camping. No permit required.

Hookipa Beach Park, Hana. This county Park offers tent camping.

Poli Poli Springs Recreational area. Located in Upcountry, this state park has one cabin and offers tent camping.

Honomanu Bay, Hana. This county park has tent camping facilities.

Baldwin Beach Park. This county park is located near lower Paia on the Hana Hwy & has tent camping space.

Currently the only camping rental company is Beach Boy Campers at 1765 S Kihei Rd., Phone 1-808-879-5322.(car rental agencies generally prohibit use of cars for camping) See general section under car rentals for price information.

HIKING

If you are interested in hiking, Robert Smith's book, Hiking Maui - The Valley Isle, is available at local bookstores, is what you need. It covers 29 hiking trails throughout Maui. The author also has guides to Hawaii and Kauai.

Kenneth Schmitt will be your guide with a relatively new outdoor option, Hike Maui, phone 224-7505 or reservations 879-5279. Half or full day excursions cover mountain to marine areas and range 4 to 12 miles. For example a half day trip of West Maui mountains runs $45 for adults, $25 for children or choose a twelve hour adventure into the Haleakala Crater $85 adults, $45 children. He has recently added overnight excursions. (Bring your own frame backpack and sleeping bag or they can be rented - all other food and equipment provided.) All trips are for a minimum of two and maximum of 6 persons.

RUNNING

Maui is a scenic delight for runners. For a free running map, write "Hawaii Safe Running Council", P.O. Box 23169, Honolulu, HI 96822, and tell them which islands you will be visiting. Stouffer's Resort in Wailea also provides guests with a running guide to the Kihei/Wailea area.

RECREATION AND TOURS
Horseback Riding - Shopping

HORSEBACK RIDING

Adventures on Horseback - phone 242-7445. three days and two nights run $1,500 per couple. A four-hour waterfall adventure outside Hana is $85.

Charley's Trailride and Pack Trips - feature overnight trips to Haleakala with the guide arranging cabin, supplies, and doing the cooking. Write Charles Aki, c/o Kaupo Store, Hana, Maui, HI 96713 or phone 248-8209.

Kau Lio Stables - near Lahaina offer two-hour trips leaving at 8:30 a.m., 11:30 a.m., and 2:30 p.m. They travel up mountainsides, through cane fields, and the kukui nut forests. $33 per person includes refreshments. Call 667-7896 for reservations. They will pick you up at Kaanapali, as they are located across private farm land. Write: Kaanapali Kau Lio, P.O. Box 16056, Kaanapali Beach, Maui, HI 96761.

Oheo Riding Stables - guided trail rides overlooking the gulch and Hana. By appointment, phone 248-7722.

Pony Express Tours - daily trips into Haleakala, weather permitting. Includes a narration of the area with expert guides $110. Phone 667-2202. A 3-1/2 hour trip is $75 per person.

The Rainbow Ranch - follow the Honoapiilani Hwy. 11 miles north of Lahaina. They tour the mountain and beach area. Trips are available for beginning, intermediate or advanced riders either English or Western style. 1 hour trip $15, 2hr trip $25, 2 1/2 hour ride with refreshments $33, beach or picnic rides $40. Write the ranch at P.O. Box 712, Lahaina, Maui, HI 96761. Phone 669-4991.

SHOPPING

To give you an idea of what to expect at the supermarket, here are some prices from the Star Market. The Star and Foodland Markets are located in Kahului and also Kihei. There is also a Foodland in Lahaina at the Lahaina Shopping Center. Safeway is located in Kahului near the Maui Mall. Most of these big grocery stores are competitively priced.

Star Market:
Eggs, large - $1.45 per dozen
Rainier Beer, 6-pack - $3.56
Butter - $2.09 per pound
Mild Cheddar Cheese - $3.51 per pound
Frozen Peas, 20 ounce - $1.45
Hamburger, 30% fat - $2.69 per pound
T-bone Steak - $5.09 per pound

RECREATION AND TOURS
Shopping

Heinz Ketchup - $1.79
Milk, 2% - $1.03 per quart
Bread - ranges 89 cents to $1.89 per loaf

You'll also find a large and unusual assortment of Oriental foods including azuki beans and dried smoked octopus!

A Few More Unusual Markets:

Paradise Fruits - in Kihei is open 24 hours and is an open-air market with a variety of fresh fruits and vegetables, also available for shipment home.

The Farmers' Market - is a group of young people who bring fresh produce down from the Kula area. They set up roadside shopping. You can't find it fresher. Look for them Monday at Front and Baker Streets in Lahaina, Wednesday at Napili near the Napili Kai, and Friday in the parking lot of Suda's Kihei Market (60 Kihei Road). Look for their green sandwich board signs that are roadside.

Azeka's Market - in Kihei is where you can pick up the world-famous marinated Azeka ribs for cooking at your condo. Also fresh Maui beef from Hana.

Lahaina Fishery - located in Lahaina Shopping Center next to the Nagasako Variety Store. Phone 661-3933. They have a wide variety of fresh island fish and their friendly staff can help you make your selection. They also sell beer and wine.

Lahaina/Kaanapali

Front Street in Lahaina offers not only a lengthy row of shops to browse, but has maintained its historical atmosphere. See the Lahaina section for specialty shops. You'll find them keeping long hours, from early morning, until late, late night. The Wharf Shopping Center is located at the south end of Lahaina and is a three-story shopping complex with an abundance of shops and restaurants.

The Whaler's Village Shopping Center is located at Kaanapali and was recently refurbished. The whaling memorabilia on display here is also very interesting.

Again, as in Wailea, the Kaanapali resort hotels offer shopping malls. You may want to visit the Sheraton Hotel, the Maui Surf, the Marriott, and most of all the Hyatt Regency's selection of excellent shops.

The Lahaina Shopping Center is at the north end of town. It's a sprawling complex that offers a lot of parking, however, it's usually packed by mid-morning. The Lahaina Fishery is one store you'll find here, located next to Nagasako Variety. It's a good stop to pick up fresh fish to cook at home. Phone 661-3933.

Lahaina Trade Center is a little hidden, but rapidly growing. Turn by the Pizza Hut just outside of Lahaina. You'll find the bakery here which offers nice pastries and also a very large Hilo Hattie's. The prices are better at this Hilo's, and

RECREATION AND TOURS
Shopping

check the free publications found about town for discount coupons which can provide additional savings here.

Kahului

There are three large shopping centers in Kahului: the Kamehameha Mall, which has a good selection of large department stores and is a pleasant mall; the Maui Mall, which has several grocery stores, restaurants, and smaller shops; and the Kahului Shopping Center, which is the oldest of the three and features a single grocery store and small shops. All three malls are located along Kaahumanu Avenue.

Wailuku

No large shopping malls here, but there are some interesting shops along their main street. Interested in some eel skin, also called "leather of the sea", check Maui Wholesale Gold at 11 Market St., in Wailuku, phone 242-5546. They sell a variety of eel skin items, from wallets to handbags. They also sell gold jewelry and perfumes.

Kihei/Wailea

Wailea Shopping Center is located near Stouffer's Wailea Resort. A Party Pantry for groceries, a few eateries, and the usual clothing and gift stores comprise this shopping center.

Kihei Town Center has the largest drug store on this side of the island. A sporting goods store, grocery store, and an assortment of other shops are located in this mall on South Kihei Road.

Azeka's Place shopping center offers a good bookstore, several novelty stores, a sports shop, two grocery stores, a Baskin Robbins ice cream parlor, and several restaurants.

There are two major grocery stores in Kihei, the Star Market and Foodland. At Azeka's Market you can select from local meats and pick up some of Azeka's ribs to take home and cook.

Rainbow Mall is a small, newly built mall, located on South Kihei Road. A novelty store, clothing, and restaurant occupy this shopping center.

The Nani Kai on South Kihei Road offers very limited shopping.

The Wailea Resort and the Maui Intercontinental both have very nice shopping malls that include Liberty House. They are open daily.

BIBLIOGRAPHY

A Sunset Book, A Guide To All the Islands. California: Lane Publishing. 1983.

Ashdown, Inez. *Stories of Old Lahaina.* Honolulu: Hawaiian Service, Inc. 1976.

Barrow, Terence. *Incredible Hawaii.* Vermont: Charles Tuttle Co. 1974.

Birnbaum, Stephen, *Hawaii 1984.* Boston: Houghton-Mifflin Co. 1983.

Bone, Robert, *The Maverick Guide to Hawaii.* Gretna: Pelican Publishing. 1984.

Boom, Bob and Christensen, Chris, *Important Hawaiian Place Names.* Hawaii: Bob Boom Books. 1978.

Clark, John, *Beaches of Maui County.* Honolulu: University Press of Hawaii. 1980.

Daws, Gavan, *The Illustrated Atlas of Hawaii.* Australia: Island Heritage Ltd. 1980.

Fielding, Ann, *Hawaiian Reefs and Tidepools.* Hawaii: Oriental Publishing Company.

Fodor's Hawaii 1983. New York: David McKay, Inc. 1982.

Gleasner, Bill and Diana, *Maui Traveler's Guide.* Honolulu: Oriental Publishing Co.

Hammel, Faye and Levey, Sylvan, *Frommer's Hawaii on $35 a Day.* New York: Frommer/Pasmantier Publishers. 1984.

Haraguchi, Paul, *Weather in Hawaiian Waters.* 1983.

Hazama, Dorothy. *The Ancient Hawaiians.* Honolulu: Hogarth Press.

Holiday Guide to Maui. New York: Random House. 1982.

Judd, Gerrit. *Hawaii, an Informal History.* New York: Collier Books. 1961.

Kyselka, Will and Lanterman, Ray, *Maui, How it Came to Be.* Honolulu: The University Press of Hawaii. 1980.

Lahaina Restoration Foundation, *Story of Lahaina.* Lahaina: 1980.

Maui Condominiums. Guidelines Corporation. 1984.

Maui Historical Society, *Lahaina Historical Guide.* Tokyo: Maui Historical Society. 1971.

Mrantz, Maxine, *Whaling Days in Old Hawaii.* Honolulu: Aloha Graphics and Sales. 1976.

Mrantz, Maxine. *Women of Old Hawaii.* Honolulu: Aloha Graphics. 1982.

Nickerson, Roy. *Lahaina, Royal Capital of Hawaii.* Hawaii: Hawaiian Service. 1980.

On The Hana Coast. Hong Kong: Emphasis International Ltd. and Carl Lundquist. 1983.

Randall, John, *Underwater Guide to Hawaiian Reef Fishes.* Hawaii: Treasures of Time. 1981.

Riegert, Ray, *Hidden Hawaii.* California: And/Or Press. 1982.

Smith, Robert, *Hiking Maui.* California: The Wilderness Press. 1979.

Stilwell, Beverly and Kenneth, *The Book of Maui.* Maui: Lollipop Press. 1983.

Thome, Chuck, *50 Locations for Scuba & Snorkeling.* 1983.

Wallin, Doug, *Exotic Fishes and Coral of Hawaii and the Pacific.* 1974.

Wisniewski, Richard A., *The Rise and Fall of the Hawaiian Kingdom.* Honolulu: Pacific Basin Enterprises. 1979.

Wurman, Richard, *Hawaii Access.* The Access Press. 1982.

READER RESPONSE

Dear Reader:

We hope you have had a pleasant holiday on Maui. We would like to hear about it from you. Our book expresses our own opinions and experiences on restaurants, recreation, and accommodations. You may have similar or different experiences and we would appreciate your sharing these with us. Any updates and changes since this edition was published, as well as any items that you can correct us on would be welcomed as well. Please mail to:

Paradise Publications
8110 SW Wareham Circle
Portland, Oregon 97223